REFLECTIONS
ON THE MERSEY

FRANK UNWIN

Gallery Press

Leighton Road, Neston, South Wirral.

ISBN 0 900389 20 6
©Frank Unwin 1983
First published by Gallery Press 1984
Reprinted 1985, 1986.
Printed by Leemancolour Ltd., Neston, South Wirral.

REFLECTIONS ON THE MERSEY

MEMOIRS OF THE TWENTIES AND THIRTIES

by

FRANK UNWIN

Gallery Press
Leighton Road, Neston, South Wirral.

ACKNOWLEDGEMENTS

The Author and Publishers wish to make acknowledgement and offer their thanks to the following:—

Margaret Davie for permission to use extracts from Malcolm Munro's book 'A Dancing Life'.

Messrs Frederick Muller Limited, London, for the extract from Bud Flanagan's 'My Crazy Life'.

The 'Liverpool Echo', and especially Mr. Derek Whale, for extracts from articles in this newspaper.

Mr. Craig J. M. Carter for information on the Mersey and its ships.

CONTENTS

FOREWORD

It was a cold autumn night in 1969 when the lift doors at BBC Radio Merseyside's studios in Liverpool crashed open to reveal a wind-swept figure half hidden behind a pile of fragile 78 records.

The figure stepped confidently forward and told the Programme Organiser he had an idea for a radio series which could not fail.

The man was Frank Unwin. The programme was 'Music and Memories'. Frank's arguments were convincing. He had long felt that many Merseysiders would enjoy hearing the music they'd once listened to so many years ago when they switched on their radios at 10.30 p.m. to listen to an hour and a half of dance band music at its brightest and best.

With equal enthusiasm the Programme Organiser grasped the idea, and agreed to give Frank and his programme a trial run—for six whole weeks. But Frank's sheer professionalism and the warm reception given to the programme by the listeners, soon meant that 'Music & Memories' was to become a permanent fixture in Radio Merseyside's schedules. The six weeks became six years, then seven, then ten, until now the programme is in its 14th year. The title of the programme, which has now achieved the distinction of being Britain's longest running big band record programme, speaks for itself—Music and Memories.

Frank and his programme have helped rekindle those dormant memories of listeners who associate his music with some personal event in their own lives.

Over the years they have written in their thousands—wonderful letters full of praise and appreciation. And Frank has in turn been able to share their memories—some happy and some sad—with other listeners.

Now Frank is drawing on those rich experiences and marvellous memories to write a book—this book. He has attempted, and if past performances is anything to go by, largely succeeded in recapturing those bygone years. Much of the book is devoted, quite rightly, to the entertainment enjoyed in the 1920's and 30's, and especially the halcyon days of ballroom dancing on Merseyside.

It is a book which will blow away the mist of time and help you relive those joyous days. I wish all his readers many happy hours of reading, and many happy memories.

IAN JUDSON,
BBC Radio Merseyside.

Chapter One
No Chip on my Shoulder

I was born within the sound of 'Paddy's Hammer', which is an affectionate term for the bells of St. Patrick's Church, in the south-end of Liverpool. If we were inclined to 'sleep in' on Sunday mornings, 'Paddy's Hammer' always proved a rude awakening.

To be born during the first World War, nurtured in its miserable aftermath, leave school in the very depths of the Great Depression of the early 30s, and arrive just at the right age to be among the early conscripts of World War II is not, perhaps, conducive to a happy, contented life. But if that sounds like the prelude to another 'look back in anger' protest, nothing could be farther from the truth. I have no chip on my shoulder, and I can honestly confess that I look back to an extremely turbulent era with an enormous amount of pleasure, and to a life, though difficult and deprived in its early stages, that was not without its compensations.

We hear so much about the 'good old days', meaning, of course, the 1920s and 1930s. Let me emphasise right at the outset, with all the vehemence at my command, that they certainly were not the good old days. There were far too many bad ones. Fortunately, we've been blessed with the gifts of forgetting many of the bad times and of recalling with affection the good times we enjoyed in abundance when most of us appreciated, and were grateful for, the simple privileges in life.

My father, who won the Military Medal in the 'War to end wars', ended up badly gassed—so badly, in fact, that he found it impossible to work. Consequently, there was no silver spoon in my mouth, and with several hungry mouths to feed and healthy young bodies to clothe, privileges were few and far between. Breakfast invariably consisted of half a slice of bread and margarine, dinner a plate of cheap but nourishing scouse, and tea a couple of rounds of bread, thinly spread with plum and apple jam. We were always hungry.

On reflection, I've come to the conclusion that this was no bad thing, as it helped me to appreciate in full measure the little joys in life which didn't come very frequently, but which I now look back on with considerable nostalgia. My red-letter day was Friday, when I received my pocket money for the week—a ha'penny, which quickly ended up in the sweetshop till in exchange for a bag of bulls eyes or aniseed drops. And that was it—no more luxuries until the following Friday.

We lived in a not very salubrious street of old terraced houses with their front and back parlours, sculleries and cellars. Our neighbours were always hard-up, hungry and deprived. But they were warm-hearted and friendly. The old song 'Friends and Neighbours' was particularly apt in our street. There was always the friendly smile, the warm greeting and the helping hand for anyone sick or in desperate need. I often look back on those people as the salt of the earth.

I have many happy memories of my first school, a stones-throw from Liverpool's Anglican Cathedral, where the discipline was strict but kindly. There was a strict 'no talking' rule in the classroom and woe betide any boy who disobeyed this rule by even a whisper, as it usually meant four strokes of the cane from two or three of the teachers, delivered without malice but with considerable energy. Any boy who had the temerity to threaten to 'fetch me dad' suffered an additional two strokes.

Caning, however, had its lighter moments—that is, if you weren't the victim. There was always great hilarity during the caning of the 'artful dodger', an activity which took on the atmosphere of pure pantomime. Curiously enough, every class seemed to have its 'artful dodger'. It started off as a kind of circular game between master and boy, where the unfortunate boy would tentatively hold out his hand half-way, so to speak, at the same time manoeuvring himself in a circular movement of evasion. When the cane descended, down came the hand like greased lightning, and the cane swished through empty space. This little frolic was repeated several times until the now exasperated teacher seized the miscreant by the scruff of the neck, propelled him over the nearest desk and proceeded to wallop every particle of dust from his trousers.

I recall one occasion when the cane missed the quickly withdrawn hand and landed on the teacher's knee with a resounding crack. There followed the comedy of the panic-stricken boy diving frantically down the aisle between the rows of desks, with the teacher in full pursuit, lashing out with the cane at every available inch of the victim's anatomy. Such moments brightened up the dull routine of the lesson. Of course there were always the stories that if you placed a hair across the palm of the hand, or rubbed resin over it, this would break the cane. I often marvel at the gullibility of some pupils who actually believed such stories. Needless to say they never worked.

I don't subscribe to the view that schooldays are the happiest days of one's life. But at least they weren't unhappy ones when I was a pupil, and the firm discipline, much frowned on today, did much to eliminate the bullying and many of today's evils. We had to be in school on time. Punctuality was insisted upon. At exactly nine o'clock the doors were locked and bolted by the caretaker, and if we were half a minute late we didn't get in.

Then you had some explaining to do, for the attendance officer—then called the 'School Board' for some reason—was a stickler at his job and was quite a feared individual, and had no hesitation in calling at your house. Incidentally, there was one well-respected headmaster in the south of Liverpool who used to stand at the school entrance just before nine o'clock, cane in hand and ready for action. You had to show him your hands, and if they were dirty, perhaps because of playing 'ollies' in the gutters on the way to school—whack! No questions asked—none were expected—you were just walloped, short and sharp. Instant justice!

We respected, often revered, most of our school teachers. As I've said, the majority of them were strict disciplinarians, but reasonably just and humane. In those days we were expected to know the difference between right and wrong, no matter what our environment, and if we were caught in some mischief or other, fair enough, we were walloped good and strong with no ill-feeling on either side.

But there were the eccentrics. One in particular. Rumour had it that he'd been severely shell-shocked during the war, and this was certainly reflected in his behaviour. He revelled in talking about his war experiences, and with typical childish cunning, if we realised we weren't going to enjoy the lesson in progress, all we had to do was to innocently lead off with a question about the war. This got him going for the remainder of the lesson. It never failed. For this individual the cane was for use and not for ornament—and used it was. We soon lost count of the number of canes he broke, and it often meant a trip down to the Blind School in Cornwallis Street for one of us to buy him a new one. Sometimes he would man-handle a boy in such a manner that, at four o'clock, he'd order him to remain behind, and give him twopence in exchange for a promise not to tell his parents.

Often, on a warm, lazy summer afternoon, this gentleman would pull the movable blackboard until it stood right in front of the clear-glass classroom door, thus effectively screening off the view from the corridor. As an added precaution he'd lock the door on the inside. Then he'd settle himself in his high teachers desk and indulge in a really good snooze. Before settling himself down, though, he'd stack his desk with a load of books—sometimes, alas, those bulky black-covered school bibles, and if any of us dared to interrupt his 'forty winks' he'd use them as missiles. His aim with those books, as with sticks of chalk, was unerring, especially for a supposedly shell-shocked hero of the war.

He grew his own tomatoes, which he'd bring to school, place them on display on the front of his desk, and tell us to bring our ha'pennies and pennies for them. Strangely enough, we obeyed him without question, and his tomatoes were soon sold. That man was quite a character. And the odd thing is that when some of his ex-pupils talk about him now we do so with a strange mixture of awe and affection. There must be a moral somewhere.

In those days, even though the headmaster might be a just and kindly man, there was a certain aura of fear surrounding him, and he was one to be avoided, if humanly possible. Whenever we passed his study, we did so on tip-toe, and with a certain amount of trepidation. It was the 'holy of holies', and we always visualised his collection of canes which stood in the corner of his room.

I remember being sent for by the head towards the end of one term, and, very reluctantly, I slowly made my way to his study, at the same time wondering which of my sins had been discovered. Was it for filling the teacher's inkwell with blotting paper, placing drawing pins on his seat, or purloining the ribbon of a girl's hair? I needn't have worried. He was in benign mood and pointed to a pile of lovely new books set out on his table. He informed me that I'd won the class prize for the term and invited me to choose the book I preferred. Now that was a thrill—a moment to savour, as we really appreciated such things in those days. And so, on prize-giving day, I proudly collected the book I'd chosen— 'Frank's First Term' by Harold Avery. It was the first of several, I'm happy to say, and I can remember to this day the books I was awarded in subsequent terms—'Will of the Mill', 'Ivanhoe', 'The Talisman', 'Treasure Island' and 'The Coral Island'—books I carefully kept and treasured right up to the war years when I discovered they'd been handed in for salvage. I wish I had them now.

Singing lessons in my first school were often quite hilarious, especially as the teacher sat at the piano with her back to us. That was a grave error of judgement. All sorts of things went on behind her ample back—ink pellets flying across the room, duels with rulers, playing darts with pens, pulling the girls' pigtails, and so on. There were no holds barred. When order was eventually restored and peace reigned supreme, we were put through the usual routine commencing with the scale, followed by the usual well-tried and well-worn favourites such as 'Cherry Ripe', 'Who is Sylvia?', 'Shenandoah', 'Blow the Man Down' and, of course, 'John Peel'. Needless to say we had our own words for some of them. In every class there was the music teacher's nightmare— the 'grunter'. She'd walk round the class as we were singing, ears alert, in an attempt to detect the offender, who was quietly but firmly led out by his ear and banished to a corner of the room, to sin no more. We enjoyed some great fun during those singing lessons.

On a more sombre note, some of the children were so poverty-stricken that they came to school in their bare feet, often without a shirt underneath the tatty old pullovers they were wearing, and trousers with their seats hanging out. That was the era of police clothes. If a child had no clothes, he or she could apply for police clothes, which were issued at the police station. The clothes and clogs were not only very unattractive, but also very distinctive.

The boys' outfit was a corduroy jacket and trousers, with clogs, of course, while the girls' consisted of a navy-blue dress with red piping round the hem and collar. They were so distinctive, in fact, that most of the children felt very embarrassed at having to wear them. If a mother felt tempted to pawn the clothes they were specially marked to warn the pawnbroker that they were public property and must not be accepted. I always felt sorry for the boys and girls who arrived at school clad in brand new police clothes for, young as they were, they must have had the feeling of being set apart. The most that could be said for those garments is that they helped to keep out the cold.

The School Meals Service was, of course, many years away. Yet some children, who were obviously under-nourished, went at mid-day to a dinner centre where they were given a plate of stew or bean-scouse. For this they were given tickets by their teacher and released from class a few minutes before the others.

The cry would ring out: 'Dinner place children!' and out they'd shuffle for their hot meal. Thank heaven there were such facilities, although the scheme could have worked in a much more discreet and less humiliating manner.

Unfortunately, not a great deal of understanding or sympathy was shown to the deprived youngsters of those days. For instance, there were boys and girls who'd been up at six or seven o'clock in the morning to deliver milk or newspapers, or who'd spent the previous evening walking the streets selling bundles of firewood. After a tiring day in the classroom they might doze off and be severely chastised, or even caned for not paying attention. Many children arrived home from school only to be given the task of chopping wood into small pieces, tying it in bundles with thin wire, loading it into a small cart on pram wheels and then tramping the streets trying to sell it. Fortunately, most of them had regular customers. Even so, they could be out for hours. What kind of a life was that?

Schools didn't boast the luxury of their own playing field at that time, and we never looked forward to our so-called games periods, as it always meant a long walk to Jericho Farm, in Otterspool, and back. There was no transport laid on—it was 'Shanks pony' all the way there and back to school again—a distance of eight miles or more. There was always an argument as to who was to have the honour of carrying the case-ball. Certain boys carried the goal posts on their shoulders, and they'd be relieved by others after a mile or so. By the time we arrived at Jericho Farm, planted the goal posts in the ground, and divided ourselves into teams, there was usually no more than ten minutes for football—about 25 on each side, by the way. Then came the long trek back with many a boy sneaking off home on the way. The teacher was inclined to turn a blind eye on this.

On dark evenings, I remember being afraid to pass St. James's Mount, next to the Cathedral, on my way home from school, as we'd been told by some bigger boys with vivid imaginations that it was the haunt of the dreaded 'Black Hand Gang'. There was another fearsome character whose statue occupied that area. To quote from the old song: 'On the mount there stands a lady— who she is I do not know'. With the passage of time her nose and mouth became so thick with moss that she eventually became known as 'Ginny Green-teeth'. She became an object of terror for young children of my age, especially if we suffered from a nervous disposition. One day some children playing there found a rain barrel and a woodman's axe. So, with youngsters' imaginations as they were, the legend was born that if they approached St. James's Mount after dark, Ginny would chase them with the axe, chop off their heads and throw them in the rain barrel.

During the summer, an ice-cream merchant was always waiting outside the school gates at four o'clock, and if we had a ha'penny to spare it always went on a cornet. There were none of the gaudily-painted vans of today with their lively jingles. It was usually a man pushing a small handcart containing a kind of pail with lumps of ice packed round it. The ice-cream was atrocious, to say the least, and how we managed to stomach it I'll never know. The only thing it had in common with ice-cream was that it was cold. But there were the better ones, such as the 'Stop me and buy one' vendor, dressed in uniform and riding a tricycle with a large box at the front. But his ice creams cost a penny, and we couldn't afford that. And then there was the 'Okey-Pokey' merchant who also rode a tricycle as he cried out: 'Okey-Pokey, penny a lump!' To which we children would gleefully reply: 'Just the stuff to make you jump!'

Chapter Two
The Streets were our Playground

I've already said that my weekly pocket money in my childhood days was a ha'penny, and that it was something to look forward to every Friday night as it was good for two ounces of boiled sweets or a bar of toffee. My ration for the remainder of the week consisted of pressing my nose against the sweetshop window, eyes popping and mouth watering at the tempting delights displayed mostly in those big glass jars.

I'd debate in my mind what I'd buy if I had a shilling. There were sherbet dabs—triangular bags of sherbet or 'kayli' with a little tube of liquorice sticking through the top with which to suck out the sherbet. There were 'lucky bags' containing a little toy, a few chalky sweets and a piece of locust bean. Gobstoppers were always firm favourites as they lasted a long time and had the added attraction of changing colour as you sucked them. Then there were tiger nuts, Spanish laces, sweet tobacco, cinder toffee, pear drops, creamy whirls, and those dainty little sweets called 'Fairy Whispers', with a romantic message printed on them. We'd give the best of these to our childhood sweethearts. Spanish laces, by the way, were long strips of liquorice. And I mustn't forget the joys of 'sticky lice'.

As Christmas approached, with what must be considered admirable self restraint, we put our ha'pennies into the sweet club. 'Join Our Sweet Club' was the notice displayed on every sweetshop window. The amount aimed for was a shilling, and when Christmas Eve arrived after what seemed an eternity, we rushed round to our little local shop with our precious cards to collect our goodies. This was one of the many joys of Christmas Eve.

Our little shop was owned by an ex-soldier—a kindly old man with a distinct military moustache and bearing, and with loads of time for children. He dubbed his shop 'John Carver's New Dug-Out'. He must have had loads of patience as well, as we kept him fully occupied with our requests for a ha'porth of this, a ha'porth of that, and a ha'porth of the other. He would weigh them with a generous eye on the scale, and then carefully put the various sweets into lots of separate paper bags, and the whole lot into a cardboard box together with our bonus for having saved up a whole shilling—a bottle of ginger pop. I remember that kindly old soldier with a great deal of affection.

I often read today of the many and varied excuses offered in mitigation of children falling foul of the law. They are deprived. They come from poor social backgrounds. There isn't enough entertainment provided for them. While there may be a grain of truth in this, I have little sympathy for such excuses. Many of my generation were desperately deprived. We came from poor backgrounds. The only entertainment we enjoyed was the Saturday matinee at the local cinema, the school play centre or the Band of Hope. We made our own entertainment in those days, and we didn't go round smashing things up or mugging old ladies. Admittedly, the streets were far safer to play in; there wasn't a great deal of traffic, so we simply revelled in our street games.

Lamp-post cricket was possibly the favourite. Even Test Match cricket didn't have so many rules—invented by ourselves, of course. For instance, the boy who owned the bat was the boss, and he decided what time to commence play. He was also 'first in' and brooked no argument. He and the boy who produced the ball selected their teams from all the would-be participants. They tossed up for first choice. 'I'll have Bill'. Bill stood behind his skipper. 'I'll have Jack'. Jack took up position behind his captain. 'I'll have Tommy'. 'I'll have Joe'. And so on and so forth until every boy was lined up in his team. If there was an odd boy they tossed up for him with no great enthusiasm, as he was obviously the 'rabbit'.

The ball was preferably a tennis ball, as the rubber ones bounced too much. A chalk mark was made on the lamp-post to indicate the height of the bails. And so the game got under way. Hitting the ball over a backyard wall was 'six and out'. If you hit the ball against a wall and it was caught you were only 'out' if it was caught with one hand. Everyone fielded even though your own side might be batting. So you were put on your honour to catch the ball safely even though the batsman might be one of your own team. And if the owner of the bat was given 'out', unjustly in his opinion, there was no argument. He promptly took his bat home and that was that. Match abandoned.

Another popular game was 'Kick the Can', and good use was made of condensed milk and syrup tins. A similar kind of game was 'Release'. The boys were divided into two teams and a suitable area chosen as the 'prison'. The team that guarded the prison had the task of capturing the members of the team that were out of prison. Capture simply meant touching a boy, and he was then honour bound to accompany his captor to prison, where he had to wait until all the members of his team were caught, or until he was rescued. All the prisoners could be rescued if one of their team still not caught could run past the prison shouting 'Release!'. Approaching the prison area without being seen called for a certain amount of ingenuity, and hiding behind the voluminous skirts of an old lady was a good idea. Both 'Kick the Can' and 'Release' were played with enormous enthusiasm.

'Ton weight heavy on' was a particular favourite and was played this way: One boy stood with his back against the wall as a 'cushion' while the other members of his team bent down with their heads between one another's legs, thus forming a continuous long 'back'. The first boy of the opposing team had to take a running jump and land as far as possible on the line of backs. The second boy followed, then the third, and so on until every boy was safely on the 'back'. There was great deal of groaning from the team 'down under'. If the back collapsed under the strain they'd lost the contest. If they withstood the weight for an agreed number of seconds it was their turn to jump. Certainly no game for weaklings and most of us had bruises and sore ribs to show for it.

Needless to say, street football wasn't neglected and, with as many as fifteen boys on each side in a narrow street, it can well be imagined that there was more brute force than skill in evidence. A ball wasn't essential. Old newspapers or an old shirt screwed up tightly and fastened with string served the purpose admirably. Coats were used as goal-posts. Speed was of the essence in street football, especially when a policeman appeared on the horizon, and then feet couldn't be seen for dust.

A similar burst of speed was required when a window was broken during the course of street football or cricket. There'd be a crash of broken glass and you just scarpered. If you were unfortunate enough to be caught by an irate householder, you all clubbed together to replace the broken pane of glass. I can remember some of those street football games ending up with a score like 56-43. They were never likely to produce a Stanley Matthews.

Playing marbles was a favourite pastime, too. The marbles, or 'ollies' as we called them, were made of clay, and painted. We played this game in street gutters or on waste land. There were several variations of the game which would take too long to describe here. Most of us had hoops which we propelled along the streets at great speed with the aid of a stick. If it was an iron hoop, we used a kind of hook, which served the purpose of accelerator and brake. But they were mostly wooden hoops, and it was an unwritten rule that girls must be content with the wooden variety and must never aspire to a metal one. The inequality of the sexes!

Good weather would bring the children tumbling out of their homes to transform the streets in which they lived. Scuffling boys would revel in 'Cops and Robbers' or 'Cowboys and Indians'. Their sisters would solemnly play at 'House', and proudly parade their 'babies', which were, of course, their favourite dolls in prams. Others would bring out skipping ropes—a length of old clothes line, one end tied round a handy lamp-post would do, and the air would be filled with the sound of shrill voices. Easter-tide was the turn of the tops. Suddenly the pavement would come alive with tops of all shapes and varieties.

You could get the top spinning in two ways—by winding the cord of the whip round and round the top and then whipping it out of its base in the soil between the pavement stones. Or you could set it spinning around with a quick tweak of the fingers and then keep the momentum going with the help of your whip. A simple little pleasure which called for a certain modicum of skill, and it was great fun.

Hop Scotch and Cherry Wobs were played by both boys and girls, too. You flicked the cherry wobs up the drain-spout and they'd come rolling down and along the narrow gutter. If one cherry wob hit one of the stones already in the gutter the owner claimed the lot.

There was a game we used to play called 'Tip Cat'. This was played with a heavy stick with which you struck a piece of wood, sharpened at each end, causing it to somersault in the air. You then had to hit it as hard as you could with your stick before it reached the ground—the further it went the better. As this game was played in the streets with terraced houses on either side, many windows had narrow escapes.

There were several cigarette card games. Perhaps the most popular one was flicking the cards against the wall, with the nearest to it the take-all winner. Collecting cigarette cards was an enjoyable pastime. Children kept out of mischief by going out in search of cards. You'll remember the plaintive cry: 'Any cigarette cards, please, mister?' And delving into waste paper baskets for empty cartons which might contain a nice new card—perhaps even the elusive 50th to make up your complete set. Sport was always a popular series, and others were 'Famous Ships', 'Film Stars', 'Railway Locomotives', 'Wild Flowers', 'RAF Badges', 'British Dance Band Leaders', 'Stars of Radio', 'Uniforms of the British Empire', 'Flags of the World', 'Household Hints', 'The History of Transport' etc. Some sets are quite valuable now.

I dare say many readers will remember those small, octagonal-sided metal objects called 'Put 'n Take'. There was a little handle on the top to enable you to spin them round, and they'd come to rest with one of the instructions facing upwards—'put one', 'take two', 'put four', 'take three' etc. And, being tremendous little gamblers, we used to have enormous fun playing 'Put'n Take' with cigarette cards. I wonder whether those innocent little toys were responsible for giving children their first gambling urge? I haven't seen one for many years but I'm sure there must be some still around.

Yo-yos enjoyed a brief, though hectic, craze around 1932. It swept the country and almost every boy and girl had one. Some of the children were amazingly skilful. Home work was neglected, and this was the excuse for dads to confiscate them. But if you chanced to creep upstairs and peep into the bedroom you might have seen many a dad in a heaven of delight practising his ups-and-downs on the confiscated yo-yo. If you couldn't afford the couple of coppers to buy one they were often made from two large buttons sewn back to back with a strong thread for the string. And girls had a crazy for working wool through a cotton reel—weaving this around four nails in the top, and a fancy cord would issue forth from the other end. Shoe boxes could be converted into peepshows, and steering carts made from orange boxes and four pram wheels.

What marvellous skipping games the girls used to enjoy. As a boy I secretly envied the skipping ability of the fair sex and longed to join in. But it would have been considered 'sissy' for us boys to take part in this essentially feminine activity, although there were one or two games in which the participation of boys was invited. Two girls would spin the rope while the others skipped under and over as it turned. As they skipped they chanted, and I often wonder how far back into Merseyside folk-lore many of those jingles went. One was 'Salt, mustard, vinegar, pepper';

another great favourite was 'Old Mother Mason broke her basin. How much did it cost? Penny, tuppence, threepence, fourpence . . . .', and as the skipping girls counted the cost the rope would spin faster and ever faster until they stumbled or became entangled in the rope. Here are just a few of the skipping jingles, which I'm sure will bring back many happy memories:—

'Eeper-weeper chimney sweeper,
Had a wife but could not keep her,
Had another, did not love her,
Up the chimney he did shove her.
How many miles did she go?
One, two, three, four, etc.'

And the counting went on until the player's 'puff' ran out.

'Dancing dolly, she had no sense,
She bought six eggs for eighteen pence,
The eggs went bad, Dolly went mad,
Ishy-ashy one, ishy-ashy two, etc.'

The next two games entailed jumping 'in' and 'out' while the rope was turning:-

'I am a sailor dressed in blue,
These are the actions I must do,
Salute to the King,
Bow to the Queen,
Turn my back on the Union Jack
And jump right out.'

'Teddy-bear, teddy-bear touch the ground,
Teddy-bear, teddy-bear turn around,
Teddy-bear, teddy-bear show your shoe,
Teddy-bear, teddy-bear out goes you'.

And the appropriate actions were made as the girls were skipping.

'Dip, dip, dip, my blue ship,
Floating on the water
Like a cup and saucer,
Dip, dip, dip, you're not in!'

'Penny on the water,
Tuppence on the sea,
Threepence on the railway,
Out goes she!'

There was one skipping game where the boys were invited to join in. Two girls would start the rope turning, while the other lasses and boys stood aside. The first girl jumped in and skipped to the song:—

'On the mountain stands a lady,
Who she is I do not know,
She has lots of gold and silver,
All she wants is a nice young man,
So call in my Freddy dear,
Freddy dear, Freddy dear,
Call in my Freddy dear
And married you shall be.'

And at the 'call in', the skipper would call in the first name of her choice, and Freddy, or whoever the boy happened to be, would enter into the skipping, holding the girl's hands, and the two girls at the end of the rope would really make it twirl. The winners were the pair who skipped the longest without tripping up.

There were many other skipping jingles in different parts of Merseyside. I trust the few I've mentioned will bring a sigh of nostalgia to many mums and grandmas as they look back to their childhood days.

I used to watch the girls playing various games with balls thrown high against the wall of a building and be caught by the hands and body in a variety of positions. There was also the game in which three balls were tossed against the wall in juggler fashion, and the girls showed remarkable expertise at this. The main thing was that these famous old street games kept us out of mischief, and we expended our surplus energy in a good and healthy way without resorting to vandalism and violence.

Before leaving our childhood activities I must mention our escapades on bicycles. We could hire a bike from certain shops for twopence or threepence an hour. But what a ramshackle collection of old relics they were! Many didn't even boast a saddle, which made sitting down a painful exercise for weeks after riding them. Most had no brakes, and they all had flat tyres. Yet we had immense fun on them, and the idea was to career down the steepest street we could find. To stop the machine we used the simple process of jamming our shoe against the front tyre. Sometimes it worked, and sometimes it didn't, especially when our shoe happened to make contact with the spokes, and then it was disaster and a mass of cuts and bruises for weeks after. Life was very dicy on those old wrecks but how we enjoyed ourselves. My own favourite place was a very steep lane in Gateacre—Gateacre Brow I think it was. I used to race down it at about sixty miles an hour. How we survived I just don't know.

Finally, those electric shock machines. We used to go into the herb shop, buy a ha'penny glass of a liquid called Vantas and have a go on the electric shock machine affixed to the wall. They had two knobs, and when you placed your ha'penny or penny in the slot the knobs became alive and emitted a pleasant tingling electric current. Several of us held hands—the end two holding the knobs, and the current would pass through from one to another.

Chapter Three
Last Tram to the Dingle

Entering a new school for the first time is always something of an ordeal. When I reached the age of eleven I was fortunate enough to pass the 'scholarship', as we called it then, and with mixed feelings I had to leave the school I loved so well and continue my education at St. Margaret's School in Anfield—Essemmay.

The only drawback was that this school was several miles from my home, and entailed a considerable journey on the No. 27 tram, and the No. 26 home again—the old outer circular route. So, resplendent in a smart new uniform, and feeling decidedly nervous, I reported one Monday morning to my new school. My nervousness was misplaced as it proved to be a really first-rate school in every way, and we were fortunate enough in having a fine staff of teachers who quickly gained my respect and confidence. I spent several happy years at S.M.A., and when my 'time was up', it was with no pleasure at all that I took my leave and embarked on the difficult task of trying to earn my living in the middle of the Great Depression of the early 30s.

My school was but a stones-throw from Wolverton Street, the scene of the notorious Wallace murder of 1931, while I was in my third year at the school. When the crime had been discovered, with all the morbid curiosity of youth, we made our way to the scene of the crime after we were dismissed at lunch-time and at four o'clock. Naturally enough, as we knew the street so well, it became a rather macabre talking point among us boys, and we followed the events with intense interest.

We all had our own pet theories as to who had committed the crime, and I used to read every single word of the trial proceedings in the Liverpool Echo and Evening Express. Many books have been written about this particularly brutal murder, and many theories propounded, but it seems certain that the truth will never be known. Did the rather timid, inoffensive-looking William Wallace batter his wife to death on that grim night in 1931? If so, with what motive? Did he meticulously plan the perfect alibi? Was the circumstantial evidence against him so overwhelming that the verdict of 'guilty' was perfectly correct? Or, on the other hand, did a remarkable series of coincidences occur that pointed an accusing finger at a perfectly innocent man? Did Julia Wallace meet her tragic fate at the hands of a person or persons unknown? Young as we were, these were the questions that were being asked as we tried to concentrate on our English, French and Mathematics.

Some people claim to know the real murderer and have actually named him. But most folk remain completely unconvinced. On the other hand, I've asked myself over and over again—how on earth could Wallace commit such a messy crime and then clean himself up so completely in so very short a time? It was dangerous to condemn a man on the evidence that was available. To this day I have an open mind on the subject.

There were no school dinners provided in those days, and some of us used to eat our mid-day sandwiches in a little shop just round the corner from our school in West Derby Road, where we could buy a cup of hot oxo for a penny. We all knew what Wallace looked like as we'd seen his picture so many times in the local papers. And some of the boys actually knew him. One day, after his release, we were sitting in the shop eating our 'butties' when, to our complete astonishment, in walked William Wallace to purchase some tobacco or cigarettes.

There was a hushed silence as he quietly pocketed his purchase and walked out again. Had we come face to face with a savage murderer who'd managed to escape the rope? Or was it just another case of mistaken identity? Two or three of the local boys who knew him insisted that it certainly was Wallace. Yet it could easily have been someone who bore a passing resemblance to the man who'd created legal history. We shall never know. But I must confess that that historic murder case still intrigues me, and I remain entirely unconvinced one way or the other.

Week-day football matches were played in the afternoon in those days, and when Liverpool F.C. had a home game at the nearby Anfield ground we were always on tenterhooks throughout the final lesson of the afternoon, our eyes glued on the clock and longing for four o'clock to come. As soon as we were dismissed we broke all records in our dash to the ground because at three-quarter time the gates were thrown open and we could watch the remaining quarter of the match free of charge and, quite often, a few late goals. They were the days of Elisha Scott, 'Parson' Jackson, Tiny Bradshaw, and suchlike Liverpool stalwarts. The only drawback was that at the end of the game there was such an almighty queue for the No. 26 tram that it often meant walking the five miles home. But it was all well worth while.

And those trams! It seemed to us that on the outer-circular route, and the No. 3 route from Dingle to Walton, they sorted out the oldest and most ramshackle cars in existence. Not for nothing were they called 'boneshakers'. They were the open balcony type, but I must admit they were very popular with us schoolboys. When we jumped on board we were up the stairs like lightning, through the enclosed top deck, and out to the front open balcony. If that was full we settled for the back, although that wasn't quite as interesting. I always felt sorry for the drivers of those trams, especially during the winter months when they were exposed to the icy winds, rain, hail, sleet and snow. They usually wore two heavy overcoats, and were muffled up to the eyebrows with thick woollen scarves. A huge pair of leather mittens covered two pairs of ordinary gloves. We could hear the driver stamping his feet on the platform to get the circulation going. They had to be tough—mighty tough to drive those old tramcars in the winter and they deserved every penny they got—and more.

An entire book could be written on the rich variety of Liverpool tramcars down the years. There was 'Priestley's Pet', a single-decker nicknamed after the General Manager of the time. There was the 'Monkey Box'—the tram with the cage-like compartments at each end. Then there was the 'Bogeyman', the first eight-wheeled bogey car, the 'Oceanic'—a huge tram with a doorway in the centre, and then the ultimate in luxury, the famous 'Green Goddess'. The 'Oceanics' were built in Philadelphia and they weren't at all popular with the drivers as they were fitted with air brakes. Of course, they had entrances at each end as well as in the middle. The bogies of these vehicles had a bad habit of going diverse ways. On one occasion the No. 12 turning from Aintree into Harlech Street caused enormous chaos to race traffic when the forward bogie went into Harlech Street while the trailing one carried on down County Road.

On one bitterly-cold day during the winter of 1927, an open-fronted No. 3 Dingle to Walton tram was travelling up London Road. Another tram, immediately in front, had just started to turn into Norton Street. Suddenly the heavy trolley head of the preceding tram came hurtling over the shoulder of a passenger who was occupying one of the front seats of the open-deck car, and landed with a loud crash at the feet of the policeman who was directing the traffic at the road junction. The officer, smiling broadly, dismounted from his rostrum, and stooping, scooped up in his gloved hands the fallen trolley wheel. Smoke arose at the contact. Screaming like a Dervish, the unfortunate policeman flung the object away from him and disappeared with the speed of an Olympic Games sprinter in the direction of the Pier Head. The poor fellow had received a terrific shock and was later treated for severe burns.

There were many humorous moments, too. Some of the conductors had that typical Liverpool sense of humour. On one occasion, a very stout old Mary Ellen, who was struggling to reach the steps of the tramcar, discovered the effort was beyond her. The conductor got his hands under her shoulders and tried to heave her up, but without success. 'Hang on a minute, Ma', he said, and gave the handle of his destination board a few turns. 'Try that now, Ma', he suggested. This time she made it. She beamed at him. 'God bless yer, son. Nobody ever lowered a tram for me before!' That man was wasted on the trams. He could have made it on the stage.

A real boon for us children who rarely had two pennies to rub together were the old penny return tickets. They enabled us to make four journeys a day—distance no object, and we took full advantage of them during the long summer holidays. The most popular trips were to Woolton Woods and Calderstones Park. We always loved going there. With a few jam butties and a bottle of water we set off early in the morning and didn't return until dusk. To add to the fun we used to wait at the tram terminals for key imprints to be stamped on our arms by obliging conductors after they'd inserted their keys into the time clocks. And a boon for our elders were the trams in which they could post a letter late at night and be sure of delivery by first post next morning.

Our route to school took us through the narrow Lodge Lane, where there was only a single track with a short stretch of double track at the stops to enable the trams to pass each other. The tramlines swung in almost to the kerb. I seem to remember they were called 'pinches'. This system worked well on normal days, but during the 'pea-souper' fogs there were problems, and a safety system was essential to avoid collisions. A box was attached to the tram stop posts at these 'pinches', with a ring inside. If the driver was unable to see up to the next stop and the ring wasn't inside the box he had to wait for the oncoming tram to arrive, the driver of which would hand him the ring and he was able to proceed. This procedure in foggy weather inevitably caused delays and we were often late for school.

On one occasion a lorry driver tried to race a tram to the 'pinch', but he wasn't fast enough, and the tram scraped the whole length of his vehicle, causing extensive damage. In his accident report the lorry driver claimed that 'without any warning, the tram driver pulled over on me and caused the accident'!

The Great Tram Race took place in 1934. This was a thrilling battle fought out by speeding double-decker tramcars driven by the most ruthless drivers ever produced by the sport of tram racing. One reporter described the event vividly: 'I shall never forget that race—the four trams seemingly locked together, iron clashing and shrieking against iron, the drivers crouched over their controls, the conductors bracing themselves out from their platforms in an effort to add a tiny last ounce of stability, the sparks burning from the trolley poles, the air full of the ozone smell that was uniquely tram-racing's, the now hushed crowd. Nothing could match the excitement of these 'tall ships' swaying and lurching round the bends at thirty miles an hour'. It was all very thrilling and breathtaking. But, alas, this was just a figment of one writer's vivid imagination—an April Fools Day hoax— the tram race that never was! And yet there are still many people in Liverpool who read about that tremendous race and believe that it actually took place.

The Liverpool Echo once ran a competition called 'Poets Corner'. I thought one of the entries was particularly nostalgic and descriptive. The poem went like this:—

'I remember that old tram that was my boyish delight,
To school within we'd tightly cram, and home again at night.
The open front of upper deck was always prized position,
To face the winds that tried to wreck our scribbled
        imposition.
Along the gleaming, snaking rails our carriage boldly ran,
Regardless of the fog and gales, as no other transport can.
With clanging bells and shaking bones, we made a happy
        band.
'Pass down the car!' the conductors yell, 'There's room
        on top for four!'
And, 'Hold tight, please!' he yanked the bell, then off
        we'd go once more.

What pleasure those old tramcars gave—the monsters of the
  track,
For children who would even crave to ride the giant's back'.
Which nicely sums up my own journeys to and from school by
tram. Many were the times I hastily scribbled out my hundred
lines imposition on the No. 27 tram.

There was disaster on January 3rd, 1934. When passengers
boarded tram No. 181 on its way to Liverpool city centre they
little knew they were on a journey to tragedy. For the tram, with
35 people on board, ended up on its side at the bottom of
Paddington Hill. Three died and many were seriously injured.
It was the worst tram disaster that Liverpool had ever known.
The tram was on the No. 4 (Wavertree) route. As it travelled down
the steep hill at Paddington, round about mid-day, it collided
with a horse and cart. It left the rails just before the corner of
Crown Street, turned across the road, struck the kerb of the
pavement and overturned, blocking the entrance of a grocer's
shop. It crashed into the milk-float, knocking the horse over and
sending milk bottles all over the street.

The final disappearance of trams from Liverpool's streets was
hastened by the worst fire in Britain's tramway history. It
happened at the Green Lane sheds on November 7th, 1947, and
it destroyed 66 trams. But its effect was decisive in speeding up
the bus era. The fire started with an electrical fault on tram No.
295 at 2.50 a.m., and spread rapidly as the flames eagerly engulfed
the wooden cleaning stages and the roof. Night staff drove
fourteen cars to safety, but then the current had to be cut, to
enable firemen to use their hoses. Other towns quickly offered
assistance, including Blackpool and Belfast. It was refused, and
a slight difference in track gauge and wheel profile was mentioned
but the real reason for the refusal was that the Corporation had
already made up its mind that it wanted buses. One alderman
was heard to say that the fire had been a blessing in disguise.
A misguided opinion, in my view. Although rather noisy and
cumbersome, a modernised tramway service would go a long way
in solving some of the many problems besetting the passenger
transport set-up of today.

Chapter Four
Scouse, Spare Ribs and Spiceballs

It's a far cry from today's gigantic, unattractive supermarkets to the humble little shops and stores of pre-war days. Shopping in those days was something of a pleasure. 'Service with a smile' was the slogan, and the customer was always right. How very different from today's 'take it or leave it' attitude which, alas, is all too common. And there was none of the modern packaging of food that adds considerably to the price of things today.

When you purchased a quarter of tea it came straight out of the crate. Sugar was stored in large sacks, weighed on the old scales with their metal weights, and supplied in blue paper bags. The butter and margarine was on a large, white marble slab—a huge mound of it with a fancy pattern. It was slapped into shape with two wooden patters, which left a pattern of indentations on it. The dexterity of the assistant as she used those patters always fascinated me whenever I went to the Maypole or the T.S.B. Store. I presume the T.S.B. stood for tea, sugar and butter. Similarly, when you bought half a pound of cheese it was cut with a wire from a whole cheese. Hardly anything was pre-packaged. Unhygienic it might have been, but we managed to survive. I always looked forward to 'going on the messages' to our friendly little shops where there was always a welcoming smile, and the shop-keeper usually managed to produce a couple of biscuits for me. He knew my favourites—custard creams.

The little local dairy served the milk from great metal churns or from large milk cans, which were oval-shaped and had hinged lids. We used to collect the milk in our own jugs, and a long, iron measure was used, which disappeared into the churn to reappear with the lovely creamy milk. There was one measure for a pint and another for half a pint. Honesty compels me to confess that, after a few sips on the way home, there was rather less than full measure when I arrived.

Making your own bread was the regular thing for many folk. The dough, left to rise during the day, was taken to the public bakehouse by the youngsters of the family when they came home from school. They'd be given a tally, and the loaves would be collected later on that night. And how well we remember the delicious aroma of oven-baked bread—and how good they looked with their golden crusts. Today's bread seems so tasteless in comparison. And in winter, we kept warm by standing over the warm grid of the bakery cellar.

Typical Merseyside delicacies in bygone days included tripe and onions, pigs feet or 'trotters', cowheels, spice balls, and even sheeps' brains. A popular purchase for many families was a pig's cheek—sometimes even a pig's head, with the well-known request to the shop-keeper to leave the eyes in so that it could 'see us through the week'. I'm sure that little joke must have palled on him. A remarkable variety of tasty dishes could be served up from a pig's head, or a sheep's head, and they were very, very cheap.

A favourite Sunday dinner was stuffed, roast cows heart. But for many Merseysiders it wasn't Sunday morning without salt fish—indeed, Sunday without salt fish was akin to Christmas Day without turkey or plum-pudding. They were large, flat fish, so liberally salted that they were as hard as a board. And what a handy weapon! Bought on Saturday night, it's been said that many an errant pub-crawler arriving home late was swiped across the head by an indignant wife with one of those formidable salt fish.

For many, the most delicious dish of all was spare ribs and cabbage. The ribs, containing plenty of meat, could be bought for a few coppers—the cabbage for a penny. Cooked, as perhaps only Merseyside housewives could cook it, it was a meal fit for the gods. Even today, when I discuss the favourite dishes of bygone years, someone will give a sigh and say: 'You can keep all your fancy meals. Just give me a plate of spare ribs and cabbage just like mother used to make'.

I need hardly say that Liverpool's most famous dish was scouse—lovely thick scouse as only Liverpudlians could make it. Need I add that it was a kind of thick stew made with potatoes, meat and vegetables—'pot herbs' possibly—all boiled together and allowed to simmer until it was thick and tasty and beautiful. It was even better with the addition of dumplings—or 'dough-boys' as we used to call them. 'Blind Scouse' was the humorous Liverpool term for the same thing, but without any meat. On a cold winter's day, arriving home from school freezing and hungry, what a glorious sight to see on the table a large plate of steaming, appetising scouse.

Some people loved cowheels, which could also be made into a tasty meal. Here, from the 30s, is one recipe for stewed cowheel:—'The ingredients are—one cowheel, one ounce of butter or margarine, one ounce of flour, one teaspoonful of chopped parsley, half a lemon, salt and pepper to taste, and four rashers of bacon if you wish. This makes enough for four people, and it should be cooked at a low temperature for about four hours. Cleanse and scald the heel and cut into four, putting the pieces in a saucepan, covering them with cold water, and simmering them gently until they are tender. Remove them and season the broth with the salt and pepper. Make a paste of the flour and butter, stir it in, and go on stirring until the mixture has boiled for five minutes. Add parsley and gradually the juice from half a lemon. Remove the bones from the meat and put the meat into the sauce. Heat until very hot, then serve. The rashers of bacon should be fried. They go very well with this dish'. Yes indeed, another dish fit to place before a king.

How well I remember coming home from school, being handed a jug and a few coppers, and told to go to the local cook shop for half a dozen spiceballs. They were the equivalent of today's 'savoury ducks'—in appearance, that is, but not in taste. None of today's products could get anywhere near the delicious taste of those pre-war spiceballs. On leaving the house, jug and money in hand, the final instruction would be: 'And tell them not to forget the gravy'. This was important as the gravy was just as delicious as the spiceballs themselves.

Unlike the supper bars and 'take-away' establishments of today they were just 'chip shops' in my childhood days, and sold only chips, fish, peas, and 'scallops'—sliced potatoes fried in fat, with batter. We obtained a goodly portion of chips for a penny in those days. Two penn'orth provided a meal for half a dozen hungry children. A twopenny fish was always a luxury, but it was always a massive one. Many a workman's favourite 'carrying out' was a package of chip butties. A common order at the chip shops was 'a penn'orth of chips with plenty of salt and vinegar, and a ha'porth of mushy peas'. So for a penny-ha'penny we could obtain a quite satisfying meal. We weren't choosy in those days. We couldn't afford to be.

And who could ever forget those famous 'Wet Nellies'? Or, to give them their more dignified title—Nelson Cakes. In a way they resembled Chester Cakes, but were much bigger. The central layer consisted of stale bunloaf, soaked in treacle, and as hard as a rock, but when they were exposed to the sun in the shop window, the treacle would melt and run down the sides of the heap of Wet Nellies until the bottom layer was soaked in treacle. Thus, when you bought them you always asked for them to be taken from the bottom. The wettest 'Wet Nellies' were always on the bottom of the pile. Old customers of such pre-war cocoa rooms as Stan Waters, and Thorn's, used to order a large mug of tea and—not a Wet Nellie but a 'Wet Nella'.

In the old days, many working men never realised what penny-pinching wives dished them up for dinner—out of sheer necessity. One Liverpool shop assistant said she used to have a stack of orders for two-penn'orth of catfish, and she knew wery well it was for their husband's dinner. The pudding was usually boiled rice covered with syrup, or a substantial bread pudding with plenty of dried fruit in it. I always preferred my rice pudding baked in the oven with evaporated milk. It was really scrumptious, and we used to take turns in having the delicious brown skin on the top.

A distant relation of Wet Nellies was the 'pudding cake' on sale in many of the cheaper shops—even in sweet and general shops—for a ha'penny. Pudding cakes were, I surmise, a mixture of stale bread and left-over cakes—made moist by the addition of syrup or treacle, and baked into hefty, soggy squares of pudding. Two of these pudding cakes were enough to sink a battleship, I know of one person who used to eat four of them in one go. If he'd been foolish enough to go swimming just afterwards, he'd have immediately sunk to the bottom of the bath like a stone.

Glancing back at food prices in the 1930s, it's rather revealing that for a whole decade New Zealand butter remained at around 1/- a pound, and lard 6d a lb. Margarine could be bought for around 6d a pound—in fact 'Pier Head' margarine in 1939 was only 4d a pound. Self-raising flour was 2d a pound and tea 10d a lb. Fry's and Cadbury's chocolate was 2d for a two-ounce block. Bourneville cocoa was 6d for a quarter-pound tin, and mincemeat cost 6½d a jar. If you shopped around you could buy a 2lb. jar of plum and apple jam for 4½d. And why not? To the many hungry children of the 30s plum and apple jam butties were just fine. Furthermore, if you took the empty jar back to the shop you got a ha'penny or a penny on it. It sounds incredible now, doesn't it, but that's how many of us got our picture money— by taking empty jamjars back.

What sounds even more incredible is that there was one period in the golden age of silent films and the children's Saturday afternoon matinee when, at one Liverpool cinema, you could gain admittance for a couple of jamjars. But all traces of the plum and apple jam had to be removed first. Consequently it was common to see queues of youngsters outside the picture palace, armed with a couple of jamjars, busily engaged in removing all traces of jam by the simple expedient of wiping sticky fingers all round the inside of the jar and transferring them to their mouths. 'Sweet' memories!

Some more prices—in 1939 milk was 6d a quart, sugar 2½d a pound, eggs 2/- a dozen—a penny each for the smaller ones—a four-pound loaf 9d, cheese 10¾d a pound, bacon 1/3¼d a pound, potatoes 7 pounds for 3½d, cereals 7½d for a large carton, and sweets 2d and 4d a quarter pound, depending on the quality. Oh yes, the farthing was a popular and much-used coin in those days. Bent's ale was 2½d for half a pint of mild and bitter. You could enjoy Digger flake tobacco at 2/- for a quarter pound. Wills' Gold Bar tobacco was 1/- an ounce. Club, Woodbine and Players Weights cigarettes cost you 2d for five, and Players Navy Cut cigarettes and similar brands were ten for sixpence. Incidentally, on October 1st, 1938, there appeared this warning in the Daily Herald: 'Unless there is a reduction in the price of flour, the price of bread will be raised on Monday week, October 10th, from 8d to 8½d for a four-pound loaf'. A rise of a whole ha'penny on a four-pound loaf. Whatever next? Galloping inflation with a vengeance!

In 1930, a tick was found by a purchaser in a pound of butter. He sent it to the Natural History Museum and it was there pronounced as a kind of tick 'entirely unknown in Europe, and clearly of Asiatic origin'. It caused such a furore that questions were asked in Parliament about the matter, and indignant letters appeared in the Press.

It's interesting to recall that after the Munich agreement had been announced in 1938, and the immediate crisis over, there was a news item about food hoarders—'The people who have been rushing around from shop to shop for several days, ordering stocks of food, are sorry now they were so selfish. All day yesterday, all over Britain, they were hurrying again from shop to shop, trying to return food they had bought. Those who have made extensive and unreasonable purchases of perishable provisions deserve no sympathy'. And the secretary of the Retail Distributors Association said: 'They may atone for their unpatriotic action by giving the food at once to hospitals and charitable relief organisations'. A worthy suggestion, but I wonder how many were killed in the rush? We'll always have our food hoarders.

The Budget of 1938 makes interesting reading when compared to the efforts of successive Chancellors of the Exchequer in modern times. It pushed up prices of premium petrol to 1/7½d a gallon. But the biggest shock was when income tax was increased by 6d to 5/6d in the pound. Only once had it been higher—from 1918 to 1922 when it was 6/-. And yet the cost of living throughout the 30s remained remarkably static. Unlike today, you could put money in the bank in 1930 and you could feel secure in the knowledge that it would not depreciate before the end of the decade. It was indicative of the steadiness in prices in the 30s when cigarettes were twenty for a shilling in 1930 and exactly the same in 1939—cheaper if you used the cut-price shops. A day return from Liverpool to London was 10/6d throughout the decade. The trip by North Wales steamers from Liverpool to Llandudno was 6/-, and it was still 6/- eight years later. Many prices even fell, and the price of a pint of mild in 1939 was still only 5d.

So there's little doubt that housewives of today who can remember the 30s look back to that decade as the time when prices rarely altered from one year to the next. In spite of low wages, high unemployment, there are many who will claim that the 30s were the good old days when money seemed to go a good deal further. Package holidays were available for £1 a day—the S.S. Doric cruise to the Mediterranean in 1933 was twelve days for £12, and in 1936 an eight-day tour of Belgium was £8—all in. Nine days in Switzerland cost £8/12/6d.

With regard to houses, I can quote an advert in a 1938 newspaper for a new three-bedroomed house, with two large living rooms, a separate kitchenette and bathroom—price £435 freehold, or £20 deposit and 11/6d weekly. Or, if you preferred a detached three-bedroomed bungalow with garden and garage, you had to go up to £550. If you wanted to rent a modern furnished bungalow there were plenty to be had for two guineas a week.

Houses and flats to let were advertised in large numbers every night in the Liverpool Echo in the 30s. Taking one at random, I notice that flats were being let in Sefton Park in 1930 for 19/6d a week. Five years later, Princes Park flats were going for 16/- a week, and in 1939 unfurnished flats in West Kirby were 17/6d a week. Houses were on sale in West Derby for £445 in 1935, and in 1938 private houses in Roby and West Derby were rented for 15/6d a week. In one 'Echo' just before the war there was the advert: 'Four semi-detached houses in the Ormskirk district—all modern conveniences—on main bus route—decorated to suit—13/- a week clear'. And in Maghull, near the Dodds Lane bus stop: 'Semi-detached villas—Low Rental including water rate—12/6d a week'. If you wanted to buy a bungalow in Heswall there was one near the shore with mains drainage, electric and water—yours for £100.

The full page furniture adverts offered: 'Four foot figured oak bedroom suite comprising four-foot wardrobe fitted with rods and sliding hooks, three-foot triple mirror dressing table with three spacious drawers, and 2 ft 6 in. three-drawer chest—beautifully finished—£8/15/0d. Free with £30 orders—handsome figured oak sideboard. With £20 orders—luxurious well-sprung easy chair. And with £10 orders—figured oak 24-piece canteen of Sheffield-made cutlery.'

Of course, as I've said, folk didn't earn big wages by today's standards. But a little seemed to go a long way. Food, fuel, clothes and rents were reasonably priced. Continental holidays were strictly for the minority, but bus, train and boat excursions to the sea and country were cheap. It was only 2d to Seacombe Sands on the ferry. My regular evening trips on the Overhead Railway from Dingle Station all the way to Seaforth Sands cost me 2d return. If you lived in Seaforth a return trip to Skelhorne Street by Ribble bus cost you 7d.

The humble penny would buy a large portion of chipped potatoes, a bottle of lemonade or ginger ale, two ounces of sweets, three Crayol cigarettes, a large ice-cream, a long ride on the tram, and the Liverpool Echo, Evening Express or Daily Post. A penny stamp would take a letter anywhere in the United Kingdom.

Sixpence or a 'tanner', would buy ten top quality cigarettes, or five Woodbines with twopence change, a pint of best beer with a penny change—and, what's more, the beer seemed to taste much stronger in those days. You could get into the Boys' pen at Anfield or Goodison Park and also have your return tram fare. Sixpence would get you a really classy haircut, or a modest seat in the 'gods' at the Empire Theatre. And you'll remember with a nostalgic sigh the famous Woolworth slogan—'Nothing over Sixpence'.

On King George VI's Coronation Day, a tanner bought a meal of cod and chips in the big Woolworth's restaurant in Church Street. Customers were invited to choose from a menu of more than a hundred different dishes, including fresh salmon, lobster salad, roast beef and Yorkshire pudding, baked gammon, and steaks, followed by steamed treacle sponge with egg custard, or something similar from a large selection of ices, cakes and fruit. All for sixpence. And tea was a penny a cup. If you were lucky enough to have ten shillings to spare you could buy one of those ten-shilling L.M.S. Holiday Contract tickets, and enjoy a week's tour, by rail, of North Wales and other places. Merseysiders used to travel to North Wales on a monthly return ticket which cost a penny a mile. What's more, you could travel by any train you wished, and break your journey anywhere along the route. When you reached your destination—say Colwyn Bay or Llandudno, you paid ten bob for your Holiday Runabout Ticket which gave you the freedom of the line for a whole week. You travelled where you pleased, and as often as you wished, with no restrictions.

An evening excursion to Morecambe Bay or Rhyl from Liverpool cost 2/1d return, Blackpool 1/10d, and Wigan 1/1d. A holiday apartment in Douglas, Isle of Man, would cost you only five shillings a day full board. If you wished to travel a little further you could have eight days in the Isle of Wight for £4/18s. Blackpool, as always, was a popular holiday resort, but it was becoming so crowded in the 30s that the House of Commons were actually debating the problems of crowds so dense that, in the words of one M.P.—'you could walk on their heads'.

Tea dances were all the rage in the 30s, so, to dance to the music of one of our local dance bands over a nice pot of tea and a plate of buttered scones, you ladies might have worn an ankle-length softly-clinging, long-sleeved tea gown for which you might have paid 39/11d. They were the days when you never went anywhere without a hat, and they were all shapes and styles, and usually worn at an acute angle. The fully-fashioned stockings you wore cost you 3/11d the pair, but if you'd taken the trouble to queue up at the many sales, you'd have got them for 8½d the pair.

A handbill of the early 30s shows some startling prices—large Turkish towels at the amazingly low price of 4½d each, pillow cases at 3¾d, table-cloths at 1/0½d, and innumerable other bargains. One of the kitchen novelties of those years was the whistling kettle, and the price of this remained a static 1/3d, year in, year out. Even the price of cars remained steady. Ford, Morris, Austin and Vauxhall all managed to keep their prices on an even keel right through the decade. For example, the highly popular Baby Ford was launched in 1932 at a price of £120. By July, 1937, the price

had actually fallen to a mere £105. This was a wonderful little car—
8 h.p. and did 62 miles per hour.

There was consternation in the wash-house in 1939 when those
big galvanised dolly tubs went up from 4/9d—the price they'd
remained since 1930—to 4/11d, an increase of two whole pence,
old pence at that, in almost ten years. And it must be remembered
that in those days there were 240 pennies to the pound. When you
got a rise in those days, and it wasn't automatic every year as it's
expected to be now, it came in shillings, and often, in the case of
office boys and such like, even in pennies. I remember how I
gleefully welcomed a sixpence a week rise when my birthday came
around.

By today's standards, things seemed to be ridiculously cheap,
but, even so, many of the necessities of life were beyond the reach
of the very poor. Unemployed men lounging on street corners, or
playing pitch and toss with the few ha'pennies they could muster,
were an all too common sight. There were many debates in the
House of Commons on the dole, and many of the greedy bosses
argued that holidays with pay would be absolutely ruinous for
industry. The N.U.R. fought desperately for a minimum wage of
three pounds a week. So it's perfectly obvious that price
comparisons, though interesting, are rather meaningless. However,
one of the things that could be argued in favour of the hungry 30s
was that Mr. Rising Price was almost unknown.

What a delightful shop Coopers in Church Street used to be.
I felt a deep pang of regret when it closed down some years ago.
They used to advertise in the newspapers: 'Where shall I get it?
When something out of the ordinary in food is wanted and you
consult your friend as the best place to buy it, the answer will
invariably be—get it at Coopers. Everything rare and exclusive
is almost always in stock. If not, and it is procurable from any
known source, neither time, trouble, nor expense is spared in
securing it. We mention this not in any self-lauding spirit, but to
let you know that Coopers service goes far beyond what is the
ordinary conception of serving a customer'.

Which was all very true. As a boy I used to love going on errands
there, if only to see the section with the singing canaries and to
savour the delicious aroma of freshly-ground coffee. That lovely
smell always pervaded Coopers. Whenever I was in town I always
crossed over to savour its delight. What used to fascinate me were
those little metal money-boxes which were slung across the store
on overhead wires. You paid your ten-bob note, which the assistant

placed in the box with the bill—she pulled a handle and the box zoomed along the wire to the cash office high up in the corner, and you waited for it to come zooming back with your change and stamped receipt.

Customers at Coopers were given the red carpet treatment before the war. Shopping was carried out to their cars by assistants, page boys were stationed on all the doors to lend a hand with the heavy parcels, and chairs were provided at all the counters. Delivery of the weekly shopping by Coopers special van was commonplace. Some people would get the most ridiculous things delivered—like a cod's head or two penn'orth of cats meat, according to Miss Florence Nightingale, the former welfare and personnel officer. Usually, orders were given by phone, and one woman in a very posh voice asked for 'two nice larm chops', and had two alarms clocks sent her. And there was the person who ordered two ducklings and ended up with two dustbins on her doorstep. That was Coopers in the 1930s. Now the unrelenting march of 'progress' has given us 'Supermarkets'. I've nothing against supermarkets personally but it was places like Coopers that were 'super'.

And just one more memory of that delightful store. I used to earn, and 'earn' is the operative word, twopence a week pocket money for doing the Saturday morning messages for a strange little woman who lived just round the corner from our house. This included, to my acute embarrassment, a surreptitious visit to the pawnshop to redeem a bundle of clothes, a trip down to Crane's in Hanover Street to pay her weekly instalment of a shilling on the piano she couldn't afford, and then from Crane's to Coopers for 'three penn'orth of bits of bacon'. Now that was a real bargain, for the 'three penn'orth' consisted of a nice, fat parcel of tasty pieces of bacon that must have lasted her through the week. She'd obviously been enjoying this privilege for years as I was instructed to say: 'Three penn'orth of bits of bacon, please, for Mrs. So-and-so'.

A most welcome event in Liverpool in the 30s was when the famous 'Fifty Shilling Tailors' hit town. They did a roaring trade, as, for fifty shillings, you got a brand-new good quality suit. In addition, and without any extra cost, you received an extra pair of trousers free of charge. It was exceptional value and there must be thousands of Merseysiders who sported one of those 'fifty bob' suits. It surely won't be long before someone else, feeling they're giving excellent value for money, opens a similar chain of shops.

39

Unfortunately, it won't be the 'Fifty Shilling Tailors' but the 'Fifty Pounds Tailors'. And I'll wager they won't be offering a free pair of trousers.

Chapter Five
They all Deserved a Medal

Most women have more than enough household chores to get through today even with the latest and most expensive appliances. And yet they should consider themselves lucky compared with the enormous amount of work housewives were obliged to do in the old days. Incidentally, I often wonder why we call them 'housewives'. 'House slaves' would have been a more fitting description in the 20s and 30s.

I can remember my mother going through the morning ritual of cleaning and polishing the fire irons, as they were called. First of all the fire-grate and surroundings were beautifully blackleaded, then the hearth carefully whitened with a large lump of chalkstone dipped in water, and the huge brass fender polished like a mirror with emery paper and brasso. The same with the hearth companion set which contained the poker, tongs, etc.

Also blackleaded were iron figures of animals and little funny men that used to clutter up the hearth, and the oven door and the hob. Even the great iron kettle, which was boiled on the open fire, was cleaned and then carefully polished with blacklead. The more well-to-do folk boasted beautiful copper kettles. There was a sort of ledge appliance which could be fixed on to the top bar of the fireplace on which the kettle rested when it had boiled. The teapot was on the hob right next to the fire, so there was an awful lot of stewed tea in those days, as those hobs were very hot. Hence the expression—'as hot as the hobs of hell'.

All the baking was done in the oven next to the fire. The hot coals could be raked underneath the oven to make it even hotter. Often, the hot shelves of the oven, covered with newspaper, were taken to bed to keep people's feet warm. I can recall going along to the chandler's shop for a large chunk of chalkstone for the hearth. These chores alone occupied the best part of the morning, let alone the daily scrubbing of floors and stairs. Carpets were too much of a luxury for the poorer people, and it was either bare boards or very cheap linoleum.

Another daily routine was the sandstoning of the front steps. Even in the worst slums of Merseyside most people took an immense pride in the outside appearance of their homes, and it was a regular custom to brighten the front steps with a lump of sandstone moistened in water. This always left a clean, pleasant appearance. Like the chalkstone, you could buy a lump of sandstone for a ha'penny or a penny.

In those far-off days, when only the 'posh' folk could afford the luxury of electricity, gas mantles were essential, but they were so fragile that they didn't last very long. When you went to the shop you were asked whether you wanted a tall upright mantle or a small reverse one. The bigger mantles were for the main light in the centre of the ceiling, and the smaller ones for the wall lights. Those incandescent mantles were made of silk, and, when you fitted a new one you had to set fire to it. It flared up in a bright bluish flame and would then settle down to give off a bright, warm glow. They quickly developed holes through which the flame would flare out so it was time to buy a new one.

Many homes, especially those in the notorious old 'courts' of Merseyside, couldn't even boast gas-light, and in others the gas supply didn't extend to the bedrooms, so paraffin lamps and candles had to be utilised. It comes as a bit of a shock to recall that you could usually buy your pint of paraffin oil from the little corner general shop, which sold food, sweets, and practically everything under the sun, and very often the large paraffin tank with its tap stood right next to the open trays of bread, cakes and other uncovered edibles. There was a great deal of sickness in those days especially among children, and is it any wonder?

Wallpapering in bygone days, especially the 'do it yourself' variety, wasn't exactly 'a thing of beauty and joy for ever'. Very often the new paper was pasted over the original, and it wasn't unusual for there to be four or five layers on the old walls. At least this thick layer of wallpaper carefully hid the large cracks in the walls, and it was often said that in the worst slums of Merseyside it helped to keep the bugs firmly in their holes. Bugs were the 'bug-bear' of many of the slum houses, and it was common for local council workmen to come along and smoke the unwelcome creatures out.

But back to wallpapering. The paste was usually made out of flour and water, and when the paper was up the wrinkles and bubbles were very much in evidence. Possibly the most surprising thing of all was that in the days of the massive old 'dressers' and other heavy furniture, the paper was hung around these objects. They were too heavy to move. Why waste good wallpaper, some argued, by pulling away these heavy items of furniture which stood in the same place for a lifetime? Perhaps the argument had some merit. And let it be whispered that in one particular house I used to visit, which displayed a massive oak-framed 'Stag at Bay' picture above the mantelpiece, the occupier had pasted the paper all round the picture. Economy was the by-word in the 20s and 30s.

A few years ago, rag and bone men pretended they were doing you a favour by taking away, free of charge, your old iron bedstead, with knobs on. Now they're in demand as antiques, and there's a steady market for them. Apparently it's rather trendy to own one of those old relics now, and some of them are fetching quite a lot of money. Those brass knobs could be unscrewed, of course, and I remember using them as a hiding place for little items I wished to conceal. Slumbering in my old iron bed, fifty years ago, I never realised that in the 1980s it might become a trend-setter and a status symbol. On this subject, I also remember the occasion when we bought a new portable gramophone and threw away our horned gramophone which had served us well for many years, and was still in good condition. I wish I had it now, for they, too, are fetching enormous prices. It all goes to show that you should never throw away anything that's likely to become a valuable antique in years to come.

The public wash-houses were a boon to the busy housewife, when the possession of an electric washing machine and a spin drier was just an impossible dream. If they couldn't be bothered going to the wash-house, the boiling of the clothes and bed linen, etc., had to be done in a large copper boiler, either in the cellar or in the back yard. Most old houses had a bricked-in boiler with a small fireplace underneath, and I've known them to be used also for boiling the massive Christmas puddings of those days.

The washing was thoroughly scrubbed on an old table, then put in the galvanised dolly tub and then pummelled around with one of those large, wooden, peculiar-looking dolly pegs. After which it would be wrung through an enormous old mangle with two heavy wooden rollers. There was an iron screw on top of the mangle for tightening or loosening the rollers, and a heavy iron wheel at the side for turning them. That in itself must have been sheer hard labour, but most of the hardy womenfolk of Merseyside in pre-war days were fully equal to the task.

Public wash-houses were scattered all over Merseyside, and it was common to witness weary, red-faced women lugging their huge baskets of washing through the streets, or bundling them on to a tramcar, after a few hours energetically scrubbing and mangling in the wash-house. There were no such things as launderettes. Even the old flat-iron had to be heated by jamming it between two bars of the firegrate. Some women today complain about the extent of their household chores, but it seems a mystery how those mums of the 20s and 30s got through their heavy day's housework without the aid of any of the modern labour-saving devices. They all deserved the O.B.E.

Even Saturday night wasn't free. For that was bath night. With no bathroom or adequate facilities this created problems, especially with a large family. The usual procedure was to boil large pans of water on the kitchen fire and pour it into a large, galvanised bath or tub which was set in front of the fire. Each child took its turn—the water continually being topped up from the pans. There was no such luxury as scented soap—it was a large block of carbolic, and there were cries of anguish as it got into the eyes. After five or six youngsters had had their bath in the same water, it became pretty slimy, to say the least. One half of Merseyside never knew how the other half lived.

Chapter Six

'We've got Hens in our Backyard'

Although only a permanently hungry, ill-clad youngster in the so-called 'Roaring Twenties', I was always keenly interested in and aware of events that occurred in my own environment, in the country and in the world at large. I used to 'devour' the Liverpool Echo, which cost a penny in those days—surely the finest provincial evening newspaper in the country. I always read it from cover to cover after my parents had finished with it. On Saturdays I'd spend a couple of hours in the public library, reading as many of the national daily newspapers I could lay my hands on, after the 'old codgers', as we disrespectfully called them, and who spent most of their lives sitting in the public library reading rooms, had read them. I was a great reader.

One thing I distinctly remember—the libraries always made a point of blacking out the horse-racing forecasts, and the results of the previous day's meetings. Not that I had the remotest interest in that sort of thing, except for the Grand National. Strangely enough, my main interest, apart from sport, but excluding racing, was politics, and even at that tender age I had very forthright views on what I considered to be the party that worked in the best interests of Britain. I could always rattle off without hesitation the names of the members of the Cabinet and the posts they occupied which is more than I could do now. I had a fierce pride in being British, and I used to marvel how such a small nation could have gained such a vast Empire. I was also interested in local politics and our local political leaders, but that was long before their antics gained Liverpool the unflattering nickname of 'Toytown'.

Sport had an enormous attraction for me, and my heroes were Malcolm Campbell, the racing driver; Walter Hammond, the Gloucestershire and England cricketer and most cavalier of batsmen; and Elisha Scott, the goal-keeper, and one of Liverpool F.C.'s immortals. Scott had the agility and reflexes of a cat, but, at that time he was approaching the end of his illustrious career. I also had a great admiration for his equally brilliant rival across the park—the immortal Dixie Dean who, to me, is the finest player British soccer ever produced. Scott and Dean were friends off the field, but deadly rivals on it, and some choice language was exchanged between the two during the local 'derby' matches. The story's told on innumerable occasions of the day Elisha passed Dixie in Bold Street, when Dean nodded in recognition and Scott dived through a shop window. Completely untrue, of course, but indicative of the immense respect a legendary goalkeeper always has for an equally legendary centre-forward.

The 1920s were the days of the 'flapper'. I'd heard the word often, but I wasn't sure what it meant. It was only in later years that I learned that a 'flapper' was one of the ultra-modern, high-spirited young ladies who, after a long and bitter war, and with a dire shortage of eligible young men, were determined to get as much fun as possible out of life. Consequently, many of them were wild, noisy, and at times positively outrageous in their behaviour. Their exploits, though innocent enough in the main, brought howls of protests from their elders. But some of the Oxford-bagged young men were more than willing to pander to their whims.

I remember reading in the newspapers of the eccentric behaviour of the so-called 'Bright Young Things'—their amazing 'Pyjama and Bottle Parties' and their zany 'scavenger hunts' in which they had to procure the most fantastic of objects. The papers gave them short shrift. I read about the notorious night club queen, Mrs. Meyrick, and her constant brushes with the law, of rich Americans pouring into Britain and buying up almost everything in sight, including ancestral homes, because they thought the 'old country' was finished, of the many eccentrics that only the 20s could have produced, and of the nightly wining and dining in London's posh clubs and restaurants. But as this kind of thing was only for the idle rich I never took much interest.

It was with more amusement than interest that I regarded the changes in women's hair styles—from long, flowing locks to the 'bob', 'shingle', 'Eton Crop' and even the 'Dartmoor Shave', the advent of long heels, and the frivolities of fashion when hemlines went up and down like yo-yos. As a healthy, normal schoolboy, I felt nothing but contempt for some of the foppish young men the 1920s produced, and I used to smile to myself when I turned the handle of our old gramophone and listened to the record by the famous Savoy Havana Band—'Masculine Women and Feminine Men'.

But what a revelation it was to read how 'the other half' lived. It was all such a far cry from the slums of Merseyside, where the proudest possession of many a woman was a shawl, where most boys and girls were clad in 'hand-me-downs' from older brothers and sisters, where all too many children were wearing the despised police clothes, where dad's Sunday suit, if he was fortunate enough to have one, lay for six days of the week on a dusty pawnbroker's shelf, and where there were only two hair styles for boys—cropped, with a fringe, and a 'tuppenny all off'.

More often than not the twopence wasn't available for a visit to the barber's shop, so dad became the barber, and that was quite an ordeal. The clippers were always blunt and pulled the hair out by the roots in clumps, evoking agonised howls and squeals from the unfortunate victim. The scissors were even blunter. The end result was very much like a coconut with a fringe. I never saw the proverbial basin being used, but I believe it was standard practice and even this was better than the 'tuppenny all off'.

The stylish young men of the 20s wore the ridiculously wide and flapping Oxford Bags, and straw hats which we in our part of Merseyside called 'Straw Cadies' or 'Straw Gussies', worn at a rakish angle most probably in imitation of Maurice Chevalier. I often wonder now why the mere sight of a man wearing plus fours always caused us boys such merriment. We always thought them highly comical, especially when worn by a very small man. Perhaps the magnificent socks that went with them had something to do with it.

In the tougher areas of Liverpool in the 20s it was as unlikely to see a policeman on his own as it is to see them in pairs on foot today. Painful experience necessitated them patrolling the streets in pairs and even in threes. They had to be as tough as nails, but most of them were kindly men who treated wayward youngsters as a responsible father would have treated a son. Any act of vandalism or having a sly smoke in the street meant a few painful belts from a heavy hand over a hefty knee. Swift justice but most effective, as I knew to my cost.

At the tender age of nine I decided it was time to sample my first cigarette—a Woodbine, given to me by a pal. After cadging a match from a passer-by I lit up and was puffing away merrily in Renshaw Street until I came face to face with a burly policeman who towered above me. They seemed to be much more beefy and hefty in those days. I nearly swallowed what was left of my Woodbine.

Assuming his sternest expression, he demanded my name and address. He then removed his heavy leather belt, unceremoniously pulled me over his knee and proceeded to hammer all the dust from my trousers. After which he warned me not to smoke again, or else if he caught me, he'd escort me home to face my father. That would have been far worse! It was a good lesson well learned. That was my first cigarette—and my last for a good many years. And I certainly did not grow up with a chip on my shoulder in regard to policemen. Those Liverpool bobbies were among the finest in the world. They probably still are, but they don't seem so awe-inspiring to children nowadays. I often think that the short, sharp punishment meted out to me when I was nine years old might well be used today with immense benefit to society.

One of my biggest pleasures as a child was watching the May Day parade along Princes Boulevard. The beautifully decorated horses and wagons were a joy to behold, and there was a wonderful sense of competition between different firms to win the coveted first prize for the best decorated horse and cart. There was also the Bootle Horse Parade—a gorgeous and thrilling event, never to be forgotten. Hundreds of the most magnificent horses bedecked with plumes and garlands of flowers, their brasses polished and shining like gold, would pass along drawing magnificently decorated wagons depicting scenes and tableaux of every description.

I can't, in all honesty, claim to remember very much about the General Strike of 1926. I was a young boy, and as my family and all our neighbours were already deprived, it must have had little effect on our daily lives, or our standard of living. The one thing I remember clearly was the coal shortage, and that's only because I was sent with a bucket to our local coalyard for six pennyworth of coal dust. That's all there was to be had, but it was as precious as gold dust at the time. I've since learned that the nation was as close to civil war as we've been for hundreds of years.

The strike had a dramatic effect on Liverpool. Rigid and inflexible attitudes were adopted on both sides. Shortly after it was realised the workers meant business a woman called at Liverpool Town Hall to offer her services as a driver. This was in response to an appeal for people to man essential services, and she was the first of the volunteers. She was quickly followed by others, and very soon the queue stretched round the Town Hall to Exchange Flags. Among them were 150 students from Liverpool University. Special constables were enlisted at the rate of 50 an hour, and many people offered their cars and motor-cycles to the authorities. By the end of the strike, more than 20,000 people had offered their services in Liverpool alone.

There was great hardship—coal, gas and electricity rationing, no newspapers, a skeleton transport system manned by volunteers, and great difficulty in buying food. So serious did the situation become that troops were landed at the Pier Head, and two battleships entered the Mersey. And yet there was humour to be found even during such a grave crisis. There were many frivolous posters and notices, such as one on a bus, manned by volunteers, of course—'To stop bus, ring conductor's neck once!'.

Elections were far more fun in those days, and the election meetings and rallies were always crammed to the doors with people cheering and jeering, heckling and counter-heckling. During the campaigns we children used to march behind makeshift bands, using bin lids, old biscuit tins and all sorts of things to make a noise, waving printed slogans given to us by the local party officials, and singing 'Vote, vote, vote for Mr. Swindells', and ending up by throwing an effigy of the candidate we didn't approve of into Brunswick Dock. Talking of effigies, I often wonder whether the south-end of Liverpool was the only place where the ceremonial burning of Judas took place on Good Friday. A bonfire was lit and 'Judas' was consigned to the flames.

'We've got hens in our back yard—we feed them on Indian corn'. So went the lines of the old song. And it was particularly true of certain parts of Merseyside where it was considered 'the thing' to keep hens in the back yard. They were kept in a pen against the wall and allowed the freedom of the yard on occasions. The hens were pretty scruffy, and decidedly smelly and noisy. Many neighbours objected. The old cockerel ruled the roost in no uncertain way. How well I remember visiting a pal whose family kept hens, and whenever I opened the back door the cock immediately flew at me with evil intent. And how people used to curse those cocks with their early morning symphony, especially on Sundays. There were four hens at this particular house—Henrietta, Harriet, Hilda and Hannah. I think the unfortunate Harriet was the first to go, ending up on the dinner table one Sunday. I hope she didn't taste as tough as she looked.

A strange thing happened in Liverpool on July 7th, 1926. Some children reported seeing 'ghost pictures' on the windows of Harrington School, in Stanhope Street. During the evening, vast crowds gathered round the school staring up at the windows. Imaginations began to run riot and one woman claimed she could distinctly see the figure of Christ carrying the cross, and the crowds didn't disperse until the next morning after claiming to see more 'ghost' pictures. It was left to the headmaster to dispel the rumours when he explained that the window-glass had previously been used as shop windows, with traces of the coloured adverts still remaining, which, for some reason, had become more distinct on that particular day. It caused a lot of excitement at the time, and many people were rather disappointed at such a logical explanation. I think they were far more superstitious in those days.

One of the sights that used to fascinate us children some fifty years ago was the resurfacing of roads. It was the steam-rollers that attracted us. Approximately every thirty yards or so there'd be a huge pile of gravel on the pavement. Along came a gas-tar boiler drawn by a horse—no gleaming harness for this job—and one of the workmen would operate a large handle that let flow a stream of hot tar which was quickly spread over half the width of the road. The rest of the workers then took over with their heavy shovels, spreading the gravel over the tar, followed by an enormous steam-roller to roll it flat. How we loved to watch those steam-rollers at work, levelling off the gravel and tar. But that sort of road surface used to play havoc with our bicycle tyres.

On many occasions we used to see gypsies passing through the streets in their beautifully-painted caravans with four very large wheels. The caravans had a rounded top similar to the Wild West type we used to see so often in cowboy films, and were drawn by a pony. Sometimes a team of six caravans would form a trail, their cooking utensils lashed to the rear of the 'vans', tinkling away and creating their own type of 'music'. A few days later, the gypsies would call at all our houses plying their wares of clothes pegs, boot-laces, and artificial flowers. Those picturesque gypsy caravans were always a pleasant sight, and they conjured up ideas of a romantic life which just did not exist. On the contrary, it must have been a very tough life for most of them.

I know that many people won't agree with me, but I'll always maintain that the decline and fall of the British Empire was a great tragedy for Britain, and for the world. It seems to me that everyone's entitled to be patriotic except we British. At school, in the 20s and 30s, we celebrated Empire Day in a big way. The Scouts, Girl Guides and Boys Brigade all wore their uniforms. The playground was decorated with flags and bunting, and it was a colourful scene of red, white and blue. After morning assembly we all marched into the playground, weather permitting, where there was a pageant of boys and girls dressed in the national costumes of the various countries of the Empire. We sang all the patriotic songs including 'Land of Hope and Glory' and the National Anthem as the Union Jack was unfurled. A half-day holiday followed. And it always seemed to be sunny and warm on Empire Day. Jingoism? Nonsense! We were just proud to be British.

Chapter Seven
The Roaring Twenties

Quite a number of Liverpool women will recall the happy days enjoyed by them as members of the British Women's Temperance Association way back in the mid-20s. Meetings were held on Tuesday evenings at No. 92 Sheil Road. Deryck Guyler's mother was on the committee, and a Miss Dobson was secretary. At that time Deryck's parents owned the Green and Guyler jewellers shop in London Road. There were dances and concerts, tennis, and walks in Sheil Park and Newsham Park. Picnics at Knutsford and Pickmere Lake, with farmhouse teas, were arranged by this club at a charge of 4/6d. inclusive. Deryck Guyler was then only sixteen, and he and his friends would form a small band and play for the ladies at the club, which they used to dance to for one old penny, including tea and biscuits.

Birkenhead played host to a League of Nations when Arrowe Park was the place chosen for the World Jamboree to celebrate the 21st birthday of the Boy Scout movement in July/August, 1929. Forty thousand scouts from all over the world crammed into the park and in the surrounding countryside. They represented 42 nations from 71 different parts of the world, and it was officially opened by the Duke of Connaught. Unfortunately, to the discomfort of all concerned, the heavens opened—it rained nearly every day, and the camp soon became a quagmire.

Baden-Powell, the Chief Scout of the World, was there, of course, and the Prince of Wales, who spent a night under canvas, gave him a letter from King George V which conferred a peerage on him. The overseas scouts swarmed into Liverpool and elsewhere on sight-seeing trips, and they loved the ferry boats with their 1½d. return tickets. The Flanders-like mud failed to dampen the spirits of the scouts, and many solved the conditions by tying large bully-beef cans to their boots. Many friendships were made, and it must have been saddening for Lord Baden Powell of Gilwell when many of those friends were forced to fight against each other in the war that was to come just ten years later. I was a member of the 200th Liverpool Troop at the time, and I recall that we shared a camp with a Camberwell group from

London, next to the boys from Czecho-Slovakia. Right opposite us were the Dutch boys. It was a memorable occasion and hundreds of thousands of visitors poured into Arrowe Park during the Jamboree.

A year before the Jamboree a picturesque event took place in Liverpool. During the city's annual civic week in 1928 the opening event was a charming and symbolic ceremony founded on an old Venetian custom, intended to celebrate Liverpool's 'marriage' to the sea—the partner of her prosperity. A procession of civic leaders, with representatives of the church, the armed forces, shipping companies, and other interests, wended its way to the river front, where the Lord Mayor dropped a ring in the Mersey as a symbol of the 'marriage'. This was followed by an impressive and colourful symbolic pageant.

One great civic occasion, honoured by King George V and Queen Mary, was the consecration of the cathedral in 1924. The city was lavishly bedecked, £1,000 being voted by the City Council for civic decorations, and the city's businessmen contributed generous amounts of money for office, bank, and street decoration, including three miles of festoons at five shillings a yard. Their Majesties, in their progress to the consecration of the completed choir and east transept of the Cathedral, passed between tall pylons topped with golden crowns, festooned in white and gold, and later were seen by the huge crowds along streets with scarlet-draped barricades, buildings hidden behind scarlet hangings, and the largest flags that money could buy. Speeches, banqueting in the Town Hall, a review of the men of the 55th West Lancashire Division of the Territorial Army, mustered at Wavertree Playground, and a return to Knowsley's green peace and quiet, to be ready for the next day and to the Cathedral, this time for the dedication of a memorial transept.

As my school was just opposite the Cathedral, I decided to take a personal interest in this occasion, and I was determined to catch a glimpse of the royal procession. The trouble was that there was little chance of a small boy getting anywhere near, as the crowds along St. James's Road were particularly dense. However, where there's a will there's a way, and I wriggled my way through the legs of the people standing there and managed to reach a position at the front with my nose touching the draped barricades, just in time for the royal carriage to pass. It was my one and only glimpse of King George V and Queen Mary.

There were several royal visits to Merseyside during the 20s.

The Prince of Wales came in 1921 to unveil the war memorial in Liverpool Town Hall. Several informal visits were made to the Grand National, and these were always followed by lavish house parties at Knowsley Hall. Lord Derby was a past master in organising shows for his royal guests. One year he was able to show a film of the afternoon's Grand National, and, to suit all tastes, a fight between the great Georges Carpentier and an opponent, followed by a nature film. Reading about it in the newspapers the next morning, Merseyside folk were highly indignant. How could Lord Derby have subjected the royal ladies to such a demoralising spectacle as half-naked men battering each other in a boxing ring? However, the nature film of a duck's private life in the park lake had been suitably vetted. In order not to offend Princess Mary's modesty, the part showing the duck in the act of laying an egg was cut.

In 1926, York House, in Nile Street, which was sponsored by the Liverpool University Settlement, was officially opened by the Duke of York. As Nile Street was only a few yards from my school, we were escorted by our teachers to a suitable vantage spot, where we stood waving our tiny Union Jacks and cheering. York House was a boys' club which proved to be an enormous success in providing all sorts of healthy activities for the needy youngsters of the area. I have fond memories of playing some highly enjoyable games of basket-ball on the roof of York House, which was completely enclosed by wire mesh.

Then in July, 1927, Liverpool again exploded in colour as King George V and Queen Mary rode under triumphal arches in scarlet and gold, between red obelisks topped by gold lions—through Church Street and Lord Street with blue liver birds poised on tall aluminium obelisks, and golden crowns on ultramarine pillars— hundreds of children massed on flag-draped pyramids, and little girls firing volleys of coloured balloons, as their Majesties made their triumphal way for the grand opening of the new Gladstone Dock at Seaforth.

The Royal Family have always been popular on Merseyside, irrespective of race, creed or colour, and the people were saddened to hear of the death of Queen Alexandra on November 30th, 1925. The BBC gave the news at 7 p.m. and then closed down for half an hour when a studio service was broadcast. It then closed down again until 10 p.m. when that doyen of announcers, Stuart Hibberd, read the general news. That was the end of broadcasting for that day. The following night, T. P. O'Connor broadcast a talk about Queen Alexandra's life. This proved to be his one and only broadcast for he died very soon after.

On the brighter side, Merseysiders and the whole nation and British Empire were delighted when the Duchess of York gave birth to a bonny, bouncing girl at No. 17 Bruton Street, London, on April 21st, 1926. Just another little princess named Elizabeth. Little did we know that the dramatic and historic events of ten years later would mean that she was destined for a life of duty and dedication as Queen Elizabeth. And what better Queen could we have wished for?

Many people will remember those cosy, noisy little parties Merseysiders used to enjoy in the back parlour in the days when anything was an excuse for a hilarious 'knees-up'—Christmas, New Year's Eve, birthdays, engagements, weddings and christenings. There was always the willing musician with his banjo, mandolin, accordion or even mouth-organ. But the guest who could play the piano was the most welcome, and he was always willing to tickle the ivories all night long provided the top of the piano was covered with foaming glasses of beer. One or two guests used to come armed with those bumper song albums produced by people like Lawrence Wright for sixpence or a shilling. These were a great help in keeping the party going with uproarious sing-songs. I still have many of those old song albums, and I notice they often say 'with ukelele accompaniment'—songs such as 'I'm alone because I love you', 'When its sunset on the Nile', 'Oh Donna Clara', 'When you were the blossom of Buttercup Lane', 'Good 'eavens Mrs. Evans', and 'My canary has circles under his eyes'. All the revellers had more than circles under their eyes after a noisy 'do', which went on until the following morning, or, for some, until the beer ran out.

'Coggy watchmen's' huts were a common sight in the 20s—sited of course, where road repairs were being carried out, and where there was always the risk of some of the materials being pinched. All the coggy-watchmen I knew were elderly men who sat in their little wooden huts, warming their hands on the glowing coke of their braziers. On particularly cold nights they always welcomed the company of us children, and we, in turn, very much welcomed the warmth of the glowing fire, helping to stoke up and sharing the watchman's sandwiches (chip butties?) as he related some lurid and patently untrue stories from his past. We'd also roast the potatoes we'd manage to purloin from home. During those wintry nights, we'd often be joined by a couple of bobbies on the beat, who thawed out frozen limbs. The winters seemed to be far more severe in bygone days.

Winter ailments were far more common at that time, when sometimes half the class was absent with coughs, colds and bad chests. Herbal remedies for various complaints were all the rage then. Some people swore by them. There were many old-fashioned and well-tried remedies, as well, such as a paste made from soap and sugar for boils and suchlike, and a hot bread poultice which was also applied to boils and festering sores. Many a child was sent to school with a huge red flannel bandage soaked in camphorated oil round his or her chest, and the classroom positively reeked.

There were iodine socks for tired feet, and if you had a wart the best way to remove it was to tie a piece of cotton round it. If a child had whooping cough the recommended thing was to take him to one of those tar-making machines. A good half-hour's whiff of the boiling hot tar and the whooping cough would be gone. But prevention is always better than the cure, so, to keep a child healthy, the usual drill was a spoonful of cod liver oil first thing in the morning, a dose of emulsion in the afternoon, and a good table-spoonful of castor oil before going to bed. If people were fortunate enough to have a goose on Christmas Day, the goose-grease was carefully kept in a large tin and regularly rubbed into the chest throughout the winter.

If such simple remedies worked, then they were absolutely essential during that terrible winter of 1929, when there was a prolonged deep freeze and, not only did the sea become ice-packed off Kent, but I seem to remember that parts of the River Mersey were frozen up as well. I distinctly remember that winter. We hated to go out into the playground for our morning and afternoon breaks—after ten minutes our hands and feet were almost frost-bitten and many children were in tears as, clad in their pitiful clothing, they really suffered. It was all right for the teachers sitting upstairs in their nice, warm staff room.

It was during the 20s that the sea dealt a fatal blow in Blundellsands, when practically the whole of Burbo Bank North, a select thoroughfare comprising a number of fine old houses, some of them the best residential property in the district, was swept away. At that time the position looked very grave indeed, and the old L.M.S. Railway authorities were very worried concerning the safety of their line to Southport. The chief cause of the trouble was the River Alt which, in its former course, used to hug the coastline and run along the beach some three miles southwards to Blundellsands before turning into the Mersey. Shortly before the last war the Alt was diverted about half way between Hightown and Blundellsands.

A mystery that has always intrigued me is whether the two Merseyside climbers, George Leigh Mallory and Andrew Irvine, succeeded in reaching the summit of Mount Everest in June, 1924. The last man to see them alive—a geologist—said they were only eight hundred feet from the top, and going strongly. After that— complete silence. Did they make it to the summit and then, on the way down, shelter under some rocks and die of exposure? Or did one of them make a fatal slip and carry both of them to their doom thousands of feet below? In 1960, a body, wearing clothing with a British trademark, was discovered just below the North Ridge of Everest. It could have been either of the two intrepid climbers. Before that, in 1933, Irvine's ice axe was found just below the summit. It's one of the great mysteries of the century, and I avidly read any scraps of new evidence that comes to light. I incline to the belief that these two Merseysiders reached the summit and were lost on the way down. One day, perhaps, we shall know for certain.

A mysterious disappearance of a far different nature took place in Liverpool more than fifty years ago. Victor Grayson, the Liverpool-born M.P., and a brilliant speaker, walked out of his mother's home in Northbrook Street, Liverpool, turned the corner into Princes Avenue, and was never seen again. The mystery of the disappearance of Grayson, who'd been born in near-poverty, discovered in youth that he had a remarkable gift of oratory, and rose to eminence in the Labour Party, with even the prospect of one day becoming Prime Minister, has intrigued many people over the years. Did Victor Grayson disappear intentionally? Was his disappearance an accident? Or was he murdered? Those questions remain unanswered to this day.

April 3rd, 1928, was an important day for Merseyside when Miss Margaret Beavan, Lord Mayor of Liverpool, dressed up like a deep-sea fisherman, and Alderman F. Naylor, Mayor of Birkenhead, met each other from opposite sides of the Mersey and shook hands under mid-river through a hole which had been excavated by Sir Archibald Salvidge, the inspirer of the Mersey Tunnel, using a pick-axe and a sledge-hammer. The completed job had entailed the removal of more than a million tons of rock, all carted to Otterspool to make the foundations of the new promenade.

At a more frivolous level, in 1928, Southport citizens were up in arms about Adam and Eve. As far as they were concerned, Southport was no Garden of Eden, and there was no place in the town for William Roberts' controversial painting of the original lovers. All Mr. Roberts had to say when his painting was banished to a private room from the public gallery was: 'What do town councillors know about art, anyhow? And why have they kept my painting in a private room instead of sending it back to me?' Not surprisingly the official answer was 'No comment'.

That same year a report appeared in the Liverpool Echo of a woman who boasted 16 children, 70 grandchildren and five great-grandchildren. And she was only 65. She deserved far more than her old-age pension. At the same time, a church magazine note to parishioners was published in the Echo: 'If the gentleman who dropped his eye-glass into the collection bag last Sunday instead of a coin will call at the vestry, it will be returned to him'. And I like this report in particular: 'At a conference on housing in Liverpool, a woman delegate complained of the style and quality of some of the new houses being built. She told the conference she could hear the man next door kissing his wife'. Now surely that complaint was tinged with just a little jealousy!

There was also this report in an Echo of 1926: 'A private individual handed in a telegram addressed to Mars at the London G.P.O. yesterday, and it was sent into the void from the high power station at midnight. An attempt to signal Mars was also made from the Daily Post and Echo Exhibition in Liverpool, and astronomers and wireless enthusiasts were busy last night trying to get in touch with the planet. The report at midnight was that Mars had sent no message'. I suppose it was worth a try.

And during his stay in Liverpool in the 20s, it was reported that Charlie Chaplin observed a man cleaning the face of the Liver Building clock. He signalled the man down frantically, and the chap, fearing some calamity at home, hurried down and over to Charlie, who asked, in the inimitable Chaplin manner: 'Have you got the time, mate?' Only Charlie Chaplin could have got away with that.

We had our share of disastrous fires on Merseyside during the 20s. There was the fire and explosion which swept through the French steamer, Oklahoma, in Sandon Dock on October 15th, 1929, soon after the ship had arrived from the west coast of South

America. The vessel was completely gutted, and sank to the bottom of the dock. Before she could be removed, the dock had to be pumped dry, and the ship patched up to make her watertight. When the dock was flooded again, the Oklahoma refloated, and in February, 1930, she was towed across the river to Tranmere beach, and broken up.

Two years before that, a ship came to grief on the Mersey revetment. She was the cargo liner, Lochmonar, a Royal Mail ship of 9,412 gross tons, built by Harland and Wolfe at Belfast in 1924. After breaking her back on the revetment near the Crosby lightship on November 30th, 1927, the stern half of the ship, with engines intact, was salvaged. The bulkheads were strengthened and the half ship was towed away to have a new fore part built on to her. The Lochmonar was inward bound from Vancouver at the time and, happily, her six passengers and sixty crew were rescued, and her cargo of canned and dried fruit salvaged. Lochmonar survived the Second World War but her two sister ships were both war casualties. It was also in the late 20s when the coaster, Jennie, crashed into Woodside Ferry and sank, taking a large section of the pier with her.

As regular scheduled air services became an essential feature of travel in the 20s, Merseyside business men realised the potential value of establishing an airfield. In 1926, an organisation was set up with the specific intention of developing an airport on Merseyside. In an article in the Echo dated November 25th, 1927, Commander Boothby, the celebrated airship expert, predicted: 'Within the next few years, air transport will begin to compete seriously for a share of the overseas passenger and mail-carrying business. As far as Liverpool is concerned, the main interest will be in airships. If Liverpool is to become an air-traffic centre, it must provide an aerodrome with a good surface for aeroplanes, and be equipped with mooring masts, sheds, and gas plants for airships'. An interesting idea, but Commander Boothby was a little too ambitious in his vision of Liverpool's future airport.

The Roaring Twenties came to an end with a terrible crash in 1929. One famous historian said prosperity ended in the autumn of that year. With the financial crash on Wall Street, economic depression spread like a plague across the world. There were fifteen million unemployed in the United States, six million in Germany, and well over two million in Britain. Merseyside suffered grievously. The Roaring Twenties went out with a helpless whimper.

Chapter Eight
Down Scottie Road to Paddy's Market

For most expatriated Liverpudlians the mere mention of a familiar place or thoroughfare brings an instant sigh of nostalgia and an excuse for a heart-warming chat about old times. It's a strange fact that while there are many folk wishing to leave the area and settle elsewhere, it's the actual leaving of Liverpool that tugs on the heart-strings. Once a Liverpudlian, always a Liverpudlian, and 'scousers' who have pulled up their roots and made their homes in other countries and other climes still regard Liverpool as their home town and swear allegiance to their beloved city, in spite of all its faults and failings.

Scotland Road is known all over the world. The old Scottie Road was always a flurry of activity, with its many shops and pubs, its street musicians and barrel organs, its shawlies, its Indian seamen on their way to and from Paddy's Market, its Saturday night street battles, its drunks, and its warmth and hospitality. It was regarded with so much affection that even the main 'road' that ran through many of the famous liners was known as 'Scotland Road'. If a passenger or a new member of the crew wasn't sure of his bearings and wished to reach a certain part of the ship he was told to go along 'Scotland Road' and turn left or right, depending on the ultimate destination.

The real Scotland Road was noted for its 'Foo Foo Bands'. Members of the ships' crews also had their Foo-Foo Bands which provided plenty of entertainment for passengers and the members of the bands alike. The 'Foo-Foo', incidentally, was a sort of 'kazoo', a simple little instrument that made a similar noise to that of the comb and tissue-paper 'music' of our childhood days, and used with good effect in some of the very early jazz bands. Members of the Foo-Foo Bands held regular practices and many parades—up and down the ships' 'Scottie Road', naturally. Many a celebrated passenger was played ashore to the music of those bands.

A friend of mine belonged to a certain Foo-Foo Band in the 30s called the Mayfair Jazz Band, and they practised in the back yard of a house in West Derby Street. He then joined the Laguna Revellers Prize Jazz Band, whose hall was behind No. 22 Chestnut

Grove, off Marsh Lane, Bootle. They used to compete for silver cups at carnivals all over the north-west. Their tableau was a large aeroplane, while their rivals, 'The Bootle First', made a liner with smoke coming from the funnels. Oh yes, they took themselves very seriously indeed.

But back to Scottie Road. Mention 'Paddy's Market' to seamen in almost every port in the world and they'd immediately know where it was and how to get to it when their ships docked in Liverpool. The Indian seamen in particular made a bee-line for Paddy's Market the moment they left their ships. The stall-holders called them 'coolies'—simple, friendly men who loved to strike a bargain, and would haggle for ages, until they walked away happily with their purchases. They always walked in single file— some with bundles of clothing, often carried on their heads, some with bird-cages, some with as many as half a dozen trilby hats on their heads, and others with the most peculiar of objects, including chamber pots. I'm told that the one who walked in the middle of the file always carried the money. Much of the stall-holders' trade was done with the coolies.

I once received a few lines of verse from a Liverpool man, who wrote it when he was a soldier in the Western Desert. Like so many of us at the time, he was convinced that he would never see Liverpool again, and at times he'd wallow in sentimental reminiscence. In his mind's eye, he told me, he'd walk back to Liverpool seeing places that once seemed squalid and ugly, but were now shining and beautiful, made so by an aching nostalgia:—

'Paddy's Market! Paddy's Market!
All the world has learned to say,
Including all the dusky seamen
Come ashore to shop today.
Hats and trousers, coats and blouses,
Pictures, kettles, fenders too!
Bits of china, here's a dance dress.
Late one summer it was new.
Maggie wore it at a wedding,
Now Ben Achmed takes it far,
To grace a darker maiden
'Neath the sun in Zanzibar'.

There was a large room with wooden tables and benches in St. Martin's Hall, off Scotland Road, which was one of the cheapest eating places in the city. 'Scouse Alley' they called it, and hundreds of plates of steaming hot scouse were served every day at a penny a time. For a little extra, hungry folk could buy a delicious plate of spare ribs and cabbage, or even roast beef and two veg. The latter cost sixpence, and a 'Wet Nellie' could be bought for a ha'penny. Spare ribs and cabbage, followed by a Wet Nellie, and washed down with a large mug of hot sweet tea—all for around sixpence. What more could you wish for?

I've often been told about a certain clock-towered pub in Scotland Place called the 'Morning Star', presided over by an engaging character affectionately known as 'Dandy Pat'. His real name was Paddy Byrne, and part of his attire was a sealskin waistcoat and a white top hat. I suppose this was why they called him 'Dandy Pat'. Pat fought tooth and nail on behalf of the ratepayers in the Town Hall—for he was a city councillor. He was regarded with such esteem that when he died they erected a fountain to his memory just opposite his pub. Scottie Road expatriates still talk about Dandy Pat and his pub.

Another champion of Scotland Road was 'Champion Whate', who ran what was possibly the most famous doss-house in the world, called, of course, 'Champion Whate's'. If you happened to peep through the basement window of his place in Scottie Road you might have seen the strange spectacle of a line of sleeping men draped across a thick rope which was slung across the room. I suppose it was better than sleeping on the floor, but how they managed it heaven only knows. Apparently the men who slept on the rope were the human derelicts who couldn't afford to pay for a proper bed. It seems the rope was called a 'flop', so the doss-house was often known as the 'flop-house'. For those lucky enough to be able to afford a bed they could be had for 4d, 6d, 9d and 1/-.

No-one seems to have met Champion Whate, but what is known is that his real name was Walter Whate—a tough, stocky little man who'd once upon a time distinguished himself in the wrestling ring. Whether he'd ever been a champion at this sport is a moot point, and is of little consequence. For hundreds of homeless men his lodging house was 'champion'.

Many an exiled Scottie-Roader will claim that the famous thoroughfare was the original course for the noble game of marbles called 'Three Holes'. It was played on some waste ground near Mile End opposite the offices of Jacob's, the biscuit manufacturers. Three holes were dug in the ground with a specified distance apart and the contestants tossed a penny for the right to be first away. Standing at the first hole, the opening player would 'knuckle' his marble towards the second hole. If he potted it first time, all well and good—he'd then go for the third hole.

But his marble might end up just a few inches from the hole, and if his opponent holed successfully this gave him the right to knock the other marble as far away as possible before going for the next hole. The complete game consisted of an agreed number of rounds in each direction. There was always keen competition, as the winner usually got a free pint. The games always attracted a large number of spectators, and produced some champion marble players—worthy rivals to their equally skilful counterparts in Princes Park. It's been said that if they'd had a Cup competition for marbles, either the Princes Park or the Scottie Road players would have won it with ease.

During the Depression of the 1930s, many of the unemployed men of Scotland Road organised themselves into football teams. They'd have their meetings in the cellars of houses. Funds were raised by bingo sessions, which were illegal in those days. Matches were played every Sunday afternoon on a large area of land adjoining the Leeds and Liverpool Canal in Lightbody Street— known as the Lock Fields. There must be men all over Liverpool who remember that hallowed ground. There was a certain referee named Jack Rooney, who had only one arm, and, because of his disability, he was respected by all the teams taking part. There was never any bad language used towards Jack, and his decisions were rarely disputed.

Many Scottie Road exiles will remember characters like Dave Moody, an agent of the Friendly Society, and known as the 'clubman'. He took the meaning of the word 'friendly' so literally that he decided to live in the area among his clients, and he became a well-known figure. There was also a character named Paddy Kelly, who'd lost both his legs, and he'd sit in a wheel-chair at the top of Cranmer Street all day long. He had a cheery word for everyone, and also a keen sense of humour. For instance, when asked by mischievous children: 'What are you waiting for, sitting there all day?' Paddy would promptly reply: 'I'm waiting to skip a lorry to Southport!'

Scotland Road really came to life on Saturday nights, and for the policemen of 'D' Division it was no easy ride. They had to be as tough as nails, and only the toughest 'bobbies' were used on that dreaded beat. Drunken brawls were common, and some of the women could throw a left hook as well as any man. Many a policeman woke up in hospital on Sunday morning. 'D' Division had its headquarters in Rose Hill, with sub-stations in Athol Street and Chisenhall Street. If there were three busier stations anywhere in Britain I'd be very surprised. For Saturday night resembled a battlefield, with numerous fights going on simultaneously both inside and outside the pubs.

The men were decent enough in themselves, but they lived in shocking conditions, and when they'd had a few drinks they became aggressive and violent. Consequently the police of 'D' Division always awaited Saturday night with considerable trepidation. It was no place for weaklings, and only bobbies who knew how to handle themselves were sent there. They often needed three pairs of hands, and even when they grabbed a drunken brawler and shoved him in the Black Maria they'd be attacked by dozens of jeering people throwing stones and bottles. A policeman's helmet perched on top of a chimney pot was a common sight on Sunday morning.

P.C. 'Tiny' Edwards was a real character in a force full of characters. He was a tough ex-soldier, who'd distinguished himself as an amateur heavyweight boxer while in the army. One Saturday night, Tiny and a colleague, Bill Forman, found themselves outside the 'Morning Star', otherwise called the 'Blood Pub' because of the amount of blood spilled during the drunken brawls. A large crowd had gathered, and in the middle of the circle two navvies were hammering the living daylights out of each other.

Tiny, always a man of action, decided there was only one thing for it. He stopped the fight by offering to take on any of the men in the crowd. After a brief, surprised pause, one hefty bruiser offered to have a go. The chance of beating up a policeman was too good to miss. Tiny calmly removed his tunic and awaited the navvy's first attack. It was the first and the last for, with one single punch, Tiny felled him. Two or three more volunteers suffered the same fate, and peace was restored. The crowd loved a fighter and looked on in awe. Whether the superintendent would have approved is another question.

There was a happy sequel to this event. There was always a pint of beer waiting for Tiny whenever he went to the 'Morning Star'. And it was paid for by one of the toughies who'd been knocked out cold by Tiny. Apparently they became good friends. Even so, the police continued to walk in pairs, and sometimes three, for their own protection.

There were many humorous moments. There was the occasion at a fairground in Scotland Road one Saturday night. 'Hit it on the top to win!' cried the man in charge of the coconut shy. Burly dockers and tough ships' firemen found the target with well placed throws. It went a little awry but still retained its position.

An angry murmur came from the crowd as someone suggested that the nut was 'doctored'. One burly 'scouser', after seeing the third of his 'three balls a penny' bounce harmlessly off the defiant target, jumped angrily over the roped barrier and, grabbing the hairy top of the stubborn target, held it aloft like some decapitated head. 'It's as so-and-so heavy as so-and-so lead!' he roared. This was the signal for the incensed spectators to help themselves to coconuts reserved for the winners, the stall-holder beating a hasty retreat.

Then there was the prisoner from Scotland Road who was up before the 'beak' for being drunk and disorderly. He was pleading for leniency:—

'Yer 'onour, oi've a bayonet wound in me back'.

'Do you mean you were wounded in the trenches?'

'Oh no, yer 'onour—in Scotland Road!'

Humour, as well as blood, flowed in Scottie Road!

Chapter Nine
The Cassie and Other Places

The Landing Stage was a part of my childhood. On Sunday afternoons a walk down to the famous Stage became almost a ritual. For they were the golden days—when beautiful liners queued up for a berth, and we looked with admiration on ocean-going ships such as the Aquitania and Mauretania, the Britannic and Georgic, not to mention the glorious Duchesses and Empresses. We awaited with eager anticipation the arrival of the great little ferry boats from Woodside, Seacombe, Egremont, Rock Ferry, and Eastham, and the busy little tenders helping to speed up the movement of passengers from the liners—the Bison, Moose, Wapiti, Skirmisher, Magnetic, and Flying Breeze. What a wonderful place the Landing Stage was in the 30s. It seemed to be the very centre of the world.

I could have spent every day of my young life there, watching another majestic liner coming in almost every day of the week, and if it had been possible to obtain the autographs of the hundreds of celebrities embarking and disembarking it would have been a fabulous collection of some of the most famous people in the world. It seemed there could have been no more exciting place in the whole world than Liverpool's Landing Stage. How very different now!

After long years of bitter opposition, the Liverpool Zoological Gardens were opened on May 4th, 1932, and proved a most popular venture. Countless happy hours were spent by youngsters and their parents at Otterspool's Zoo. Unfortunately, it didn't enjoy the best of luck and suffered a whole chapter of accidents. It wasn't long after it was opened that a visitor was attacked by the rather fearsome-looking lion, Nero, and was severely injured. This was particularly unfortunate as, not long before, that same lion had savagely mauled its keeper in Manchester, with fatal results. Then a leopard attacked its keeper in June, 1937, and the badly injured man died on his way to hospital.

Probably the most popular of the animals was Mickey the chimpanzee. He was playful and unpredictable, and you had to treat him very warily indeed, especially as he'd bitten quite a number of unsuspecting visitors who got too near to him. My most vivid recollection of Mickey was his unerring throwing of a football. You'd toss him a ball and he was so strong that when he threw it back, if you were unlucky enough to be in the way, you were almost knocked off your feet. This contrary animal was never happy in captivity and escaped on four occasions. He was always recaptured, but only after a great deal of trouble. On one of his escapades it took more than a dozen policemen, his keeper, a lion-tamer, several police vehicles and an ambulance to hunt him down. One amazed and terrified coalman was uncere-moniously seized by Mickey and hurled across the road.

One would have thought that after these escapes the zoo authorities would have seen to it that he was made so secure that it couldn't possibly happen again. But escape he did, and this time there was no return. He got out on March 24th, 1938, and was determined to make the most of his freedom. He made his mischievous way to Sudley Road School, in Aigburth, where a class of boys were doing their physical training exercises in the playground. Imagine the terror of those children when they saw a fearsome-looking chimpanzee making his way towards them. They ran, panic-stricken, but in vain. Mickey grabbed one of them, whereupon the schoolmaster courageously went to the rescue, and was viciously attacked, suffering quite severe injuries. Happily, none of the boys was badly hurt, and the master was later given a well-deserved award for his bravery.

Mickey, by now, was in desperate mood. He climbed on to the roof of a house, pursued by a number of policemen who decided that enough was enough. The crazed chimp had reached the end of the road. Fourteen shots were pumped into him before he fell with an almighty thump into the back yard of 29 Lugard Road. It was all rather sad. He'd always been a great favourite with Liverpool children and, in spite of his many unfortunate escapades, they were very sad at his passing. Under the circumstances it was necessary for Mickey to be shot, but the whole affair left me with an uncomfortable feeling that it seems utterly wrong to keep animals caged up and denied the freedom they're entitled to. Ever since Mickey met his doom I've never really enjoyed a visit to the zoo. Liverpool Zoo was closed down in the late 30s, much to the disappointment of countless children.

One of Merseyside's most familiar sounds in bygone days was the famous one o'clock gun which used to boom out day by day to the relief of thousands of workers who knocked off for their lunch break, and for countless other folk who synchronised their clocks and watches to it. Merseyside without its one o'clock gun seemed almost as unthinkable as London without the sound of Big Ben, but, for several reasons, on October 20th, 1932, the Mersey Docks and Harbour Board decided to dispense with it.

This offended public opinion so much that the protests were loud and long, and the Dock Board bowed to this outcry and relented. It was an ancient 34-pounder cannon which was a veteran of the Crimean War—perhaps even earlier wars. As it was so old, the decision was taken to replace it with another, so, in 1933, a new 32-pounder arrived from Woolwich Arsenal. This continued to boom out over the River Mersey until the outbreak of war when, for security reasons, it was silenced for the duration.

It's of interest to mention that people on the Liverpool side of the river would allow about four seconds for the boom to travel across the Mersey. A third gun was installed after the war, but Merseysiders heard it for the last time on July 18th, 1969. The one o'clock gun was a welcome sound to everyone except the startled seagulls and pigeons—as welcome as the five o'clock whistle.

Liverpool abounded in cheerful, cosy pubs. Everyone had his or her favourite, of course, and each pub had its own individual character. It would be impossible for me to describe them all here but some were rather special. One universal favourite was 'The Eagles', situated behind the Empire Theatre, but internationally known as 'Ma Egerton's', and was the favourite haunt of the many musicians and performers at that theatre. Dear old Ma Egerton used to hold court, surrounded by her adoring subjects, her head always crowned by one or other of her many magnificent hats.

All the famous in the theatre were her friends and customers, and their photographs adorned the walls. It seems Ma Egerton was a wonderful person, and, during the war, was especially kind to her old customers who were serving in the Forces. It was obligatory to call in and see her when on leave. There was always a gift from her—cash, perhaps, a carton of American cigarettes, and sometimes even a joint of precious meat or a parcel of foodstuffs. During my many chats with famous dance band leaders, musicians and singers on my BBC Radio Merseyside programme 'Music and Memories', whenever we talk about the Empire they all refer to Ma Egerton's with genuine affection, as it was there they all gathered after their performance at the theatre.

There used to be a pub situated opposite Liverpool's Royal Infirmary called 'The Royal Hotel', and this was a popular haunt. For some reason it changed its name several times, and it became 'The Pembroke Hotel' and later 'The Daulby Hotel'. Perhaps it's best known as 'The Wireless Hotel' because it happened to be the very first pub in Liverpool to boast a handsome cabinet wireless set situated high up in one corner of the lounge. The manager even had his photograph in the Echo because of this. When the time came when practically every household possessed a wireless set, it reverted to 'The Royal Hotel'.

Most publicans were characters. They had to be. But the one at the Royal Hotel was, in addition, a practical joker, whose victims were left either highly embarrassed or splitting their sides with laughter. But practical jokes often backfire. One night, during a particularly severe winter, the rag and bone man, who was a regular customer, came in for a quick pint or two. There were few people on the streets as a blizzard was raging.

Greeting the rag and bone man in his customary jovial manner, the publican remarked, in jest: 'You don't mean to tell me that you're going to leave that poor horse outside in this weather while you drink that? Bring the poor devil in and warm him in front of the fire'. Perhaps the rag and bone man realised his leg was being pulled. Perhaps not. At any rate he immediately jammed the wide pub door open with a stool and dragged the pony in, cart and all. I don't know who was the more astonished—the customers or the now red-faced publican.

An interesting letter to the Echo came from a man who used to work in a pub in Christian Street, on the corner of Springfield Street. He didn't mention its name, as I recall, but it was destroyed by bombs during the war. This man recalled that they used to get all sorts of characters in there—Street buskers, 'knock off' merchants, organ grinders, and 'tatters', who, of course were the rag and bone men. In the 30s, beer was fivepence a pint, so they could usually manage the price of a pint or two.

'A chap came in one night', he said, 'and I served him a pint. I was doing my job when he called me over and said: 'Barman, this is a funny pub'. 'Is it?' I said. 'Do you know', he went on, 'I've been looking round and you and I are the only people here with two good eyes'. I glanced round the bar. 'You're right', I said. For apart from him, the customers were three blind men, one blind woman, one man with only one eye, and two women with one eye each. One night two of the blind men had a set-to, and the third tried to separate them. This one, that is the fellow who tried to act as peacemaker, was an old sailor who used to sit outside the 'Tam o'Shanter' pub in London Road with his begging bowl.

Tourists visiting London always make a point of visiting Madame Tussaud's famous waxworks. Once upon a time, Liverpool also boasted its waxworks.

In 1860, a certain Alfred John Reynolds decided to settle in Liverpool, bringing his travelling waxworks. His intention was to find a permanent site for his wax effigies, and when the old Freemasons Hall in Lime Street became available he decided this was the very place he was looking for.

At first it was just a dining room, but a couple of years later he began to instal his effigies which grew in numbers to such an extent that it soon became enormously successful as 'Reynolds Waxworks', which was to enjoy a stay of sixty years. The most popular section was down below in the basement—a section which contained the wax figures of famous criminals and called, 'The Criminal Chamber'. Charlie Peace was probably the best-known figure among a host of notorious murderers.

Reynolds decided to celebrate the 25th anniversary of the opening of his waxworks with a lavish banquet in the Great Hall. Three hundred guests assembled to eat and drink beneath the brightly-flaring gas-lamps. There were some very important people including the guest-of-honour, the then Prince of Wales, and Prince Von Bismarck from Germany. The banquet was the most important event of its existence, as, with silent films quickly growing in popularity, the waxworks was declining in popularity. A brave attempt to keep the flag flying by installing a bioscope, which gave two shows a day, was made, but it was all to no avail and, regrettably, Reynolds was forced to close down in 1922.

There are many Merseysiders who still retain fond memories of the waxworks. They may recall how, as they entered, a dummy nurse would curtsy and nearly startle them out of their skins. During the afternoon the lights would be dimmed and the audience would sit on their wooden seats to watch one of the film shows. It's said that, being surrounded by some particularly brutal murderers, the nervous ones would hold hands and pray for the lights to go up again. When the end came for Reynolds

Waxworks it was replaced by a billiards room, with a tea room on the ground floor.

One place in Liverpool that was always crammed to the doors was the old Pudsey Street Boxing Stadium. It's often been claimed, and not without justification, that most professional boxers of the 20s and 30s fought, not just for fame and fortune, but because they were hungry, and using their fists was the only way of earning a few pounds—very often just a few shillings. And this was the reason why those fighters served such a long apprenticeship to become top-class pugilists and brilliant champions. The finest fighters were always the hungry fighters.

Not for them a mere handful of contests and the chance to fight for a British title. That was unheard of in those days. Some of them had hundreds of fights before they were given the smell of a title contest. But they gave the customers their moneys-worth. Pudsey Street Stadium used to almost burst at the seams in those days, and it staged some of the finest shows in the country, and produced some of the most brilliant boxers in the world. Pudsey Street's last show was on March 5th, 1931, the bill reading: Dom Volante v Teddy Brown, Bert Wallace v Benny Howells, Billy Byron v Franky Hughes, Os Parry v Johnny Driscoll, and Billy Cooke v Stan Higson. The new stadium was never quite able to recapture the atmosphere of Pudsey Street.

I feel sure that there are quite a few Merseysiders who enjoyed a cup of tea in Ma Anderson's cafe in Dale Street, especially if they were city office boys, as it was the office boys' favourite rendezvous. But it was also frequented by hundreds of the city's clerks, secretaries and cashiers who went there for their penny cup of tea and bun.

It's perhaps remembered best as the 'Old Hare Soup Shop'. For Ma Anderson's soup was quite delicious, and became famous all over the world. Many foreign sailors had heard about it and made a point of coming to the restaurant for a bowl of the exquisite soup. Some of the customers would tease the assistants as to whether it was hare soup or merely rabbit soup, and the proprietess would promptly declare that if they were too ignorant to know that rabbit meat was white, whereas hare meat was darker and redder, she certainly was not. Many ex-policemen will remember this restaurant as, for many years, it was a bridewell dinner cafe. For many people it was a sad day when Ma Anderson shut up shop in January, 1930.

There was also Harry Petty's famous cafe, which was also

known for forty years or more as the office boys' cafe. Scores of now elderly Liverpool business men will recall the days when they could buy a hearty meal of meat and potato pie with chips at that cafe in Tempest Hey for 5½ old pence. Office boys were the main customers and such was Harry's fame that, during the First World War, the bloody beaches of Gallipoli became a free advertisement for his cafe when the Liverpool men erected over their mess tent the legend 'Harry Petty's Tea Rooms'. And in the legendary ITMA shows on radio, Tommy Handley frequently referred to the famous cafe.

The original building was a warehouse, which Harry converted into a restaurant with three floors. There were spotless white tablecloths on all the tables except those on the top floor. There was an excellent reason for this. Liverpool's office boys, then as now, were as full of tricks as monkeys. They'd throw sugar at one another, put salt in the sugar bowls, mix the salt and vinegar, and blow cigarette smoke into the sauce bottles. Consequently, the top floor was set aside for the mischievous youngsters, and it was distinctly spartan with no cloths on the marble-topped tables. Up there they could eat their meals without getting into too much mischief or causing too much of a mess, but the thoughtful Harry provided draughts and dominoes for them. As they grew older, and a little more responsible, they graduated to the lower floors.

The average weekly wage for an office boy in 1932 was around 7/6d, so he had to watch his pennies. At that time he'd pay 6½d for a three-course lunch at Harry's, or he could get a plate of sausage and mash for 4d. If he couldn't afford that he could get by on a bowl of hot soup for 2d. Many of today's business men bless the day when Harry Petty decided to open that cafe, where, as office boys, they could enjoy a large meal on a small wage packet.

There were, in fact, two Petty's cafes for the youngsters. There was one run on similar lines to Harry's just over the road, and run by his brother, George Petty. It was popular enough but Harry's was much better known. After a while George joined forces with his brother and he continued to run the cafe after Harry's death in 1932. Office boys continued to enjoy good meals for a low price until 1954 when Harry's son decided to close down. But Tommy Handley's catch-phrase, which must have puzzled a lot of listeners up and down the country—'See you at Harry Petty's!' lived on for many years.

One of the most picturesque areas of Liverpool was Pitt Street, commonly called 'Chinatown'. Many of the Chinese wore traditional dress and pigtails. It was fascinating to look in the shop windows with their Chinese food, chopsticks, oriental vases and curios. On Chinese holidays, colourful banners were hung outside the shops and clubs. But even though the vast majority of the Chinese population of Pitt Street were decent, upright, law-abiding citizens, I always felt there was a rather sinister aspect about the place in the 20s and 30s. Perhaps I'd seen too many films of Doctor Fu Manchu.

However, there was a time when opium smuggling into Liverpool's Chinatown was rife. There was also a thriving trade in cocaine bound for America. Constantly waging war against the opium dens was Detective-Sergeant Burgess, a dedicated policeman, who's still remembered in Liverpool. It's a great pity the Chinatown we once knew now no longer exists.

For those people who loved their greyhound racing, it was a red letter day when the White City Greyhound Track in Lower Breck Road was opened in 1932. And they didn't just go for the dog racing. Over the years it became a rendezvous where friends met and enjoyed a chat and a drink, and they found this just as agreeable as watching the racing and having a little flutter. One tattered old programme from 1932 shows that at the White City there were eleven races in the afternoon and another twelve at night—enough to satisfy the keenest punter. Those halcyon days of greyhound racing in Liverpool have now long gone, and even the popular track at Seaforth has long since disappeared.

What simple little things used to entertain my generation when we were children! I was always fascinated by the clock outside Russell's, the jewellers shop in Church Street. It was a facsimile of a Nuremberg clock which carried the gilded figures of Father Time and two sailors who struck the chimes. I used to hang around Church Street for hours just waiting for the chimes to strike. I enjoyed seeing beautiful things, and that clock was beautiful. Russell's Building, on the corner of Church Street and Church Alley, was destroyed in the 1940 Christmas blitz, and the chimes were silenced. I wonder whether that clock was destroyed with the building?

A far more famous building, of which I knew almost every nook and cranny, as my duties as an office boy used to take me there several times a day, was Liverpool's old Custom House. I would never claim that its exterior was beautiful, but its interior, with the famous Long Room, was magnificent. An added attraction for a thinly-clad office boy on a particularly cold winter's day was its warmth. Getting customs documents through the various departments—they called them 'seats'—was often a lengthy business, but I didn't mind that one little bit. I think I spent more time in the Custom House than I did in the office. In 1941, this splendid old building was gutted by fire bombs. I was a long way away when it happened, and many other famous buildings were destroyed with it, but those who saw the burning Custom House say the flames attracted the enemy raiders like moths round a candle.

One great landmark of Victorian Merseyside—the David Lewis Hostel, escaped the wartime blitz, but was a victim of the planners. It seems a pity that such a fine building was demolished. I can remember it in the 30s as a cheap, comfortable hostel for men of limited means—and there were many of them in Liverpool. The David Lewis was built on the corner of Great George Place and Upper Parliament Street in 1907 from money left by Liverpool philanthropist David Lewis, who was the founder of Lewis's Stores and the David Lewis Northern Hospital. The hostel also incorporated a once popular theatre. I can also remember a thriving boys' club there, and the warden was a well-liked man named Mr. Crean. Right at the back of the David Lewis Hostel, with its entrance in Rathbone Street, there was an out-building which was the headquarters or 'den' of the 200th (Liverpool) Scout and Rover Group, whose leader for many years was the popular George Lees.

And how many Liverpudlians retain happy memories of Hutchinson Hall, at the south end of Mill Street, Toxteth? I remember 'Hutchy Hall' best as a place where we could enjoy a good cowboy film for a penny. But the film shows were the least important of this popular mission's functions. Its story goes right back to the 1880s when a small group of dedicated young men felt the need for a Sunday School in that area of south Liverpool. They started their work with just one scholar, but they refused to be discouraged and the numbers steadily increased, and, many years later, the big new school was built in the amazingly short time of 42 days.

Anniversary time was a very special occasion for the children, especially if they were included in the 125-strong choir—the girls in their new white dresses and the boys in smart new suits. For Sunday School treats the youngsters were taken to such places as Eastham Woods—over a thousand of them getting on the ferry boat at the Herculaneum river wall, and disembarking, after a happy day, at the Landing Stage because of the tides, and walking all the way home to Dingle. Sefton, Maghull, and later, Helsby, were other popular venues for the annual summer outings. Saturday afternoons saw some sixty or more boys and girls rambling all over Wirral. Wednesday evening was 'pictures night' or 'the breaks', so-called because there was a lengthy break of film after each two parts. What the children didn't realise was that there was only one projector, and the projectionist had to stop to take out a reel and put in the second one.

Summer holidays were spent on the Cast Iron Shore, when the children discarded shoes and stockings and went everywhere barefooted. What a magic and exciting place the 'Cassy' seemed to be for children in days gone by! They'd go to the local fish shop and ask for a cod's head, which was fastened to a good length of string, and off they'd go to the 'Cassy'—the cods-head owners to fish for crabs, while the others sat on the Black Rocks at Dingle Point.

A useful apprenticeship was served there. The younger boys collected firewood from the oak trees nearby, and kept the fire burning while the older boys fished. The red crabs were boiled on the fire, and the 'green 'uns' were thrown back into the water. In the spring they stole home through Brown's Field and collected bluebells for their mums.

Alas, as folk moved away from the locality or grew older, numbers severely declined, and with the arrival of the 'age of the vandal' the church and premises were wrecked. Regrettably, the good old 'Hutchy' was demolished a few years ago. Many adults today have good reason to be grateful for the training they received at that old mission hall.

There used to be plenty of good-humoured heckling at the 'Smith Street Lamp'. This was an area around an underground convenience where open-air political and religious meetings were held. Some of them were very lively indeed. One typical 'scouser', who didn't agree with a speaker, had a stock retort: 'Ah go an' put yer 'ed under the tap!' The person who reminded me about the Smith Street Lamp added that, some years later, when passing along Scotland Road, he saw the faded photograph of this heckler in the window of a certain political party shop, with a row of other photographs. There was a note underneath which said, simply: 'Killed in Action—Ebro Front'. This was of course, in the Spanish Civil War. My friend never knew who he was but he felt rather sad because he recalled his chirpy and cheerful manner of goading speakers with a humorous sort of good-natured aggression.

Incidentally, I'm sure many folk will recall the advertisement outside the signwriter's shop in Brunswick Road—'I was making signs before I could talk'. And the one near Parliament Street— 'Get off that tram—it will never be yours. Use your fares to buy a bike!' The latter seemed to be sound logic to me, so I took their advice and bought a second-hand bike, which saved me quite a lot of money as I had it for many years. The power of advertising!

Talking of bikes, before the war, many of the bicycle shops sold many other things as well. I used to buy my 78 gramophone records and needles there. Some of the old record sleeves are a mine of information. Taking just one as an example, showing pictures of now ancient phonographs, gramophones and bicycles, it proudly claims: 'Repairs to any make of cycle or talking machine. Agent for Raleigh, B.S.A. and Rudge Whitworth cycles. Incandescent mantles and fittings, rubber pads, footballs, mouth organs, watches, novelties, etc. Enamelling and plating at reasonable prices. Edison four-minute attachment fitted free of charge'. I can clearly remember buying gas mantles from some of those cycle and gramophone record shops.

Happily, religious tolerance is very much on the increase on Merseyside nowadays, and all the churches, no matter what their denomination, seem to be working together in harmony and friendship. It wasn't always so. Even as children we were the victims of religious intolerance. Walking home alone from school, I was often seized by a gang of boys demanding: 'I or O?'. Now we all know what that meant—'Irish or Orange'. If you were a Roman Catholic you were assumed to be Irish, for some strange reason, and if you were a Protestant, you were automatically labelled 'Orange'. The trouble was I never knew to which group my captors belonged. So I had to tread very warily and try to weigh up the opposition in an effórt to give the answer that pleased them. Invariably I failed lamentably and gave the wrong one. Next morning I'd arrive at school sporting two black eyes and a squashed nose. One against half a dozen wasn't a fair match.

Before the war blitzes destroyed large areas of Merseyside and dispersed the population—a matter to be regretted—it was a real pleasure to tour places like Essex Street and Toxteth Street in South Liverpool, around Orangemen's Day and see every house newly painted and lavishly decorated. The streets were a blaze of colour and pageantry. The same can be said about the predominantly Roman Catholic streets on their special religious occasions—every house spick and span, marvellously decorated, and even the pavements scrubbed clean, and the kerbs whitewashed. And, as with the Orange Lodges, it was a delight to see all the children in procession, dressed completely in white, even down to their pretty shoes.

I've already mentioned the 'Smith Street Lamp'. There was also the 'Edge Hill Lamp'. This was the name given to the small island at the top of Paddington, close to St. Mary's Church. The place acquired its name from the Tall Victorian lamp which stood in its centre. It used to be the local Hyde Park, where soap-box orators spouted their beliefs. If you'd been there in the 20s you might have heard some lusty singing from a group of shabbily-dressed men, standing in front of the speaker. And you'd have recognised the tune—'Tell me the old, old story'. This was in response to the claims and promises of a political speaker of the Right,—for the area was a Labour stronghold, and the speaker encountered formidable opposition from the very many unemployed men.

By and large it was never bitter opposition—rather was it good-humoured banter from men seeking a brief respite from the monotony of a drab existence. They'd invariably strike up with, 'Tell me the old, old story—of Tanner and his lies', to the well-known hymn tune. When the speaker alluded to the subject of unemployment, they'd change it to, 'When the dole is on the counter I'll be there', to the tune of 'When the roll is called up yonder'. Six roads converged on the Edge Hill Lamp, and the vastly increased stream of traffic meant the requiem of this popular Speakers Corner.

The old St. John's Market was a bustle of activity on Saturday night. Mary Ellens cried their wares of 'sage-a-mint-a-parsley', and proffered bags they'd made from potato sacks they'd picked up. These had handles made from the straw ropes of orange cases. McCormick's stall is well remembered for live fowl, and customers would use this type of bag to carry away their clucking purchases for backyard breeding. We children weren't very interested in the main part of the market—we always made a bee-line for the back street where the puppies, kittens and canaries were on sale.

And then there was Birkenhead Market. The outside market on Saturday night with oil lamps hanging on the stalls. What a great free show that was! Bob Strong, stripped to the waist on the coldest nights, performing his feats of strength and so enabling him to sell his special medicine. Professor O'Toole, who claimed to be able to grow hair on a snooker ball. Wasn't he completely bald? Symond's sweet stall, where for sixpence you could get a huge bag filled with chocolates and sweets. 'Beat the Goalie!', with the footballs soaked overnight in water to make them as heavy as lead. And the stall where you could buy a ha'penny roast potato about the size of a grapefruit. Birkenhead Market on Saturday night was quite a place!

There must be many folk living around Queens Drive, Stoneycroft, who don't realise that the piece of land opposite Sandfield Walk and Alder Road, now incorporating schools and a playing field, was once a deep sandstone quarry. This was called 'The Delf', and children used to play in the quarry in bygone days, when one side was enclosed only by an easily-climbed wall, over which a narrow ledge of tangled undergrowth concealed a sheer drop of fifty feet or so.

Injuries and fatalities there are recorded. Queen's Drive, between Mill Bank and the present Black Horse Lane, was officially opened on June 2nd, 1926. So that this road could be built at this site, it was decided to fill the quarry, and for about ten years up to 1930, thousands of tons of domestic and industrial waste were tipped into it. The youngsters used to have a great time, sliding down the steep slopes of the tip on corrugated-iron sheets, with the ends turned up like sledges. Better still, for the smaller boys, a bin lid, with handle removed, was just the thing. Tarzan-like swinging from dangerously tatty ropes fixed to a high tree was another popular quarry game. Wherever there was a chance of adventure, children of those days were sure to find it.

With typical 'scouse' humour, Liverpudlians very quickly found nicknames for many of the city's well-known places. Ullet Road Recreation Ground was called 'The Greasy Fields', probably because of its usually muddy condition. Princes Park Boulevard soon became 'The Bully'. 'The Cassie', needless to say, was the Cast Iron Shore and 'The Monkey Rack' was the main path in Sefton Park, very popular with courting couples. There was a path overlooking Herculaneum Dock known as 'The

Cinder Walk'. Nearby, off Harlow Street, there was a large area of waste land which provided an ideal playing field and known as 'The Millerfields'. Most people knew the Landing Stage as 'The Stick', and the playing field in Princes Park, on which I must have enjoyed hundreds of games of football and cricket, was dubbed 'The Baldy Pitch' because of the complete absence of grass.

I can't leave out Merseyside's 'jiggers' or 'jowlers'—the back alleys, which were slum children's playgrounds in the old days. The handy gutters were great places for playing ollies. The games were often interrupted by coalmen staggering along with hundred-weight sacks of coal on their backs, or by the dustmen with their special iron implements to unhook the bins which were flush with the walls, and the rag and bone men with goldfish and balloons in exchange for woollens and jamjars.

The back entries were also the scene of backyard concerts, produced, directed and acted by children for children, provided the audience paid their admission fee—a ha'penny. There was some great talent among those entry entertainers—the boys with their dads' bowler hats, or 'blockers' and walking sticks, and black moustache painted on for their Charlie Chaplin acts, and the girls with most of ma's wardrobe trailing along the damp tiles, and a few ricked ankles from high-heeled shoes. The alley was the dogs' domain, and the wall tops made ideal runs for all the cats, or 'jigger rabbits' of the neighbourhood.

And what of the Dock Road? That amazing panorama of events—the heavy waggons, packed high with boxes, crates, sacks, and bales of cotton wool, and drawn by those magnificent Shire horses. What beautiful creatures they were—the direct descendants of the old English war horse, to which they owed their immense strength and size—having been carefully bred to be capable of supporting a knight in full armour on their broad backs. The cloppety-clop of their hooves on the cobbled road almost drowned every other noise.

There was the clatter of the Overhead Railway above—the 'Dockers Umbrella'—that cheap, efficient railway that used to run from Dingle to Seaforth Sands, and trains every few minutes. It's not so many years since it closed down—a very short-sighted decision in my opinion as it would be invaluable now with the present fuel problems. The amount of money needed for repair would have proved a worthwhile investment for the future. It served me best in the 30s when I was one of its regular passengers—the days when we could travel the whole distance from Dingle to Seaforth and back for a few coppers in the evening. The wooden seats weren't all that comfortable, but for cheap, speedy travel, plus an excellent view of the docks, the Overhead Railway was ideal.

Underneath, the little freight trains used to run. Hustling, bustling little trains, they were aptly named 'Puffing Billies', and they helped to add character to the rich tapestry of events which was the Dock Road.

The road absolutely teemed with vehicles of every description. There were the steam wagons—a familiar sight in the 30s. But they had their disadvantages. Their water tanks only allowed for 15-mile journeys (12½ miles for safety), and special hydrants were conveniently installed along the routes. Coal had to be loaded daily, too. Another disadvantage was the Mersey Tunnel. It was often difficult to get enough steam up to go through the Tunnel without a stop.

They were once an everyday sight, hauling their loads along Merseyside's streets. Special copper discs were used which fitted the special boxes that once supplied water for those old steam wagons. By placing the tally into a slot, the driver or his mate could obtain a tankful of water. These water boxes were located at certain points on the main routes. The tallies were obtainable from the Water Board at sixpence each. Although running out of water for a steamer was like running out of oil or petrol for a modern lorry, the steam wagon driver could at least resort to natural water supplies en route, such as village ponds, streams and ditches. But trouble often arose between carters and steamer drivers when the latter poached water from the horse troughs.

But back to the Dock Road. A common sight was ragged little urchins chasing after the loaded wagons with pen-knives in their grubby hands. They knew what they wanted, and quickly picked out those carrying sacks of brown sugar, nuts, and locust beans. They'd rip the sacks, unnoticed by the carter, shove their hands in and fill their pockets, and away they'd go as quick as a flash. Those sacks of edibles were easy prey for the hungry youngsters.

The Dock Road was never lacking in incident.

Chapter Ten
'Don't Forget the Diver!'

When we refer to a person as a 'real character' we usually mean that he or she is a little above the ordinary—someone rather special—a person who invites our amusement, or respect, or our admiration. There were many such 'characters' on Merseyside in the 20s and 30s.

Take the one-legged diver for example. For many folk, 'Don't forget the diver!' was simply a laugh line from Tommy Handley's legendary radio show, ITMA. But thousands of Merseysiders will remember that the originator of that plea was New Brighton's famous one-legged diver, Bernie Pykett, who used to dive off his high perch on the pier into the murky waters of the Mersey for the benefit of the incoming ferry crowds. Sometimes Bernie would vary his act by riding a bicycle off the pier, but he always hopped back up his iron ladder in time to catch the crowd and their coppers with a fishing net at the end of a pole. 'Every penny makes the water warmer', he used to quip.

Bernie, who taught many youngsters how to swim, was said to have played football for an Ellesmere Port club before he lost a leg in action in the Great War. I've only a vague memory of this memorable character, as I only recall seeing him once when I was a small boy, but I seem to remember that he wore a long black bathing costume with a black rubber helmet covering his head. The stump of his missing leg was wrapped round with the spare leg of his costume. Unless my memory is playing me false, on the occasion that I saw him he dived from a great height into a tub which, to my young eyes, seemed perilously small. 'Don't forget the diver! Penny for the diver!' he'd keep shouting.

On one occasion Bernie announced that he'd dive off the wing of a biplane, which in those days provided trips for the holiday crowds. Thousands turned up on the day he'd promised to dive off the plane—all waiting in eager anticipation, and some a little nervous. Unfortunately, he'd overlooked the tremendous pressure of air when the plane was in flight. Handicapped as he was with his one leg, he found it impossible to jump, and there was only one person more disappointed than the spectators—the intrepid Bernie himself. Some said it was all just a publicity stunt and that Bernie had no intention of making such a risky jump, but I've no reason to doubt the courage and integrity of the man, and if the circumstances had been favourable he would have jumped. I'm told that he last dived at New Brighton in 1929, being prohibited the following year as his exhibitions were said to be causing an obstruction.

Now there was a character if ever there was one. And it appeared there was a one-legged diver at New Brighton even before Bernie Pykett. He was a stunt man calling himself 'Pegleg' Gadsby, who would set himself on fire before plunging into the river.

There were many colourful characters around Scotland Road. Probably Scottie Road's most famous 'Mary Ellen' was the shawled lady who sold oranges for many years outside the 'Half Way House' pub at the corner of Bostock Street. She found unwelcome fame one night during the last war when she was mentioned by name on the German radio. Lord Haw-Haw, in his broadcasts, aimed at undermining the morale of people in this country, and he often mentioned people and places whenever he threatened an air raid. One night, after boasting that the German Luftwaffe had selected Liverpool as their 'target for tonight', and were actually on their way, the traitor flaunted his knowledge of the city by mentioning 'Mary Blunn—who sells oranges along Scotland Road'. This remark didn't scare Mary. Blitz or no blitz, she went on selling oranges.

All the 'shawlies' were characters in their own way. In the days when women wore shawls, a thick fawn shawl with a deep fringe was 'the thing'. It was often worn with an emerald green scarf. Some women were lucky enough to sport fur coats. They were usually the moneylenders, who kept barrows on the streets and lent money—charging interest, of course, to the many hard-up families. It was said that the women paid more for their shawls than for a coat. Many bought them from pawnshops. A shawl was the most important part of some women's wardrobe. 'Hobble' skirts were also worn, and sometimes linsey skirts, together with Russian boots and brown Valentian hats with big flowers on.

The 'shawlies' had a certain ritual concerning money. Any money changing hands on the first Monday of the New Year was thought to be lucky. They called it 'Hansel Money', for some reason which I've been unable to discover. The money given by the customer that day to a barrow-girl, for instance, was known

as Hansel Money. It was supposed to bring luck for the
the year. Some women regarded certain people as lucky, and
sure they were the first to give them money on Hansel Mc.,aay.

Lizzie Christian, the tiny barrow girl with a heart bigger than
her barrow, is part of Liverpool's folklore—one of the city's best-
known and best-loved street vendors. Lizzie knew no other life—it
was nothing but sheer hard graft for her, year in, year out. With
her layers of shawls, her boots, her cherubic pink cheeks peeping
out from under her headscarf, and her cries of 'Four for ten'
from behind her barrow, she looked as if she'd stepped right out
of a Dickens novel.

In her early days, Lizzie used to go scrubbing steps round
London Road, for which she was paid threepence. She'd take
bundles to the pawnshop, not just for her own family, but also
for neighbours who were too ashamed to be seen inside a
pawnshop. Yet surprisingly, she always maintained that she
enjoyed a happy childhood. One of her favourite games was 'jacks
and ollies', and she used to go dancing at St. Martin's Hall.

The family's clothes and shoes all came from Paddy's Market.
She became a street vendor and, to earn a little money for the
family she went to the old Cazneau Street Market, filled a big
basket with flowers, and went round the houses selling them at
four bunches for sixpence. Then she became a barrow-girl. Yet
she was never heard to utter one word of complaint. Her life was
far from being a bed of roses, but she won the hearts of countless
Liverpool folk and a place in the city's history. Lizzie Christian—
what an appropriate surname!

And what of Martin Hearn, whose name is so familiar in
aviation circles in the Merseyside area? His aircraft factory at
Hooton Park was of vital importance during World War II as
the main repair depot for Mosquito and Anson planes. But how
many know Martin Hearn for his more extraordinary— some
say crazy-exploits which entertained thousands of people back
in the mid-30s?

In those days of pioneer flying, Martin had one of the craziest
jobs imaginable. He was the famous wing-walker in Sir Alan
Cobham's Flying Circus. After learning to fly in 1928 he got a
job with one of the very first air circuses, run by a Fred Holmes.
At the end of 1931, Sir Alan asked him to join his circus which
moved from town to town giving thrilling displays of stunt flying,
mock bombing, and also joy rides to people brave enough to go

up at that early period. Martin Hearn was hired to fly these joy-riders.

One day, calamity hit the show. The man who did the wing-walking was discovered hopelessly drunk. Hearn immediately volunteered to take over, and perform the most amazing tricks hundreds of feet above the ground without even taking the precaution of wearing a safety harness. Things became decidedly dicy on occasions. He'd be walking about on the wings when, suddenly, there was nothing beneath him—when the plane dropped due to turbulence and he'd be left in mid-air. He said he didn't know who was the more scared—himself or the pilot.

One of Sir Alan's bright ideas for his show was an aerial trapeze act. Once again the performer failed to turn up. Once again Hearn volunteered, and the first time he tried the act over Colchester it very nearly ended in disaster. After completing his performance, which entailed doing tricks on a trapeze while suspended 75 feet from a Handley Page Clive plane travelling at 75 m.p.h. and 500 feet above the ground, he was supposed to be winched up into the plane. But the winch jammed at the vital moment and panic broke out. Photographers ran to the back of the plane for pictures. With all the weight now at the rear of the plane, it shot up vertically as Martin clung on desperately. Sir Alan ordered the cameramen away from the rear, the aircraft then levelled out, and eventually Hearn was hauled on board by a safety rope. But it was a very narrow escape.

There was also that versatile sportsman—Theo Cowdy, who was also a Merseyside man, and a great performer in many sports. I like the story of when, in the summer of 1939, Theo had reached the semi-finals of the County Antrim tennis championship at Portrush, and was drawn against the German star, Hans Klaus. Unfortunately, he lost the first set 0-6, and the second 2-6. There seemed little hope of staging a fighting recovery. But as the two players rested before what would have been the final set, a telegraph boy arrived and handed the umpire a telegram. It was for Herr Klaus. The German opened it, read the contents, turned suddenly, stood smartly to attention, and with arm outstretched shouted 'Heil Hitler. The match is yours!' And with that, Hans Klaus strode off the court and off to the service of Adolf Hitler. The telegram had been his call-up to the Fuhrer's forces.

One of Liverpool's most famous daughters was Miss Jessie Crosbie, the indefatigable headmistress of St. Augustine's Church of England School in Everton. In the hungry 20s, Miss Crosbie, so well ahead of her time in so many things, found it was useless trying to teach children with no food inside them. She decided there and then that all her children would have at least one substantial meal a day. She did it by employing all her charm and guile in persuading all the local shopkeepers to supply the food, free of charge. And so began the first school meal service in the country.

The scheme was officially adopted and became nationwide in the 30s, as did her play centre. Jessie was a realist as well as a woman of vision, and decided there was a real need to keep her children amused during the evenings. Quite simply, for a few hours in the evening, the class rooms were opened and used for games and hobbies. The children could read, play Ludo or dominoes, or indoor football, or skip. They could make toys and models, paint—in fact do what they wished under discreet supervision. Hundreds of youngsters with nothing else to do spent many hours there—the very first play centre in the country.

Not content with that, Jessie somehow persuaded, coaxed, or cajoled the local council and philanthropists to instal baths in her school. Not one of the houses around her school boasted a bathroom, and most of the children were happy to go through life without a decent bath, so it was no easy thing to encourage them to take baths regularly. In those days, some of the children were literally sewn into their clothes, so they were undressed with some difficulty. Jessie was a very shrewd lady. First of all she invited all the mothers to bring their younger children to the school and give them a bath. Then she and some of her staff would take care of the children and keep them amused while the mums themselves took a bath, and even did their washing. And that's how St. Augustine's School had the first meals service, the first nursery school, the first parent-teacher association, and the first play centre. Jessie Crosbie was a truly remarkable lady.

A few years ago I was delighted to hear from Jessie's niece, Mrs. M. D. Green, of Liverpool, who told me she had fond memories of her redoubtable aunt, and she was lucky enough to have all her treasures, including her MBE. Remembering all she did for the city of Liverpool, and for the nation at large, I'm convinced that Jessie Crosbie was deserving of a far higher award.

I haven't the space to include all the great sporting characters of Merseyside. The outstanding sportsmen produced in this area are probably more numerous than in any other part of the country. If I attempted to write about such legendary characters as Dixie Dean, 'Pongo' Waring, Nel Tarleton, Dom Volante and Ernie Roderick it would take up the entire book, and their stories may be read elsewhere. But because he was rather unique in Merseyside sport, I'd like to write a few words about Jimmy Jackson.

James Jackson was one of the truly great soccer players of the 20s. He joined Liverpool F.C. from a Scottish club, so he wasn't a Merseyside man. But he became a Merseysider. He later became the Reverend James Jackson, fondly known by the Anfield faithfuls as 'Parson' Jackson. Jimmy played for Liverpool for eight years as a professional in order to support himself while studying for the ministry—becoming skipper and one of the finest defenders in the game. He was known throughout the land as the 'gentleman of soccer' for his exemplary conduct on and off the field.

He studied at Liverpool University, completing his education at St. Aidan's College, Birkenhead, and Cambridge University. Jimmy was invited to be the assistant minister at Liverpool's Shaw Street Presbyterian Church in 1928. He once said: 'The footballer learns the greatest lesson which life can teach him—to play the game. I have found footballers a generous body of men. In most cases they are just grown-up schoolboys, full of fun and laughter'. Jimmy said that in the 20s. Without wishing to be cynical, I wonder whether he'd have the same sentiments in the 1980s?

The Reverend Jackson used to play in front of that legendary Irish goalkeeper, Elisha Scott, and it's generally known that relations between the two weren't exactly cordial on the field of play. Elisha's earthy language was a bit too much for Jimmy. Parson Jackson died a few years ago at the age of 79. He was, without question, one of Anfield's greatest characters and a shining example to the far more lucratively-paid footballers of today.

I couldn't possibly do better than to quote Derek Whale, of the Liverpool Echo, in describing that formidable character, Mrs. Mirabel Topham: 'The power behind the Grand National for almost half a century, Mirabel Dorothy Topham used to laugh at the names she was given during the time she ran Aintree Racecourse. These ranged from ''The Duchess'' to ''The Aintree Iron''. She had a dominant nature, was an astute business-woman, tough as any man in negotiations, and often downright blunt. Conversely, she could be charming, humorous, gentle and kind.

'Her dual personality was founded on her being an actress before she linked up with the world of racing. As Mirabel Hillier she was playing at the Haymarket Theatre in 1922 when she met Arthur Ronald Topham. Perhaps it was an omen that Mirabel saw "Music Hall" win at her first Grand National in 1922. For Arthur was soon to stand in the wings and invite his wife on to a board far removed from the stage, and from January, 1935, Mirabel became a director. Controlling some 300 acres, with numerous facilities, including 274 stables, public accommodation, stands, fences and their maintenance was a mammoth task for any woman, even with a staff of fifty. But Aintree ran like a hive. And Mirabel was Queen Bee. "I'm always too busy to sting", she would smile'. That just about describes 'The Aintree Iron' perfectly. As long as the Grand National is run at Aintree, the name of Mirabel Topham will keep cropping up.

A man who probably would not have approved of Aintree Racecourse was the compelling Pastor Jeffrey, with his wonderful gift of oratory. He was the Billy Graham of his time. Pastor Jeffrey began his work in Liverpool on May 28th, 1934, and his church was a vast marquee in Carisbrooke Road, Walton. He called it 'The Bethel Crusade of Healing and Salvation'. He drew vast crowds with his great evangelical crusade, and one of the main attractions of his ministry was his faith-healing campaign. An indication of his immense appeal was that at the start of his crusade there was a huge congregation of 15,000, and he continued to draw enormous crowds by his sheer magnetism throughout his stay in Liverpool. The pastor's assistant was Philip Hulbert, the brother of the famous Jack and Claude Hulbert. Pastor Jeffrey's crusade was something of a sensation in the 30s. I don't know what happened to him after he left Liverpool.

Undoubtedly one of Liverpool's most eccentric characters was 'Sir' Frederick Bowman, whose knighthood was either self-bestowed or, according to some, given to him while in prison by a fellow-prisoner who claimed to be the 'King of Rome'. At any rate, Bowman always insisted on being addressed as 'Sir Frederick', and I've always found it best to humour such eccentrics.

I met and talked with Bowman on several occasions in my capacity as secretary of a certain Book Club in Crosby. I can't remember whether we invited him or whether he invited himself. To give him his due I always found him to be extremely witty, charming and interesting. He was an enigma. For instance, he always claimed to be a pacifist and violently opposed to hanging. And yet at one of our meetings he gave a talk on some notorious murderers, and the hanging of them, with such obvious relish that he seemed to enjoy every word of it. To illustrate the talk he brought along with him some rather gruesome relics of various hangings, which he handled with loving care. I don't doubt his sincerity, but I often wondered why such a strong opponent of capital punishment should value such grisly souvenirs.

Bowman always turned up smartly dressed in a rather faded, old-fashioned suit, velvet beret, white silk scarf, and a rather wilted carnation in his buttonhole. He wore a monocle, though whether this was just for effect I'll never know. He used to tell us something of his amazing life—of how he started writing for comic papers while still at The Liverpool Institute, and later went on to own his own papers. I've read some of his stories and articles and the man certainly didn't lack talent. He was also an actor and appeared on London's West End stage when he was about 20, in some play or other. Many years later he hired the Pavilion, in Lodge Lane, in order to play the part of the villain in 'East Lynne'.

His obsession with murderers and hangings can perhaps be gauged by the fact that he once produced a play in which he played the part of the murderer, who was caught, tried, sentenced to death, and was hanged in the final act. He even went to the extreme lengths of buying an old gallows and hiring the public hangman, Ellis, to 'hang' him at each performance. But things went alarmingly wrong at one performance when the cushion on which 'Sir Frederick' was supposed to fall as he dropped through the trap door hadn't been placed in position—with almost fatal results.

He went to prison in 1939 for his strong pacifist views, but he proved such an awkward prisoner with his continual complaints and attempted gaol breaks that no-one was sorry when he was released in March, 1943. As I say, he was a complete enigma, and although he told us all these things with apparent honesty and sincerity, I'll never be completely certain of his true beliefs. He was a consummate actor, and life for him was just a stage. Yet we can only judge people on how we find them ourselves. On the occasions when I was able to converse with 'The Chevalier Sir Frederick Bowman', I always found him intelligent, courteous and affable. But without doubt he was the classic eccentric.

Tom Merry was called 'Liverpool's Dockside Poet'. He used to have a tea kiosk under the Overhead Railway opposite Canning Place. He kept a large blackboard outside his little kiosk on which every day he'd write a poem on one of the outstanding topics of the day, with particular emphasis on happenings on Merseyside.

Tom was well known for his charitable work, and I believe he once rented the bottom floor of a warehouse in Blackstone Street as a shelter for homeless men. You could always be sure of a hot cup of tea, a friendly word, and a helping hand from Tom whenever you entered his cafe. As someone once wrote as a foreword to his little booklet, 'Tom Merry's Rhymes', price sixpence:—

'It gives me a very high pleasure indeed to write a little foreword to this book, "Tom Merry's Rhymes", by one whom I am happy and proud to call a friend of mine, and who, I know, is also a friend of the poor and afflicted, and always ready to serve in the cause of compassion and charity. These good qualities, as virtues, you will find in his poetry, as well as humour, which sweetens the world with smiles and laughter. There is much to write about in "Dockland"—comedy and, alas, tragedy at times, and Tom Merry, the Dockside Poet, knows "Dockland" well. When first I made his acquaintance he was running a little wooden cafe near the wharves and the water and it was not only a place of refreshment but a little temple of fellowship with the good humoured and versatile rhyming Tom Merry presiding. He has given ready help to the Weekly Post Babsie Fund for mothers and children, and in the words of another poet may be written down as "one who loves his fellow men" and does his best and gives his best every time'.

Tom Merry's real name was George Robinson, and I once had the pleasure of meeting and talking to his daughter-in-law, Pat Robinson, at a BBC Radio Merseyside dance at the Carlton Rooms in Eberle Street. It was very apparent that Pat remembered her father-in-law with great affection, as did the many people who'd met this lovable character in his little wooden cafe in the heart of Liverpool's dockland.

Sir John Brocklebank, the former chairman of Cunard, was quite a character in his own way. He was a very able cricketer, having played for Lancashire and also for the Gentlemen against the Players at Lords. That was during the days when there was a great deal of snobbery in cricket. There were the professionals who, of course, played the game for a living, and the amateurs who played it for fun. The Players weren't allowed to use the same entrance as the Gentlemen. Were we to assume that none of the Players were gentlemen? It was a ridiculous state of affairs. In point of fact, there were one or two so-called gentlemen who had a nerve in calling themselves by that name. Fortunately, all that has changed.

Sir John Brocklebank was in the gentlemen category. He toured Canada with the MCC and would certainly have played for England had not the 1939-40 tour been cancelled because of the war. My good friend and former wartime colleague, Harold Wolfe, that fine and knowledgable sports writer with the Liverpool Echo, knew Sir John well, and says that many legends have been woven around him, as he was a real 'card'. There was one about the Liverpool Cricket Club player who was still trying to score his first run at the end of the season. His great moment came at last, and having cracked the ball hard, he galloped to the other end, only to find skipper Brocklebank leaning nonchalantly on his bat and be greeted with the question: 'What do you want, old boy? Change of half a crown?'

And we had the formidable Bessie Braddock. Even if you didn't agree with her politics, and she was very extreme at one time, she was full of guts, and throughout her stormy career she was always the champion of the underdog and fought relentlessly for what she believed in. Battling Bessie was a doughty fighter, and even her enemies admired her. The majority of her constituents in Exchange Ward loved her for her battles on behalf of the poor and the under-privileged. If there was injustice Bessie fought tooth and nail to put things right, and no cause was too small or unimportant for her. The sight of that ample figure getting up to make one of her fiery speeches must have struck fear in the hearts of her opponents. Contemptuous of the many politicians who rabbited on round a question without ever giving a direct reply, Bessie always called a spade a spade, and her forthright opinions impressed people of all political persuasions.

No chapter on some of the great characters of Merseyside would be complete without mention of Miss Margaret Beavan— 'the little mother of Liverpool'. It was due in no small measure to Sir Archibald Salvidge that Miss Beavan became Liverpool's first lady Lord Mayor for the year 1927-28. The appointment was warmly welcomed by the city, who realised how very fitting it was that a woman who had served her city so devotedly should become its civic head.

And, indeed, it had been a wonderful career. It was due to the efforts of Margaret Beavan that the formal opening of the babies' hospital in Woolton took place on June 30th, 1924, by no less than Queen Mary. It was also in the 20s that she hit on the idea of providing a carefree week's holiday for mothers who were worn out with the daily task of coping with large families. A large, spacious house with a lovely garden, in Allerton, was borrowed, and was soon converted into a holiday home for those mothers who'd never dreamed of taking a holiday before.

In 1926, it was fitting that her 25 years of devoted work on behalf of children should be honoured by a banquet at Liverpool Town Hall, given by the Lord Mayor. Glowing tributes were paid to this resourceful lady for her efforts in opening the Liverpool Open-Air Hospital for Children in Leasowe, the Royal Liverpool Babies' Hospital in Woolton, the Ellen Gonner Home for Convalescent Children in Hoylake, the C.W.A. Holiday Camp, and the place with the rather unfortunate name of the Tired Mothers Rest Home. I believe a more suitable name was found for this some time later.

The appointment of a woman Lord Mayor was big news at that time, and the occasion was not without its humour. Miss Beavan received an avalanche of letters and telegrams from all over the world. One French newspaper declared that it was fitting that 'La petite mere de Liverpool' should now become 'Maire' of Liverpool, and a Spanish paper wrote her a delightful letter: 'Madam—Miss Margarita Beavan—You have been the tender little mother of Liverpool children, and now you will become the mildly-stern mother of Liverpool's city fathers'.

There were several important events during her 'reign', including a visit to Liverpool by the King and Queen of Afghanistan, the completion of the boring through of the Mersey Tunnel, a spectacular Pageant of Youth on the Review Field of Sefton Park, and a remarkably successful visit to Italy, where she received a marvellous reception and even a beautiful bouquet of roses from Benito Mussolini himself.

Not only Merseysiders, but the whole nation mourned at her passing on February 22nd, 1931, at the terribly young age of 54. It was a grievous loss for the city, and tributes poured in from the highest in the land, for this remarkable lady had caught the imagination of the whole nation. King George V made a point of sending a telegram to Lord Derby, expressing the sympathy of Queen Mary and himself. She was honoured by a civic memorial service in Liverpool Cathedral. Many tears were shed at the funeral, and there were many hundreds of wreaths, including one from 'the mothers of Liverpool', another from the city's taxi drivers, and, perhaps the most moving tribute of all—at the Cathedral steps the flower girls of Clayton Square approached the cortege and humbly presented their own wreath to 'The Little Mother of Liverpool'. That would have pleased her most of all.

Liverpool had its own woman flying pioneer in the 30s. The name of Amy Johnson—wonderful Amy, had been on everyone's lips ever since her epic flight to Australia in 1930. They even wrote a song about her. But in 1931, Mrs. Trinick—then Delphine Reynolds, daughter of Sir James Reynolds, the Liverpool M.P. and cotton king, decided to pioneer air routes to Africa's west coast, together with a hoped-for record-breaking return flight from Cape Town. She recalled her arrival in Sierra Leone: 'They all went mad. Chiefs came down from the hills bearing gifts. I was presented with a Mandingo snake, which is of the python variety. It loves being handled, and I used it as a pet and left it in the cockpit. No one ever interfered with the aircraft when they saw the snake, and yet it was harmless. I flew with it curled up at my feet. I was also given three crates of rare birds and a baby gorilla'.

Strangely enough, Mrs. Trinick later admitted that she was afraid of flying. She said: 'It seems stupid to be afraid of flying as a passenger when I used to do all sorts of crazy things in the air. I even made a couple of parachute jumps. I was fearless. I pioneered the air route to Sierra Leone, flew over Mount Vesuvius, and had my engine cut out over the crater as I was looking down into it'. Many Merseysiders and others will remember the flying exploits of the former Delphine Reynolds.

I must have walked along Great George Street hundreds of times in the 20s and 30s on my way from the south-end to the Landing Stage. It was usually on Sunday, and I can remember the trams absolutely packed with people stopping outside Great George Street Congregational Church. When the conductor rang the bell again the tram would be empty, for his call of 'Paxton's Chapel' meant all the passengers disembarking and making their way into the well-known chapel. They came from all over Liverpool. And not only in trams but also in expensive cars which would be parked in the neighbouring streets.

For the main attraction of this old church was its remarkable minister, the Reverend William Paxton. Paxton, a Scot with a very powerful gift of oratory, arrived when the church seemed to be in decline and the congregations falling alarmingly. His fiery sermons, his immense personal appeal, and his superb gift for down-to-earth preaching soon brought the people flocking back. I used to see so many people crowding into the church that I'm convinced that many of them must have had to stand throughout the service—that is when they weren't on their knees.

The Reverend Paxton possessed a magnetic appeal, and it's been said that if he hadn't devoted his life to preaching he would have made a supreme actor. He knew how to put it over, and his sincerity was there for all to see. There was always a solitary beam of light from a suspended lamp playing on the features of this superb preacher, clad in his black gown, with two white tabs at his throat. His voice, starting softly, built up gradually as his theme gathered momentum, until it ended in a spell-binding climax. William Paxton ministered at Great George Street Congregational Church from 1925 to 1933, and later his son was minister of the church for ten years. Preachers like Paxton Senior are very rare indeed.

Chapter Eleven
Some Quaint and Curious Characters

The streets of Merseyside never lacked entertainment during those colourful days before the war. They seemed to be swarming with street vendors of every description. There were scores of rag-and-bone men who used to hand out balloons, toy windmills, chipped cups and saucers, and even goldfish for old rags and bones and pieces of iron. One character had a miniature merry-go-round, balanced rather precariously on an old cart, and drawn by an even more ancient nag. For a few rags we enjoyed the doubtful pleasure of a ride on the merry-go-round which seemed to go round ever so slowly, accompanied by music played on an old gramophone. The trouble was that the merry-go-round was always breaking down.

Even the pub doorways were jammed at night with buskers plinking and plonking away on their battered old banjos or mandolins. Some of the most welcome of the street entertainers, especially for us children, were the barrel-organ grinders. The distinctive sound of those barrel-organs drew youngsters like bees round a jam pot, as they churned out the popular tunes of the day like 'Valencia', 'When it's springtime in the Rockies' and 'Yes, we have no bananas'. Few of the organ-grinders that I saw in the twenties had monkeys, but if they were lucky enough to have one they certainly drew a bigger crowd and a bigger collection.

When I was a child I used to be fascinated at the sight of the women who used to come round the streets with about half a dozen large blocks of salt balanced precariously on their heads. They all seemed to be dressed the same, with enormous pleated skirts pulled in very tightly at the waist, over which was a white apron, a heavy shawl, and black lace-up boots. Their hair was taken back in a bun, and on top of their heads would be a roll of cloth with the blocks of salt on top. I used to marvel at their skill in keeping those enormous blocks in position. Sad to say, we used to walk behind them, hoping for some disaster, which never happened. Some of those women were, in fact, the salt of the earth, and they certainly earned every penny of the few shillings they made.

And then there were the street grafters. There was one rather scruffy character with a perpetually runny nose who played the zither at the end of Princes Road, backing on to the Greek Orthodox Church. He was making his living from the zither long before Anton Karas made it big with his 'Third Man Theme' and 'Cafe Mozart'. If, and when, someone dropped a copper into his hat, he didn't bother to smile or say thank you—he just kept on playing as if in a dream.

Round about the same period there was the so-called 'Masked Singer' with tatty black cape and air of mystery to match. Many were the rumours as to why the mask. Some said it was because he'd been so fearfully disfigured in the Great War that he dared not show his dreadful scars. Others said he'd once been a rich man jilted by a shrew who'd bled him white and left him in abject poverty. Still others had it that he was a former opera singer who'd become a hopeless alcoholic and who could no longer obtain work in the theatre. There could be no possible truth in this theory because he had an atrocious voice. It later transpired that he was in fact just another street grafter with an unusual gimmick. He made a fair living, particularly around the business area of Liverpool, and he used to be seen counting his daily takings in Ma Egerton's pub in Pudsey Street, minus the mask.

The 20s and 30s was the era of the street 'quack doctors' and their mysterious concoctions. I remember one in particular who bore a remarkable resemblance to W. C. Fields. He used to set up his high platform on the corner of Park Road and Wellington Road in the south end of Liverpool, and he'd extol the magic qualities of his mysterious mixture. He charged sixpence a bottle, after claiming with great eloquence that it was a certain cure for all the ills under the sun—nature's own remarkable elixir, and if you took the prescribed dose you'd never again suffer a day's illness. Naturally, there were the gullible ones who fell for his patter and parted with their precious tanners. Some said that this marvellous liquid was nothing more than cabbage water.

The Lightcake Man—I seem to recall that we called him 'Lightcake Billy'—was a very welcome street seller on Merseyside many years ago. I suppose some people would call him the Muffin Man, but he called them light cakes—a sort of pancake. Regularly every Sunday afternoon he'd walk round the streets with a basket full of those little cakes, and he did a roaring trade. I can even remember the price—seven for threepence.

Then there was the knife and scissors grinder who used to ride round the streets on a tricycle with a circular grinding wheel at the front. I've forgotten what his cry was—something like 'Knives to grind! Any scissors to grind!' We'd take out our knives and scissors and he'd pedal away furiously to spin the stone, and the sparks would fly as he put a sharp edge on the implement. It's a great pity we never see them nowadays—what a roaring trade they'd do—as would the old umbrella man who would repair your broken brolley for a couple of coppers. He'd be warmly welcomed in this wet, miserable climate of ours.

The Salvation Army bands were a great attraction in those days. They'd play regularly every Sunday afternoon or evening on the street corners, drawing large audiences. I've always had a healthy respect and admiration for the men and women of the 'Sally Army', especially during the war when, to our eternal gratitude, they brought their mobile canteens as close to the front line as was reasonably possible. They were usually first on the scene with the welcome cups of hot tea. The crowds used to enjoy singing hymns to those fine bands and they also enjoyed the warmth and friendliness of the bandsmen and women. I don't think I've ever heard one word of criticism of the Salvation Army.

Talking about friendliness, when I was a small boy, who ought not to have been playing out at such a late hour, I often received a sweet from the friendly lamplighter—the man who always made the nights a little brighter. At dusk each evening he'd appear with his long pole with a hook on the end—reach up and engage the hook into the circular wire switch at the base of the lamp, and, hey presto! the street was lit up sufficiently for us to continue our fun and games.

'Once he walked the windy town, in his hand a mysterious long pole whose faintest touch brought brilliant light'. Well it wasn't brilliant light by any stretch of the imagination. 'The childhood delight of watching the lamplighter's slender wand coax the black stems of the street lamps into golden flower'. The sight of the old lamplighter approaching was very welcome on a particularly dark night.

Another 'creature of the night'—or early morning, to be exact, was the so-called 'knocker up', but he was far from welcome. He'd roam the streets at the crack of dawn, armed with a long pole for knocking on the bedroom windows to rouse those snoring occupants who were fortunate enough to have jobs to go to. Apparently, even those massive old door-knockers failed to do the trick, so it had to be the bedroom window. I often wonder who knocked up the 'knocker-up'!.

One of the most familiar aspects of city life in those days was the enormous variety of buskers outside the cinemas and theatres, and in the busy city shopping centre. They certainly added colour to drab city streets as they sang, and played, with little talent, I hasten to add, their concertinas, accordions, banjos and tin whistles. My own favourite was the 'sweet potato piper'—the man who played the ocarina—a small wind instrument shaped something like a potato with a bulge coming out of one side, at the end of which was the mouth-piece. It was often called the 'sweet potato' and it played many a pretty tune. I suppose I liked it because it was different.

And with what joy we welcomed the one-man band. He'd play the big bass drum together with the crashing cymbals on top of the drum. He alternated between the harmonica and the flute, and he had a real variety of instruments which he operated ever so skilfully with his arms, elbows and legs. As we watched him we were filled with wonder at his skill and dexterity. Musically, it left a lot to be desired, but it was certainly spectacular and gave immense enjoyment to us children. Other buskers we'd usually ignore and get on with our street games, but when the delighted cry, 'Here's the one-man band!' was heard, we dropped everything and provided an appreciative audience.

I often wonder what became of the half a dozen unemployed Liverpool lads who were Liverpool's own version of Hollywood's 'Dead End Kids'. This happy six used to travel the streets singing, dancing, and playing the fool—anything at all just to make you laugh. They called themselves 'The Happy Gang', and their zany antics brought much happiness to a lot of people. One summer in the late 30s they were doing a knockabout comedy act in Ryan's Fair at Moreton. They had no money but they had no grievance about the world owing them a living. They deserved better things.

There was the little Italian who worked the cinema queues in the city playing his zither. He always carried with him a little fold-up table to put the zither on while he performed. And the veteran circus performer with his white shoes and heavy walking stick. He'd position the stick with one hand outstretched, and then twist his body underneath the arm which held the stick. He'd also use the stick to skip with. He was no Fred Astaire but he was pretty nimble on his feet for his age. Before his performance he told his audience that these were the tricks he used to do on the back of a saddle-less horse as it pranced around the circus ring—but in those days, he added mischievously, he was only eighty! I think his name was Tom Duff.

A 'horse' of a different colour was the self-styled 'Major Dawson', a well-known racing tipster who sold his tips on waste ground, at the docks, and on street corners. One of his favourite pitches was at the junction of London Road and Falkland Street. Oh yes, the 'major' had served in the army, during World War I, but full private was the highest rank he ever attained.

However, he'd posed as a major for so long that he began to look the part. Dawson had a veritable 'gift of the gab', and his audience were always treated to a flamboyant discourse on racing matters. One of his sales gimmicks was to claim that at the previous day's race meeting he'd spoken to 'my friend, Tommy Weston'—a prominent and successful jockey of his day, who'd given him the name of a horse—a 'sure snip', which couldn't possibly fail to win the 2.30 at Epsom the following day.

Whether it was his sales talk or his racing acumen is a matter of conjecture, but his tips sold like hot cakes. As for the 'major' having been at the previous day's race meeting, it was far more likely that he'd been no further than the Legs of Man public house in Lime Street. Certainly he made quite a good living from his tips and he always looked prosperous.

I recall with amusement the man who used to walk the back entries of Liverpool with a brush and a bucket of whitewash, shouting: 'Outside petties whitewashed for a tanner!' He was quickly taken up, and, with a sack over his head, and two holes to see through, he'd give the outside 'loo' a spanking new coat of whitewash. Then the charge went up to a shilling—then 1/6d. Imagine the furore when he increased it to a staggering two shillings! Protested one man, in a high state of indignation: 'It's absolutely scandalous. Two bob just for whitewashing the petty!' Petty? Now where exactly did that name originate? Was it another 'scouse' term, or did it come from the heart of the country where, like the fairies, the 'loo' was always at the bottom of the garden?

Very welcome were the roasted chestnut merchants, especially on cold wintry nights. And the shrimp man, who sold fresh fish and shrimps 'all-alive-o!' Also the 'kewin' seller. 'Kewin' was a Liverpool name for the common winkle. We used to buy them by the cupful, and we'd 'winkle' the little fish out of their shells with a pin. And the fellow who sold potatoes in the streets from his cart, calling out: 'Taters! Taters! Floury Taters!' Also welcome was the brandy-snap seller, the roasted peanut vendor, and the man who used to come round with trays of toffee apples—quite delicious at a ha'penny each—lovely big apples covered with a thick layer of toffee—ever so much better than their modern equivalent. Times were hard, but we seemed to get full value for money.

Many's the time in years gone by when, with little else to do, I've stood in Lime Street and watched the shoe-shine 'boys' putting an immaculate shine on the boots and shoes of passers-by. I think they charged a penny. It was a useful service in the days when men prided themselves on having their shoes brilliantly polished—and when youths had their hair shining just as brilliantly with the use of brilliantine hair oil, and often parted down the middle.

I once received a letter from a listener to my radio programme: 'Your mention of buskers brings two to my mind—one you won't believe, but I swear by all that's sacred it's true and did take place. It was a middle-aged gent clad in pyjamas, a small skull-cap and plimsolls, and carrying a small bucket. He used to place the bucket on the ground, stand on his head in it and sing such songs as "The old rustic bridge" and "Nellie Dean". I first saw him in a park one Sunday afternoon. Another was a man who came round every Saturday morning singing and playing the mandolin. When he came to a high note he couldn't quite reach he became furious and fair gave that mandolin some stick. One song of his I liked a lot was "Meet me down beside the singing waters", and I was ever so thrilled to hear it on the wireless some time later played by Troise and his Mandoliers, and sung by Don Carlos. This busker faded from the scene just before the war started, and we never saw him again. It must have been a very tough life for them for, entertaining though they were, few people had coppers to spare for them'.

Merseyside had 'groups' in the 20s and 30s—nothing like the 'pop' groups of today, but groups of young men who went busking round the streets dressed in 'drag', as we call it now. They were all unemployed, without any dole or assistance from anywhere. There was some real talent among them—singers, musicians and dancers. They usually toured the streets in groups of four—they could hire their instruments for the day from a shop which stood next to the Rifle Brigade barracks in St. Anne Street. From this shop buskers could hire any musical intrument they wished—the windows were chock full of instruments of all kinds.

Many will remember the character who walked up and down the back entry shouting: 'Tubs to mend! Dolly tubs to mend!' The dolly tub was an essential part of household equipment in those days. And the man who'd sit in your back yard and reseat those old-fashioned, rush-bottomed kitchen chairs, not to mention the chap who sold syrup from a tank on a pony cart—you'd take your cup and he'd fill it for a penny or so. All these characters were part and parcel of the Merseyside scene in pre-war times.

Before the war, Merseyside swarmed with street corner bookies—long before betting shops were made legal. They catered for the man-in-the-street's longing for a small wager on the three-thirty at Epsom and so on. They used to employ what were called 'bookies' runners'—youths who were used as go-betweens with bookmakers and their customers. They'd accept threepence-each-way bets at that time, written on grubby little bits of paper or on the back of a cigarette carton.

These bookies had to be extremely wary as the plain-clothes policemen, or 'D's', were often more than a match for them. We were often regaled with the sight of dozens of tatty little betting slips soaring in the breeze as a bookie was frog-marched to the waiting Black Maria. The police would sometimes hang around disguised as workmen, waiting for the opportunity to pounce. Sometimes, if the favourite won the big race, you were lucky to get your winnings, as some of the bookies just scarpered.

There were some 'characters' to be found among Merseyside's money-lenders—the unofficial ones, I mean. Some were kindly, understanding people, but there were others of the more shady and avaricious kind who'd suck their victims dry. In many of the poorer districts some women did a thriving trade in money-lending—an offence severely frowned on by the law, as very often the interest charged was quite exorbitant. I'm told that if you borrowed, say, five shillings, with a shilling interest for the week—so long as you paid the interest each week that was perfectly acceptable. But the capital of five shillings remained. Thus, in a full year, for a mere five shillings, the borrower could pay back £2.12s. and still owe the money originally borrowed. Easy pickings for some of the more unscrupulous.

Even in the 1940s, street musicians were a part of our city, when most of them were allegedly 'ex-servicemen'. There was one not-very-accomplished trumpet player, universally known as

'Phil the Fluter'. A friend once told me that, during the war, when he had to work in Manchester for a spell, he lodged with a very smart one-legged man who never revealed what he did for a living until later, back in Liverpool, he was seen with 'Phil the Fluter' and a group of alleged ex-servicemen grafting in Lime Street. Needless to say, the one-legged man was the 'bottler'— that is, the one who collected from a largely sympathetic public. And from the way he dressed when he was 'off duty', so to speak, it was quite a lucrative business.

The 'Sandwich Board' men were a common sight in the old days—a pathetic procession of shabbily-dressed, half-starved men treading wearily along the gutter. Recruited mainly from the doss houses around Islington, they were paid a few shillings a day. Doubtless they were grateful for the protection of their sandwich-boards during bad weather. Frequently, when out of the public eye, they'd shuffle into some back entry, prop their boards against a wall and puff away at cigarette stumps from their grubby pockets, and originally fished out of the gutters.

Many people, especially drivers, will remember the 'mechanical bobby', which was the nickname of one of 'B' Division's policemen, earned because of his rhythmic, semaphore-like, perfectly-timed point duty. A well-built man of smart military bearing, he had a healthy tan which was a memento of his army service in India. His last point-duty assignment was at the top of Pembroke Place, opposite the Dental Hospital. When he died, several years ago, the Liverpool Echo gave him an obituary paragraph headed: 'Mechanical Bobby Dies'. During the wartime threat of invasion he exchanged his point duty to guarding the entrance to Prescot Street Bridewell. Standing at the foot of the steps, thumb behind his revolver holster, every now and then he'd look challengingly up and down the street. He seemed to epitomise the famous Churchillian cry: 'We will fight them in the streets . . . !'

I mustn't forget the pavement artists—men with considerable talent who were obliged for reasons known only to themselves to display their artistic ability on some street pavement—their only reward being the odd penny or two, or, if it happened to be their lucky day, a little silver sixpence. I remember seeing some superb pavement work, and I always felt extremely sorry for the artist when it started to rain and his painstaking efforts were obliterated.

The escapologists never failed to attract huge interest, and large crowds. I recall one in particular who used to perform his apparently impossible feats near Canning Place. He'd be bound hand and foot with the most formidable looking chains—then he'd invite some of the spectators to inspect him thoroughly while he was lying on the ground. He'd promise to throw off the chains within a specified number of seconds. Then, after what appeared to be a tremendous struggle, he'd free himself, jump to his feet and take the hat round.

And who was that generous Liverpool benefactor who called himself 'A Man of no Account'? To anyone involved in a personal tragedy, or had a stroke of bad luck, and might be in desperate need of help, of which this man read in the local newspapers, he'd always send £10. At Christmas time he'd also send a generous gift to the Echo Goodfellow Fund. His good works were always hidden under a cloak of anonymity. He was truly a man of very considerable account.

There were a couple of characters who called themselves 'Jim and Jerkem'. Jim played the piccolo and Jerkem the banjo. Jim wore a large bow on his collar which he'd keep moving with the aid of his Adam's apple, even while he was singing. They usually came round the streets during the children's dinner break, and started their performance by marching up and down in military fashion until they had a crowd of eager youngsters following them.

Then they'd get the children to sit on the ground and start them off singing. Jim would knock on the front doors for pennies while the children were kept singing by his partner. When they decided to move on they'd stop the singing, and order the youngsters not to follow them. They kidded them that they'd been to their various schools and that the head teachers had told them to give them all a half-day's holiday. Then they'd ask for three hearty cheers and away they'd go. Which was all pretty unscrupulous, to say the least.

We certainly didn't lack variety in those days. Many will recall with considerable amusement the Irishman who went round singing. Unfortunately, he only knew one song, and he didn't sing that very well. Wherever he went it was the same old song. Perhaps it was from him they got the advert, 'Roses grow on you', for the name of his one and only song was 'Just a rose in a garden of weeds'.

The flower-sellers have always been a familiar and colourful part of Liverpool's city centre life. They always did good custom, and were well-liked by the public. When Margaret Beavan became Lord Mayor of Liverpool in the late 20s, one of her many human gestures was her invitation to the flower girls of Clayton Square to morning coffee at the Town Hall—a thoughtful act that not only won her the lasting affection of the flower sellers themselves, but also captured the imagination of the Liverpool public.

Liverpool folklore contains the rather mysterious names of Dicky Sam, Icky the Firebobby, Joe Soap, Joe Egg, Dick Plush, and Daddy Bunchy. Who these characters were, no one seems to know for certain but I'm told that Dicky Sam used to run a pub on Mann Island, near the Pier Head. His real name was Richard Samuels, and with the Liverpudlian habit of contracting names he became known as Dicky Sam. But who on earth was Daddy Bunchy? Some say he was a dwarf, but, as the name was often used in children's games as a rather frightening figure, there's a theory that they were threatened with Daddy Bunchy if they played truant, as he was no less than the School Attendance Officer.

Chapter Twelve
The Sign of the Three Brass Balls

I left school in 1932 and found myself in the desperate situation of being one of hundreds of school-leavers chasing after the paltry few jobs available. A decent education counted for little in the depths of that other Great Depression. To describe it as a desperate situation is to put it mildly, so I counted myself exceedingly fortunate when I obtained work in August of that year, albeit for a few paltry shillings a week. I quickly discovered that beggars can't be choosers, and that it was good policy to grab any sort of job that was offered. All my lofty ambitions had to go by the board.

My job was in an office near the docks, and I remember seeing the hundreds of men standing in as many as four queues to reach the doorway of the local labour exchange in order to sign on for their miserable pittance of dole money. They had to sign on three times a week. If they failed to do so they got no dole. They didn't appear to be bitter or resentful—just resigned and apathetic. And yet there must have been bitterness in their hearts and humiliation in their souls as they stood in those dole queues.

They were the days of the hated Means Test with its army of snoopers, whose job it was to make sure that people didn't actually earn a few extra shillings without informing the authorities, and draw their pitiful dole money at the same time. If a son or a daughter was found to be earning money, then the man's dole was reduced. This inevitably led to families splitting up, as many of the youngsters preferred to leave home rather than see their father's dole reduced or cancelled. I suppose they could claim they were only doing their jobs, but those snoopers were even more detested than the Means Test itself.

I remember vividly the half-starved men hanging around the street corners, passing a Woodbine round for each of them to enjoy a drag, until a policeman arrived on the scene and dispersed them. They weren't allowed to gather on street corners for an innocent chat. Maybe they were plotting revolution! I remember them playing pitch and toss—that is if they had a few ha'pennies in their ragged pockets. They stood in the gutter and tossed the coins against the wall, and the one whose coin ended up nearest the wall was entitled to gather up all the coins and toss them up. He was allowed to keep those that came down heads—or tails, depending on the rules of the game. There were variations of the game. In the eyes of the law this was gambling, and a boy was usually put on 'douse' to watch out for an approaching 'copper'.

The sign of the three brass balls was a familiar sight in Merseyside's poorer districts. They were almost as numerous as the pubs. Practically everything found its way to the dusty shelves of the pawn shop. Many people had to wear the same clothes day after day—they had no others. But if some folk possessed decent clothes they only allowed themselves to wear them on Sundays as, first thing on Monday morning they were pawned. On Saturday, the pawnshops were besieged by people redeeming their Sunday best, followed again by the usual queue on Monday morning.

As well as clothes, they pawned sheets, blankets, curtains, tablecloths, towels—anything at all that would fetch a few shillings for the next day's meals. I'm assured on good authority and I have no reason to doubt it, that one old lady used to pawn her false teeth regularly every Monday, and redeem them in good time to enable her to attend church on Sunday morning.

The pawnshops provided a welcome service. There was a statutory pledge period during which the pawnbroker was obliged to keep the 'popped' article and the customer could redeem it by repaying the original loan plus interest. At the end of this period—I believe it was a year and one day—'uncle' was free to put any unredeemed articles up for sale. On the other hand, the customer could prevent this happening and buy more time by merely paying the weekly interest.

Pawnshops were small, dark, musty places, which you entered by a side door, and where business was carried out in discreet, low whispers. Some pawnshops had a pen machine—a useful gadget of three linked pens. So, by writing with one, the pawnbroker or his clerk automatically operated the other two, so that three copies of the pawn ticket could be written simultaneously. One ticket was pinned to the pledge, one went into the files, and the third was handed to the customer. The shelves reached right up to the ceiling and a ladder had to be used to reach the top ones. I think it was an Echo writer who claimed that half the neighbourhood was represented on those musty old shelves, and the pawnshops were a monument to poverty—a storehouse of human hardship and misery.

If a pawnshop employee's job was secure in the thrifty and threadbare 30s, so also was the check man's. For they were the days of the check. Certain stores issued checks to needy people enabling them to purchase clothes and things and repay the amount weekly by instalments, plus interest, of course. Thousands of folk took advantage of this scheme, and the check man calling round for the weekly repayments was one of the most familiar sights on Merseyside.

The trouble was that, for some people, this was an easy way of obtaining some ready money. They'd get the check, say from Sturla's, buy some articles from the store, and immediately take them to the pawnshop where they'd be given only a fraction of their real value. In many cases they had no intention of ever redeeming these goods, so that the little money they received was quickly spent, and yet they'd go on paying the check man long after the goods had ended up on the pawnbroker's shelves. It's easy to say that such people were stupid, but desperation leads to many foolish actions, and there were hungry little mouths to feed. For many such folk they were horrible, hideous times, and many mothers went hungry in order to see that their children were reasonably fed.

Many houses in those days had penny-in-the-slot gas meters, and a penn'orth of gas seemed to go a long way. The collector, or the 'gas man', as he was called, would come round at certain periods to empty the meter. And what a welcome sight he was for many people in the poorer areas. He'd empty the pennies on to the table—hundreds of them—count them carefully and deftly wrap them, in bundles of fifty, in blue paper. And you got discount. I can't recall how they calculated it, but the precious pennies handed back often meant a couple of meals for the hard-up family. Is it any wonder that he was welcomed so warmly? In one district of Merseyside the gas man was a kindly little Welshman named Evan Evans. So it really was a case of 'Pennies from 'Evan'!

Whenever I went to Woolworth's in the 30s for my sixpenny Eclipse gramophone records there was always a group of men and women round the spectacles counter—busily trying them on in order to find a pair that would suit them. It was a pathetic sight, and a sobering thought that they had to make do with a sixpenny pair of glasses from Woolworths. I'm not blaming the store in the very least, for it was a useful service, but what damage those glasses must have caused to the eyes.

It's good to know that dockers get a far better deal these days. In the bad old days of casual labour the docker's tally became worth its weight in gold. They couldn't be employed without a tally, and they could even get credit for a meal on the strength of it. There was a system which the men called 'three on the hook and three on the book'—which meant three days work and three days on the dole. In those days the men stood around hopefully—and very often hopelessly—for the jobs that were available, and a tap on the shoulder meant they had one, perhaps for only half a day. And then it was hanging about again, waiting for another tap on the shoulder.

If your face didn't fit it was a complete waste of time, as a lot of unfair favouritism went on, so if they had a penny they consoled themselves with a hot drink in one of the cocoa rooms. For hundreds of dockers in the 30s, their hooks, which they used for moving the cargo, were neither ornamental nor useful, as they could go for months without any work at all. It was soul destroying. Chatting to an ex-docker some years ago, he reminded me of those cocoa rooms which were a feature of the Dock Road. Dockers and carters would go in for a plate of scouse, a mug of tea, and sometimes a 'Wet Nellie'. And the horses waiting outside weren't forgotten. One of the things they enjoyed most of all was a sugar buttie.

Half-starved children, many of them barefooted, would wait for the dockers coming off the ships with the plaintive cry: 'Any butties please, mister?' And many of the men, who were lucky enough to be working, would save some of their sandwiches and give them to the hungry children. Which reminds me that there was once the poor children's queue for bread on Sunday nights in Hanover Street—a charity run by a gentleman from the Liverpool Gas Company.

You'd often see shabbily-dressed men walking along the gutters, armed with long sticks with a pin or spike in the end, 'sticking' cigarette stubs and transferring them into old tobacco tins. They were the days before tipped cigarettes, and a half inch stub was more than welcome. Sometimes they were lucky and stumble on a half-smoked cigarette, and you could see the joy on their faces. Having filled their tins they'd take them home, carefully extract the tobacco from the stubs and roll it into new cigarettes. It was all so pathetic.

In those pre-war times, when two evening papers competed on the Merseyside streets—the Echo and the Evening Express, the newspaper boys' cries of 'Late extra—read all about it!' were a familiar sound. In those days, the miserably-clad boys, many in cloth caps and bare feet, had to wait on the street corners for the van to toss out a bundle of newspapers. Then, extremely fleet of foot, they'd race round their own coveted area shouting the old familiar cry: 'Echo or Exy!' and cover it in next to no time—impatient at having to give change for a bob, a tanner, or a tiny threepenny 'joey'. They certainly earned their few coppers commission. Not for them the comparative comfort of a kiosk, and very often one's heart bled as their feet bled as they raced along some of the roughly paved streets of that time.

One of the most praiseworthy charities was, as now, the Liverpool Echo Goodfellow Fund. Of necessity, it was on a much bigger scale in the 30s. Any seriously deprived family could be nominated for a Goodfellow parcel. It was a wonderful innovation. When the festive season came round, a family in desperate circumstances would receive a bumper hamper of Christmas goodies, thanks to the generosity of Echo readers and the newspaper itself. Two other charitable sections of this fund were the Cuefellows and the Gleefellows. The Cuefellows used to play billiards in pubs and clubs to raise cash for the Goodfellows. The Gleefellows, including some of the employees of the Daily Post and Echo, used to go round singing to make money for the fund.

The terrible poverty and unemployment that blighted the nation should have shamed our leaders into some positive action. But little hope was offered. I remember reading of the Jarrow Hunger March, when the men of that stricken town, whose families were in desperate straits, decided to march all the way to London. Led by Ellen Wilkinson, the M.P. for Jarrow, the very pit of depression, and to the sound of mouth organs, they went on their march to London.

There was no disorder. The ill-fed, badly-clothed men made their protest in dignified manner before catching a special train back to Jarrow, where they received a tumultuous welcome home. It was one of the great marches of history. It seems quite incredible that the Unemployment Assistance Board in Jarrow immediately deducted from four to eleven shillings from the brave marchers' meagre allowance, on the grounds that while they were away from their homes they would not have been available for work had any jobs materialised. Officialdom at its most cruel and heartless.

Chapter Thirteen
High Days and Holidays

For many of us children, going away on holiday was something the posh people did. It was not for us. We accepted the fact, and it simply didn't occur to us to feel envious of those who could afford to spend a week or two at Blackpool, Morecambe, or the Isle of Man. What we'd never had we never missed.

When the summer holidays came round, we spent our days walking down to the Landing Stage to see the ships, taking a penny tram ride to Woolton Woods or Calderstones Park, or having fun and games on the Cast Iron Shore. The Cassie! What memories that conjures up of happy days in the sunshine, playing cricket or football on the grimy, oily sand, or sheltering in our tatty little tents when it started to rain. A few jam butties and a bottle of pop and we were in heaven. Sometimes it didn't even run to a bottle of pop so we had to make do with a bottle of water. And did we just imagine that the summers were longer and hotter in those days? We left home early in the morning and didn't get back until late in the evening, tired, dirty, and happy. Who wanted Blackpool when we had the Cassie on our doorstep?

Later, we aspired to greater things such as a ferry trip to Seacombe, New Brighton, Rock Ferry, or Eastham Woods. Many a Liverpudlian's holiday was a day out 'over the water'. They were the days of dancing on New Brighton Pier for twopence, or dancing on the deck of the ferry boat to the music of the concertina or the banjo. There was the thrill of waiting with the vast crowds on the Landing Stage for our boat to come in, and of running down the gangway and up on to the upper deck of the ferry. New Brighton's sands were golden in those far-off days, and people would sit for hours in the glorious sunshine, not budging except for going for a pot of tea to drink with their sandwiches.

There's no doubt whatsoever that New Brighton's beautiful beach was spoiled by the building of the promenade. Before that there was a glorious expanse of golden sand, enjoyed by tens of thousands of trippers. It came right up to the 'Ham and Egg Parade' with its busy shops, and nearly up to the Red Noses. It even invaded the enclosure of the Queens Hotel, where the pierrots, to our delight, performed on a wooden platform laid on the sand. It was nice to have the promenade but it was the beginning of the end for the beach and the halcyon days of New Brighton as a popular holiday resort. The scour of the tides swept away the sand and silted up the landing stage. It was a sad day when the regular ferry service came to an end. For countless folk, the trip by ferry to New Brighton, and a day spent on the beach and at the famous fair was one of the highlights of the summer.

Many Merseysiders will recall with affection the old paddle steamers, and especially perhaps 'La Marguerite' which used to grace the Mersey. She was probably the finest acquisition of the Liverpool and North Wales Steamship Company. 'La Marguerite' was a 2,205-ton paddle steamer built in 1894, and the biggest and finest excursion steamer on the coast, with a speed of 22 knots. She made her last voyage in September, 1925, and was broken up later that year after carrying thousands of happy passengers. 'Mona's Queen' was the last paddle-ship in the Isle of Man Steam Packet Company's fleet, and was disposed of in 1929. The Liverpool-North Wales Company's 'Snowdon' lasted until 1931.

What memories the paddle-steamer 'Jubilee Queen' evokes. In the 30s this pleasure boat was embarking passengers for Blackpool at Princes Landing Stage. 'All Aboard for Blackpool' was the notice, and the return fare was five shillings. I remember a picture in the Daily Post showing passengers embarking on the 'Jubilee Queen', and also a happy picture with the caption: 'They're matey with the mate', showing two tiny tots in the arms of the mate of the 'Queen', and both wearing sailors hats, with the caption: 'Privileged youngsters pose for their photographs with the mate of the pleasure steamer 'Jubilee Queen' while on their way from Liverpool to Blackpool'. The smiling mate was that grand old sailor, Ted Gore, of Crosby, who could write a book about his adventures in peace and war.

Happily, the paddle steamer 'Waverley', one of the oldest operating boats in the British Isles, is still paddling merrily away. And I mustn't forget the old 'Ruby' and 'Pearl' which carried happy trippers to Eastham. They made their last trips in the spring of 1929, when, sadly, Eastham Ferry closed. Most of us know the old Eton Boating Song, but how many have heard the Eastham Boating Song during the great days of the paddle steamers?

'To Eastham, to Eastham, where music fills the air,
All nature seems enchanting, and the girls are wondrous fair.

For all seems bright and happy, and hearts go pit-a-pat,
To Eastham, dear old Eastham, I still take off my hat'.
And so say all of us who enjoyed those wonderful trips.
Incidentally I wonder how many people remember that great
attraction at Eastham—the Maze, which almost equalled the more
famous one at Hampton Court?

There must be thousands of folk throughout the country who
still cherish happy memories of the steam yacht 'Killarney', which,
in the halcyon years before the war, cruised from Liverpool to
the beautiful coasts of the Western Highlands. She was associated
with Liverpool for 54 years. 'Killarney' served in the Great War
as a hospital ship, and, later, round about 1920, was renamed
'Classic'. But her strangest name was that with which she was
dubbed when sailing as 'Killarney', the cruise vessel—'The Lady
of the Pawnshop'.

This originated from her off-season sojourn in Stanley Dock,
which was once known as the 'pawnbrokers dock' because vessels
were sometimes impounded there for failing to pay their dues.
But it is for her jolly, out-of-Liverpool holiday cruises that
'Killarney' is best known. A five-day cruise to the Highlands
would cost two people 17 guineas, inclusive of fares, board and
meals. And a 13-day 'Round Great Britain' cruise, taking in many
attractive Scottish ports like Oban and Inverness, and southern
ports including Cowes, Plymouth and the Scilly Isles, would cost
38 guineas for two passengers.

Southport has always been a happy haunt for Merseysiders and
for Lancashire folk. Back in the days before the continental
package tours became all the rage, sunshine holidays meant
Southport and the North Wales resorts. We recall the 30s when
for 1/6d we could buy a ticket at Liverpool's Exchange Station
which would take us to Southport and back, and also give us
admission to the Floral Hall for an evening's dancing. And the
time when, for sixpence, we could enjoy a Sunday afternoon band
concert there with tea and biscuits included, and served by
waitresses.

In those days the Floral Hall's manager, a Major Edward
Haines, was quite a disciplinarian. He would tolerate no nonsense.
He'd wander round the hall in a lounge suit, and if he heard any
objectionable language he'd quietly ask the offender to go to the
box office where his admission money would be refunded, and
would then be shown the door. If the offender apologised and
promised to behave, he'd be allowed back. Everyone had to be

properly dressed. He'd recoil with horror if he saw some of the casual clothes of today. For Major Haines ran the Floral Hall on superior lines so that parents could feel confident about taking their children there.

The orchestra leader had to submit the band's musical programme to the Chief Constable for his approval. Those were the days when there were long queues along the promenade for the Sunday concerts of popular music, and, for the evening concert, a dozen musicians from the Liverpool Philharmonic came along to augment the orchestra for a concert on Palm Court lines. The Chief Constable never queried the programme. But there were restrictions. They were not allowed to start until eight o'clock so that it wouldn't interfere with Sunday evening worship.

Colourful posters advertising Southport as one of the country's leading holiday resorts could be seen on many railway stations. They were the work of an Italian artist, Fortuninin Matania. One showed a man and a very attractive girl in bathing costumes—full length, of course, because trunks and bikinis hadn't arrived at that time. One of the girl's shoulder straps had slipped down her arm—totally unrevealing, but it provided that little bit of titivation. It just shows how times and attitudes have changed when, believe it or not, even that innocent poster aroused some protest.

Every afternoon during the holiday season, the crowds would flock to Southport's pier head to enjoy 2½ hours of sparkling entertainment by the local concert party—'The Pals', for the princely sum of fourpence, which, of course, also included admission to the pier.

From 1919 to 1963, apart from the war years, the more adventurous could enjoy a pleasure flight from the beach provided by the Giroux Aviation Company. Thousands of passengers were carried during its 45 years existence. The initial machines were Avro 536 three-seater open-cockpit biplanes, which left the passengers somewhat exposed to the elements—'wind and wires' flying as it was known at that time. In 1935, these aircraft were replaced by De Havilland Fox Moth aircraft—four-seater cabin biplanes which offered passengers a more comfortable trip. These joy rides were very moderately priced, even for the 30s. For a ten minute flight over Southport and its environs the charge was 2/6d, and for a twenty minute round trip to Blackpool you paid five shillings—hardly the price of a short bus journey nowadays. For a little extra you could experience the delights of a bit of modest stunting, like 'looping the loop' or 'the falling leaf'. Quite a lot of passengers took advantage of this extra thrill. One of the pleasure flight biplanes was involved in an accident in 1930, fortunately without injury to anyone. It got caught in the railway telephone lines between Birkdale Palace and Lord Street Stations, and crashed on to the railway lines. This happened just after mid-day on the Saturday of a Bank Holiday week-end. Within a few hours the line was completely cleared.

Compared with the brash, noisy, uninhibited 80s, the 20s and 30s were sedate, even at the holiday resorts at the height of the season. So sedate and strict that all the music for the Sunday concerts played by the military band in Lord Street had to be vetted too, so that it wouldn't offend people on the Sabbath. Imagine the sensation when a British Guiana Band, which had come to Britain to play at the Wembley Exhibition, came to Lord Street one Sunday in 1925, and had the audacity to play 'Horsey, keep your tail up' and 'Felix kept on walking'. Some of the ladies present reached for their smelling salts. For weeks it was the talk of the town.

Llandudno and Colwyn Bay were Meccas for those seeking a holiday in the sunshine. For Llandudno seemed to have everything—a wonderful beach, a magnificent promenade, the Great Orme and Little Orme, an attractive shopping centre, entertainment in abundance on the pier and elsewhere, and Happy Valley, that delightful little spot where a concert party provided jolly entertainment every day, weather permitting. Who could ask for more? Many holidaymakers will recall John Moravia who conducted the pier orchestra for nearly forty years. The concert hall was situated at the far end of the long pier, and it was something of a route march to get to it, often made more difficult if a stiff breeze was blowing against you from the sea. But you could always be sure that the musical entertainment made it all worth while. John Moravia came to Llandudno from Hastings to take charge of the orchestra in 1938, and he succeeded some very distinguished conductors, including Malcolm Sargent.

One of the permanent fixtures at Happy Valley during holiday time, even now, is Alex Munro and his concert party, and the crowd still flock to the enclosure, and also to 'Aberdeen Hill', over-looking the valley. 'Aberdeen Hill', so named because they were the non-paying audience, although one or two of the concert party make regular visits to the hill with their collecting boxes.

But long before Alex came to Llandudno, his predecessors,

the Happy Valley Minstrels, were drawing vast crowds. There were no microphones in those days, and the Minstrels had to 'stretch' their voices to reach up to the audience on Aberdeen Hill. Apparently the showmen never lost an opportunity. A well-known actor of the day once spotted a dead whale washed up on the shore, and, with commendable enterprise, dragged it under the pier beyond the reach of the tide, and charged holidaymakers sixpence a time to see it. This didn't last long. The stench of the rotting carcase brought the wrath of the Town Council upon him and he was forced to move it. The Happy Valley Minstrels used to serenade all the hotels along the front and lead the way to their little theatre, very much like the Pied Piper of Hamelin.

I must confess that in the 30s, Llandudno and Colwyn Bay were my two favourite holiday resorts. For all their attractions, Rhyl and Prestatyn had little appeal for me, and I must have been unlucky as whenever I went to Blackpool, it was invariably cold and windy. I loved the North Wales coast and the North Wales countryside. I'm sure I must have known every nook and cranny of Colwyn Bay and Llandudno.

One of the attractions in Colwyn Bay in those days was the quartet which played on the small stage on the pier. Musicians destined for greater things played on that pier. Reginald Stead, for instance, who went on to become leader of the BBC Northern Orchestra. Playing for them all was that most talented of pianists, Miss Dorothy M. Lloyd, who must have played professionally for close on fifty years. There was also Eric Bramhall, who found success in Eirias Park with his puppets.

It was in the 1940s that Hugh Stanhope, who was putting on a variety show on the pier, together with John Neale, then entertainments manager, gave Eric a contract to appear in Eirias Park at the end of the traditional holiday season. He was an instant success—playing to packed houses every night. His puppet show was a great novelty because the holidaymakers had seen nothing like it before. Eric Bramhall played in the open-air theatre in Eirias Park on the far side of the boating lake, before the council bought the marquee to enclose the theatre and enable the shows to go on no matter what the weather. During the first year they did such phenomenal business that the council not only paid for the marquee in double quick time, but also had enough money left over to buy a new stage and curtains.

The old Llandudno and Colwyn Bay Electric Railway, or 'Toastracks' as they were affectionately called, were popular for their 'air conditioning' as they rattled along between the two resorts, lashed or caressed by sea breezes, according to the prevailing weather. The 'toastracks' also offered a 'down to earth' ride, for their seats seemed so close to the ground that even at a gentle and sedate speed, the illusion was created of tarmac and grass verge rushing by.

The tram journeys were memorable as they invited passengers to challenge the elements, allowing sea breezes to flush colour into pale cheeks. Running on rails 3ft 6ins apart—more than a foot narrower than the standard gauge of railways, the trams took you through a magnificent visual route. The high point was the climb up the Little Orme's flanks at Penrhynside, and a swoop to the edge of Llandudno's built-up area at Craig-y-Don. It embraced a stretch of North Wales' finest three-dimensional scenery—green fields in the foreground, the beautiful bay in the middle distance, and the rugged hump of the Great Orme beyond. At any time of the day the view was glorious—at sunset it was magnificent. The conductors lurched from bench to bench along the footboards to collect fares. They were ideal holiday transport. Holidaymakers found them free of such inhibitions as doors, windows and roofs. All might have been blasted away to enhance the sense of fun and freedom.

The atmosphere of the 'toastracks' was entirely their own. It mattered little to passengers if they were delayed on the single line sections—it added several more minutes to an enjoyable journey. The longest route was 8½ miles from West Shore, Llandudno, to Llysfaen Road, Old Colwyn. That was the eastern terminus from 1915 to 1930 when the route was reduced about 1½ miles to the centre of Colwyn Bay. The last tram ran ceremonially on Saturday, 24th March, 1956. The demise of those immensely popular 'toastracks' was a matter of regret to every holidaymaker. Now, as they travel from Llandudno to Colwyn Bay by bus, many people long for those old, open trams which, on windy days, swept their hair-dos into a terrible mess, and gave such a keen edge to their appetites.

'Lobby Lud' was a popular character many holidaymakers will remember in the 30s, when competition between newspapers was intense. If you carried a copy of the News Chronicle and recognised this character who'd visit several seaside resorts each day, you'd approach him and say: 'You are Lobby Ludd, and I claim the pound note!' Unfortunately, there were many cases of mistaken identity. A friend of mine was walking along

Llandudno's promenade one day when a woman approached him and claimed the pound note. In spite of his denials she was such a determined lady that she pursued him the entire length of the prom, until, in desperation, he was forced to take refuge in a gentleman's lavatory. He half expected her to follow him even there. He dared not emerge until he was certain she had gone. He told me: 'On reflection it would have been far easier for me to have handed over a pound note in the first place!'

During the early 30s, if you were enjoying yourself in breezy Blackpool during the holiday season, you may have come across a very unusual stall at a certain spot on the Golden Mile, somewhere between the performing fleas and the bearded lady. The stall contained a middle-aged clergyman sitting in a barrel and reading a book. This rather unsavoury exhibition was more tragic than comic as the man in the barrel was the Reverend Harold Francis Davidson, who'd been convicted by an ecclesiastical court of grave misconduct. This, evidently, was his form of protest, but the exhibition was distasteful in the extreme, and many holidaymakers hurried by in embarrassment. He was, of course, better known as the Rector of Stiffkey.

There was much worse to come, but this time it was to end in tragedy. After his barrel episode, the ex-Rector of Stiffkey did something even more extraordinary. He decided to appear as a sort of Daniel in the Lions Den in Skegness Amusement Park. Apparently, the contract was for him to appear with just the one lion, but when he reached the cage he discovered there were two, a male and female. He disputed this, to no avail. He certainly didn't lack courage for he went ahead with his act. The lion-tamer opened the cage and Davidson went in between the huge, fearsome-looking 'Freddie' and his mate, who was sleeping at the rear of the den. To the horror of the large crowd of spectators 'Freddie' killed the little clergyman from Norfolk. It has always been a constant source of amazement to me that such a thing could be allowed to happen. It was all so sad, tragic, and so unnecessary.

Then, in 1935, some peculiar individuals thought up the rather crazy idea of exhibiting what was described as 'Starving Honeymoon Couples' lying in bed behind a glass window. There were indignant protests from all and sundry, but a certain peepshow impresario went on with his ridiculous 'Starving and Freezing Brides' show, somewhere along Blackpool's Golden Mile. So many of these stunts were deliberate frauds, and it was observed that the 'starving' occupants emerged at night-time and treated themselves and their friends to a slap-up feed. I never cease to be astonished at such stupid and incredible ways of making money.

Blackpool today seems pretty much as it was in the 30s with its famous Golden Mile, its even more famous Tower, and its Pleasure Beach. It still makes a big thing of its Illuminations, which are bigger and brighter than ever. But there's now something missing—the fun of crowding into those cheerful old song booths, to be led in song by a gentleman in a straw hat, with his pointer and giant-sized song sheet. We used to sing our heads off with the 'top twenty' songs of the day.

While this was going on, other straw-hatted men, dressed in natty blazers, bearing the name of Feldman, Lawrence Wright, or some such famous publisher would come round trying to sell us the sheet music of the songs we were singing so lustily. We'd take them home and hopefully thump them out on our pianos— songs such as 'Minnetonka', 'Pasadena', 'Happy days and lonely nights' and 'I'm forever blowing bubbles'.

Then there was 'Mr. Blackpool' himself—the popular Reginald Dixon, who, for so many years, played the mighty Wurlitzer organ in the Tower Ballroom. When the strains of his signature tune, 'I do like to be beside the seaside' were heard, the vast crowds in the ballroom knew they were in for a marvellous night's entertainment.

Reginald Dixon first came to Blackpool in 1930, when he was announced as Mr. R. H. Dixon. His brilliant organ playing became immensely popular, not only in Blackpool, but through-out the country because of his broadcasts and his gramophone records. The Tower was always packed to capacity when Reg was due to give one of his cheerful concerts. But it wasn't always like that. 'I remember one Sunday in June during glorious weather when there were only two people in the ballroom,' Reg said, ruefully, 'It was my first performance and, to begin with, the size of the audience depended on the weather. Then, somehow, it changed, and Sunday became my main day. It was really marvellous, and I can't believe it even now'. I wonder how many readers of this danced the night away to Reginald Dixon on the organ and Bertini and his popular Blackpool Tower Dance Band? Happy days—or perhaps I should say happy nights.

At most holiday seaside resorts entertainment wouldn't have been complete without the penny peep-show machines, which provided the menfolk with a few seconds of innocuous tittilation. They were always a source of great amusement. What the butler saw was so little that it seemed a complete waste of a penny. The action stopped abruptly just when the viewer thought he was going to see something exciting.

I read some time ago that fourteen of those machines that once graced the end of Brighton Pier were up for auction. There were all kinds of enquiries, from all kinds of people. One man wanted them for the old Gaiety Theatre, and a lady thought they'd go down well in her public house. Lots of people fancied having one in their homes. The saucy films were expected to go for as much as £500 each. So what the butler saw for free cost some customers a fortune.

That beautiful holiday haven, the Isle of Man, is still as popular as ever with Merseysiders, in spite of change. Not only did we enjoy cheap, happy, carefree holidays there, but, given fine weather, the cruise to the island was, in itself, a pleasure, with all the passengers in holiday mood enjoying a good, old-fashioned sing-song to the accompaniment of the inevitable concertina.

The first new steamer after World War I was 'Ben-my-chree', which entered service in 1927. A famous name, and one which has always been given to crack ships of the Isle of Man Steam Packet Company. This was a splendid ship. In 1930, the company celebrated its centenary, and introduced that magnificent steamer, TSS 'Lady of Mann' which, in tonnage, was the largest in the fleet. The launching ceremony was fittingly performed by the Duchess of Atholl, who was, of course, the Lady of Mann. In grimmer times those famous ships gave sterling war service— 'Lady of Mann' and 'Ben-my-chree' being mainly involved in trooping, chiefly to Iceland. That other famous steamer, 'King Orry', was lost at Dunkirk on May 30th, 1940.

Motor cycling enthusiasts used to flock over to the Isle of Man every year for the T.T. races. The very first international motor cycle race was held there in 1936. In those days the road was not closed for the race, so it was all rather chaotic. A lorry followed the race to collect the damaged machines. On one occasion a cameraman came out from behind two parked cars halfway down Bray Hill to take pictures of the massed start. Someone ran into him and the accident resulted in a pile-up of about ten riders.

There must be many people around who enjoyed the thrill of a joy ride with Sir Alan Cobham's popular Air Circus. From 1932 to 1936, Sir Alan toured the British Isles with his circus giving displays. I've little doubt that many Merseysiders who think nothing of flying to Spain for their holidays had their first thrill of flying in one of Cobham's planes. Nearly five million spectators attended the displays over the years, and a million of them took joy rides at five shillings a time, and ten shillings for 'looping the loop'. An accident over Blackpool in 1935 marred these pleasure flights when two planes collided and parts of the machines fell in the busy streets. One pilot and two women passengers were killed. But this did not deter thousands of other people from taking to the air.

Charabanc trips were immensely popular in the 20s and 30s, and Blackpool was always a popular centre for a day's outing. Stopping for half an hour or so at a countryside pub—dubbed 'the half-way house', was considered a ritual on these trips, and the day wouldn't have been complete without it. For some people charabanc trips were an excuse for a good 'booze-up'. They'd load the vehicle with crates of bottled beer before they started out, stop for more liquid refreshment at the 'half-way house', and make a bee-line for the nearest pub when they arrived at their destination.

Certain hotels and public houses on the charabanc routes catered for these parties. But they had a problem. The trippers were very welcome for the money they spent, but, on occasions, not so welcome for their behaviour. A load of trippers would arrive, take over the place, and leave behind a dozen or so broken glasses, tables soaked with spilled beer, the floor covered with cigarette stubs, and dirty toilets. Such people were in the minority, I hasten to add, but they made it difficult for others. And many of the regulars, having had quite enough of the bad behaviour, decided to take their custom elsewhere. Because of this, many pubs on the main chara routes put up a notice: 'Strictly no charabanc parties'.

Holiday camp king, Sir Billy Butlin, who died on June 12th, 1980, is said to have brought sunshine to millions. He was 80, and died sixty years after he arrived in Britain from Canada with just a few pounds in his pocket. He decided to spend this on a fair-ground stall and gave away budgies as prizes. But the sight of the miserable holidaymakers sheltering from the rain depressed him, too, and he hit on the brainwave of holiday camps where people could stay for a week, eat in communal dining rooms, enjoy a bit of dancing and entertainment, and sleep in chalets.

So Billy Butlin's first holiday camp was built on a potato

field in Skegness. The cost was £2 a week with two square meals a day. Shrewdly, he'd decided long before the opening that the expense of taking out half-page advertisements in the Daily Express would be well worth while. And his judgment paid off, as the response was immediate and enormous. Applications came pouring into his office from all over the country. The Skegness camp was officially opened by Amy Johnson, who was still a great favourite with the public after her heroic air exploits.

Billy was a master of publicity, and immediately after Len Hutton's record breaking innings of 364, Len was invited along to Skegness for one of the Butlin 'camp week-ends', which were also proving very popular. The great batsman was paid a hundred pounds for a couple of hours entertainment, which included batting with a bat made of Skegness mint rock, while two of the then leading stars of the theatre, Gracie Fields and Florence Desmond, bowled to him. It seemed that everything Billy touched turned into gold, as five thousand people paid a shilling each to watch this entertainment.

Although Butlin went into debt in order to open Skegness, he wasn't worried, as he knew very well that he was on to a money spinner. His cheap, happy holidays appealed to thousands of people who wanted a change from the boarding houses they'd been used to—and it was ideal for the children. It wasn't long before more Butlin holiday camps were springing up around the country, and Butlin's became a household name. Billy became a millionaire. Not bad for a man who'd arrived in this country with a miserable few pounds in his pocket.

Billy was quick to realise that dancing was the most popular of all entertainment in the 30s, and he made sure his camps contained a spacious ballroom and a first-class orchestra. His Viennese Ballroom at Skegness was probably the finest of its kind in the country. Only the best was good enough for him and so the first dance orchestra he engaged was Mantovani's. This was several years before Mantovani became so famous with his great, lush string orchestra. But he had an excellent dance band and he knew what the dancers wanted.

I don't know how true it is, but it was said that when 'King Billy' died, he had twelve hundred budgies. Why budgies? Well they helped him to get a start in that first hoop-la stall way back in 1920. Tens of thousands of ordinary working folk have cause to thank Sir Billy Butlin for some wonderful holidays spent in the jolly camps that sprung up like mushrooms all over the country. He always gave good value for money.

There was a time when Hoylake meant an enjoyable day out for many trippers. For children, especially, Hoylake meant lots of lovely sand and paddling, Punch and Judy, donkey rides, and the Black Minstrel. I spent many an enjoyable day at Hoylake as a child. I always preferred it to New Brighton. There was something warm and inviting about the place. The children used to run down Seaview Road, climb on to the top of the thick black railings and . . . plump!—they jumped right on to that lovely soft sand. And if they walked along the sand towards Moreton they came across the Black Minstrel with his banjo. Halcyon days indeed!

Moreton was a popular camping place. Camping enjoyed a boom in the 30s, and two favourite places were Moreton and Leasowe. It mattered little to us youngsters whether our tent was full of holes—we were optimists in those days, and half a dozen of us would pile into a tent made for two. For brewing up we used an old methylated spirit stove, and our tea was sweetened with 'conny onny'.

On a hot summer day we were lucky to find even the smallest site on which to pitch our tent, as the area was chock-a-block with campers. We existed on biscuits, tea, and lemonade, but sometimes we could buy chips—a big bag full for a penny. If we had no means of brewing up we could buy, if we wished, and more important, if we could afford it, a hot, watery liquid that went for tea. The tea cost about threepence a jugful, but there was usually a deposit of a few shillings on the jug. There were no noisy transistor radios in those days—we could sunbathe in peace, or spend the day swimming, or playing cricket, football or rounders.

We made our own entertainment in those far off days. The beauty of the countryside drew tens of thousands of young people hiking at week-ends. How I loved hiking through Wirral and North Wales! I considered it to be the most wonderful enjoyment in the world, and I used to walk miles and miles and miles in sheer contentment, resting at intervals with my head on my rucksack and gazing up at an azure blue sky—looking forward to a cheap but satisfying meal at the Youth Hostel we were heading for. You could keep your expensive holidays as far as I was concerned; hiking and camping out, or spending the night at a Youth Hostel were just for me.

For the outdoor types, the formation by the Liverpool

Ramblers Association and others of the Youth Hostels Association, and the opening of the first British Youth Hostel at Pennant Hall, in North Wales, was one of the most important events of the early 30s. Unfortunately, the water supply at Pennant Hall proved unsatisfactory, so it had to be closed. But the idea of providing the means for young people to explore the countryside cheaply had well and truly caught on, and the well-known Liverpool shipping family, Holt's, immediately subscribed money for a brand new building.

Professor Abercrombie, of Liverpool University, designed it, and his model Youth Hostel was built on land presented by the Birkenhead mountaineering author, the Rev. H. H. Symmonds, at Maeshafn in Flintshire. Many youth hostellers will remember with gratitude the splendid work done on behalf of the young people of the 30s by these men, and by that kindly, enthusiastic, and infectiously happy chairman of Merseyside Youth Hostels Ltd., the late Mr. P. J. Clark.

Maeshafn was an exciting beginning, and hostels spread quickly through Merseyside's area of influence, and thence throughout Britain. Manchester's first Youth Hostel had a water problem of a different nature from that of Pennant Hall—not too little, but far too much! Derwent Hall was opened as a huge and beautiful Youth Hostel by the Prince of Wales, in the Peak District, in 1932. Sadly, the whole valley had to be flooded to quench Stockport's thirst, and the hostel now lies at the bottom of Derwent Reservoir.

But those days were full of promise, and it was wonderful to be able to come to the end of a hard week's work at noon on Saturdays and then make for the mountains by bus, train, or bicycle, and to meet like-minded people at Llangollen, Idwal Cottage, Bala, and other Youth Hostels, share Saturday night yarns with them and revel in the glorious countryside the next day. All that for a shilling a night, plus a shilling per meal, or the use of cooking facilities if you preferred to cook your own food.

For the less energetic, the joys of the open road, with petrol at little more than a shilling a gallon, beckoned the more well-to-do who could find a hundred pounds for a brand-new family car, and the less affluent who were content to pick up an old 'tin-lizzie' for a fiver. The little Austin Seven was worth its weight in gold. The sight of those sit-up-and-beg box-like vehicles with their pram-type wheels might be a bit of a giggle for today's motorists, but it's worth recalling that many versions embodied, as part of their normal equipment, refinements which are often absent from today's cars. They had sliding roof-tops, windscreens that would open, ventilators in the roof of the saloons—all manner of useful gadgets including the precious starting handle. And they were made to last.

The halcyon days of cycling were undoubtedly the 30s, and it was common to see large groups of cyclists, each group belonging to one cycling club, on the way to North Wales and other country places. The cyclists were a mixed bunch—young, middle-aged and elderly, pedalling away furiously and obviously enjoying life to the full. There were many little roadside kiosks and cafes which supplied the thirsty cyclists with tea and cakes, and home-made lemonade. I recall some of the popular models of the 30s—Raleigh, Rudge Whitworth, Sunbeam, B.S.A., Triumph, Royal Enfield and Coventry Eagle, and if you weren't too well off you could either buy a second-hand one for a few shillings, or obtain a new one on the 'never-never'—a small deposit and half a crown a month. Most newspapers and magazines advertised bikes on those terms. And 'two on a tandem' was another popular sight in those days.

For the 'posh' people, as we used to call them, there were far more luxurious holidays. When, on August Saturday, 1931, the 25,000-ton White Star liner, Adriatic, carrying a full complement of passengers, proudly sailed down the Mersey on a three-day coastal voyage, she set a new and exciting fashion in summer holidays which took Britain by storm—the £1 a day cruise in luxury liners. For Liverpool, hard hit by the world trade depression of the 30s, and fast becoming a port of idle ships and unemployed crews, the Adriatic's voyage was to lead to a most extraordinary interlude in port activities as cruising liners, taking over from North Atlantic liners, dominated the river scene.

This cruise was an enormous success, so the shipowners, rather than see their vessels lying idle, decided to introduce popular short cruises at a price many people could afford. So, in 1932, several famous shipping companies announced luxurious 12-day cruises at a minimum fare of £12. The liners Adriatic, Doric, Lancastria, Laurentic, Montcalm, Montclare, Montrose, Voltaire and Vandyck becoming exciting cruise vessels. They made a splendid sight on the Mersey, and hundreds of holidaymakers eagerly embarked at Princes Landing Stage. With the ship's orchestra playing, their cruise liner sailed away to the magic lands of the

Mediterranean, the Norwegian fjords, or the Atlantic isles. Twelve days later, the ships would return with their happy passengers carrying loads of souvenirs, passing through packed Custom sheds and on to the special trains awaiting them at the adjoining Riverside Railway Station. By 1933, the £1-a-day cruise, which had begun as an experiment, was now a booming industry, and there was a rush to book one of these bargain cruises.

It was only an interlude. As world trade picked up and the recession showed signs of ending, the Atlantic liners were gradually diverted once again to normal service, and by 1936, the £1-a-day cruises were more or less a thing of the past. But while it lasted, hundreds of Merseysiders took full advantage of it, and they still retain happy memories of those happy, carefree cruises.

Chapter Fourteen
The Turbulent Thirties

I liked the article in the Liverpool Echo in October 1977 under the heading 'Echo Comment'. It said: 'Why does the past always seem more rosy than the present? There's no disputing the fact that it does, because whenever folk old enough to indulge in the luxury of memories gather together, the conversation invariably seems to turn to days gone by. Perhaps it's because those days have already been lived, their challenges met, their battles fought.

'All that remains are insubstantial shadows flitting across the mind. And everyone knows that shadows can do no harm. Without doubt times past were hard for some, cruelly hard, but the hardships of yesteryear, it seems, have merely been changed, in the name of progress, to a whole catalogue of new hardships of the present. Small wonder that people say: 'Things are not what they were' and find consolation in turning to memories more ordered, law-abiding, honest and stable way of life'.

And they're my sentiments exactly—sentiments that set the tone of my Radio Merseyside programme 'Music and Memories'. We don't kid ourselves that the past was a bed of roses, and we know only too well that it's the future that's important. I've enjoyed receiving thousands of letters from listeners who tell me how much happiness they've derived from some of my memories of bygone days. It's good to remember, so long as we don't wallow in the past. The writer who said: 'Happy memories are just like roses in December' couldn't have put it better.

The Wall Street Crash of 1929 and the subsequent Depression was not an auspicious beginning for the turbulent Thirties. It was one of the most momentous decades in Britain's history—a decade which was to take us to another World War, at the end of which the nation emerged victorious but impoverished, never again to enjoy the prosperity of former years. And Merseyside suffered from this decline to a far greater extent than most other areas of the country.

But the 1930s started brightly enough. There was rejoicing when Princess Margaret was born at Glamis Castle, Angus, on August 21st, 1930—one of the windiest nights for over a century, which was perhaps, for the more superstitious at least, a significant omen for a rather stormy and controversial life. Her parents, the Duke and Duchess of York, already had one daughter, Princess Elizabeth, so it was only natural that they'd hoped for a son. If their hopes had materialised, that son would now, of course, be King. But it was not to be. She certainly was a beautiful baby and was much loved by the nation as Princess Margaret Rose.

Talking of Royalty reminds me that Britons all over the Empire, not least on Merseyside, were highly indignant in 1930 when the cocky anti-British Mayor of Chicago proclaimed his intention of 'landing King George V one on the snoot' if he ever visited Chicago. I often marvel at the fact that the United States, with its huge population, and large proportion of highly intelligent people, has nearly always scraped the bottom of the barrel when it comes to choosing its leaders.

It was in 1930 that Mary Bagot Stack created tremendous interest, and not a little mild amusement on the part of the male population, when she formed her League for energetic young ladies—the Women's League of Health and Beauty. As many as 120,000 members joined up in that first year, with several hundred on Merseyside. The movement—and 'movement' is probably the right word—movement to music—spread rapidly all over the British Empire. And although the present membership is nowhere near that number, it's still going strong, and its leaders today are the same three women who took over the administration on the death of Mrs. Stack in 1935. Prunella Stack, daughter of the founder, is chairman of the League's Training Committee, assisted by her two sisters.

I remember watching a large group of these ladies performing their impressive gymnastics in Southport's Princes Park, adjacent to the Marine Promenade. They were well drilled and seemed to be enjoying themselves immensely. They performed their exercises to the accompaniment of suitable music relayed through a public address system. The League's famous emblem, 'Movement is Life', is well-known to members and ex-members, and there must be many of the original members of 1930 still alive and well on Merseyside.

In the poverty-stricken days of the early 30s, we children well knew the meaning of deprivation. So we made do with the simple little pleasures, like aeroplane spotting—tremendously exciting in those early days. When a plane was heard, the drill was to rush out into the street shouting, 'Aerio', and stab the air in the direction of the marvel. Spotting an aeroplane really was a thrill.

On May 22nd, 1930, there was an extra special thrill. There was a deep, throbbing noise of powerful engines, utterly unlike the noise of the 'aerios', rising to a tremendous roar. Then, looking up to the skies, we saw it—a truly unforgettable sight for us youngsters, and for many adults. It was the mighty British airship R100 passing over Liverpool—huge, silvery and beautiful, seemingly hovering over our heads, its engines thundering. She was on a test flight before her longer voyage to Canada. Her Atlantic crossing took 46¾ hours. A couple of years later, the mighty Graf Zeppelin flew over Merseyside, so low that we could clearly read the name on the side of this giant German airship. Another tremendous thrill, but many Merseysiders claimed that she was flying deliberately low in order to photograph the whole of the Mersey dock system.

The nearest to Merseyside the ill-fated R101 flew was over Queensferry, Parkgate and Chester, during her one thousand mile flight in November, 1929. There was quite a dense fog over Liverpool at the time. That other famous German airship, Hindenburg, crossed the coast at Hoylake and flew over Merseyside on her way to America on June 26th, 1936. It was the golden age of the airship, but it proved to be a disastrous era.

However, back to 1930, for that was the year when the Liverpool to Manchester Railway celebrated its centenary with some lavish events—from the 13th to the 20th of September. It was a memorable week, and I was just at that impressionable age to enjoy every moment of it. The weather was appalling, but this failed to dampen the spirits of the many thousands of Merseysiders and visitors from all over the world who attended the special celebrations.

Lord Street, Church Street, Lime Street, and many more of the city's main streets were gaily decorated with railway motifs, pictures, ornate arches and pylons. The main attraction was at Wavertree Playground—the 'Mystery', where there was a huge pageant with some 3,500 performers on a 100-foot stage. Collins Brothers roundabouts and switchbacks were a tremendous attraction at the Mystery, as was Bostock's and Wombwell's Zoo and Menagerie, in spite of the quagmire of a field. There was the Royal Italian Circus, with 'The Great Risko' performing a 'Turn Sixty' in mid-air. The pageant included a replica of the famous 'Rocket', and there was a magnificent firework display every night, including 'Maud the Kicking Mule', 'The Falls of Zambesi', 'Stephenson's Rocket', 'Portraits of George

Stephenson and Sir Josiah Stamp' and 'The Wembley Finale'.

The real heroes and heroines were the performers in what was called 'The Railway Pageant', as they all got soaked to the skin almost every day. In St. George's Hall there was a magnificent exhibition of some of the world's finest locomotives, which was opened by the American Ambassador, General Dawes. Another big attraction at St. George's Hall were the three Queens—Miss Molly Brown, the Railway Queen, Miss Ena Best, ex-L.N.E.R. Queen, and Miss Mary Kitson, the ex-Queen of the G.W.R. Line. Three very beautiful girls. That was a marvellous week for us children, and we seized every opportunity of getting to the celebrations. It wasn't quite so marvellous for me in the evening, though, when I arrived home from the Mystery with a large proportion of the field attached to my shoes. I wasn't allowed into the house until every particle of mud had been laboriously scraped off.

As I've said, I was an avid reader of every newspaper I could lay my hands on when I was a boy, and in 1930 I remember reading about a whale that had got itself stranded on the Mersey shore between Seacombe and New Brighton, and had died. The carcase was nearly thirty feet long, and had been left by the receding tide on the shore opposite the Mariners Home at Egremont.

The unusual spectacle attracted large crowds of people from the promenade on to the beach, and what offended my youthful sense of propriety was reading of some of the people cutting portions of the flesh to take away as souvenirs. How peculiar can some people get! This wouldn't have been so surprising ten years later, but they wouldn't have been for souvenirs, but to supplement the meagre wartime meat ration!

Another whale—a rare Risso's grampus, was stranded at Widnes in December, 1939, and the carcase cut up in pieces and dumped in the river. Then there was the one that got away. It was seen frolicking in the Mersey in September, 1942, and was stranded on a sandbank for a time, but released by the incoming tide.

And here's another whale of a tale. It's perhaps rather surprising to think that, in the 30s, the whaling industry was booming on Merseyside. The men who were sent to catch the giant mammals had to work very long hours, but they received good wages. Their biggest problem was sheer boredom from long voyages in sub-zero temperatures. Some years ago, Liverpool's

Everyman Theatre put on Claire Luckham's excellent play, 'Yatesy and the Whale'—all about the hundred-foot whales of the Antarctic, each seventy or more tons of bone and blubber, many of them hunted by men who set sail from Bromborough. The giant whaling ships of the Mersey, with their gaping stern hatches for hauling the mammals aboard, are now things of the past. They were floating factories on which the whales were cut up and their flesh boiled for oil. It was a skilled and dangerous job, perhaps something like working on an oil rig nowadays. The ships themselves were like huge butchers shops. When the slack was taken off, after a whale was harpooned, they'd sometimes leap twelve feet in the air, or turn and try to cut the line on the ship's propellor. The men would bring mementoes home with them for the mantelpiece, such as whales teeth and eardrums. And the story goes that a jawbone was once used to make a bridge for smugglers across marshy ground near New Brighton.

The names of the whaling factory ships were Southern Empress and Southern Princess—both converted oil tankers of over 12,000 gross tons, owned by the Southern Whaling and Sealing Company —a subsidiary of Lever Brothers. At the end of every whaling season they'd come into Bromborough Dock to discharge their whale-oil cargoes for the soap and margarine factories of the Unilever group at Port Sunlight and Bromborough. Sadly, both were lost through enemy action in the early 40s.

We had so many Merseyside men serving in the Royal Navy that we were all shocked when the startling news of the naval mutiny at Invergordon was announced in 1931. The country was in such a desperate economic plight that most people were forced to take reductions in their pay. I wonder what the reaction would be if a similar thing happened today? Another General Strike perhaps?

The trouble at Invergordon was that the men felt a sense of bitter injustice at the inequality of the reductions for naval personnel that had been ordered. They felt that the cuts in their pay were particularly savage. So, for the first time since 1797, Royal Navy men refused to obey orders and put to sea. It was an ugly situation that might have got completely out of hand had not it been handled with diplomacy and understanding. The First Lord of the Admiralty himself, Sir Austen Chamberlain, travelled post-haste to Invergordon to make personal investigations, and the result was that the pay cuts for Royal Navy personnel were cancelled. A highly dangerous crisis had been averted.

There was humour, too, in the hungry 30s. A headline in the Echo read: 'Hymn Singing Polly'. Polly was a Wallasey parrot who, at the age of 32, had learned to sing 'Jesus bids us shine' and, as a contrast, 'Poor old Joe'. She could only manage part of 'Rule Britannia', however, and, according to her owner, hated all men and red-haired women.

And during a Liverpool by-election, the wife of a candidate delivering campaign literature from door to door had her finger bitten through a letter-box. The dog bit the finger to the bone before he finally let go. The main lesson seemed to be that when engaged in electioneering you should ascertain the political leanings of all the dogs in the district before starting out.

During a court case in Wirral concerning alleged malicious damage to a hive of bees, a man told the court that, although he'd been stung fifty times, and needed hospital treatment, he still loved bees.

Then there was the case of the man in Moreton who announced that he'd shot a monster rat in a pond. To prove his claim he produced its body which was eighteen inches long and had a tail fourteen inches in length. Some rat! I'd seen some huge rats during my excursions to the Dock Road, but never one to compare with that, the carcase of which weighed nine pounds. Then another man in the same area claimed that the 'monster rat' wasn't a rat at all, but one of his tame South American coypu which had escaped a few weeks before.

There was also the Echo headline, which raised a few eyebrows —'Horse sits in Liverpool Music Store Window'. The horse, attached to a cart, which was standing quietly outside a warehouse in Wood Street, was startled by something which made it bolt. When it reached Hanover Street it was unable to stop and just careered straight across the road and through Crane's window. The commissionaire heard the crash and went to see what had happened. 'There was the horse', he said, 'sitting on its back legs among all the musical instruments'.

Of course, throughout the 30s, we were continually reading stories about the Loch Ness Monster. But 1933 was a particularly good year for alleged sightings of that elusive creature. It proved to be the most popular silly season story of the year. So many people claimed to have seen it that a fanciful Punch cartoon of Christmas, 1933, showed the complete monster, suitably garnished, on a fifty foot table, surrounded by mince pies, Christmas puddings, etc. The diners, thirty or more, are waiting for the monster to be carved. They'd even stuck a huge sprig of holly in its mouth.

In those years, I was an avid reader of crime stories, and my favourite authors were Agatha Christie and Edgar Wallace. I'd borrow an Edgar Wallace thriller from the library, read it from cover to cover in one evening, and then I'd be back at the library the next day for another one. Wallace quickly earned thousands of pounds from his stories, and just as quickly spent it. So I was particularly interested to read in the local papers that he appeared in Blackpool in 1931 in a yellow Rolls Royce as a Liberal candidate in the General Election of that year. Sadly, he died exhausted and in debt just a year later, having written in all 150 novels, 18 plays, and countless short stories and newspaper articles. I'm pretty certain I must have read all his thrilling crime novels.

In 1932, with due ceremony befitting such an occasion, Cupid or, if you like, Eros, came to Liverpool. Not in any spiritual form, however, but in the shape of a statue which was unveiled in Sefton Park on July 25th, 1932, by the Lord Mayor, James Conrad Cross. A great crowd assembled to witness the unveiling ceremony, as the arrival of the God of Love appealed to the public's imagination. It was a welcome acquisition for Sefton Park, which was then at its best and most beautiful, and unspoilt by vandalism. The handsome bronze statue survived through countless storms, the German bombing of Liverpool, and far more pigeon bombings.

Four years earlier, if I may return to the 20s for a moment, Peter Pan, the little boy who never grew up, came to that same park. This lovely bronze statue, sculptured by Sir George Frampton, and depicting Peter on a magic mound, surrounded by fairies, was unveiled on June 16th, 1928, by the splitting of an artificial tree built around it. The statue was presented by George Audley, together with two cannon which had once been on the Royal Yacht, Victoria and Albert.

Sir James Barrie, the author of 'Peter Pan' some 24 years earlier, was unable to attend the ceremony, and his niece, Miss Barrie, represented him. On a beautiful summer's day thousands watched a two-hour Peter Pan pageant unfold in brilliant sunshine, and 'Peter' and 'Wendy' later shook hands with five hundred delighted children from various institutions in the city. Liverpool's Lord Mayor of that year, Miss Margaret Beavan, gave a luncheon in honour of the statue's donor, Mr. George

Audley. It still gives immense pleasure to thousands of Liverpool children who've been charmed by Sir James Barrie's delightful story, but, on the other side of the coin, whenever I go to Sefton Park these days I'm pained to see the unappreciative and destructive element of our child population clambering all over it—watched, I may add, by their indulgent parents.

A statue of a far different nature was Jacob Epstein's controversial 'masterpiece', 'Genesis', which was on show in England in the early 30s. Some people liked it—other people pretended to like it, while still others loathed it. The statue was in the form of a heavy-featured woman in an advanced state of pregnancy, and it came to the chief provincial towns and cities, including Liverpool, after being on show in London and reproduced in nearly all the newspapers.

They charged a shilling for viewing it, and there were long queues to see it. It created the same kind of ribald humour as that other famous statue outside Lewis's in later years. Perhaps the two should have gone together! And although they'd queued up and paid their shillings, some people, when they came to the 'presence', modestly averted their gaze and just walked by. Things were different in those days.

Tragedy struck Liverpool in 1933. On one fateful July night, the city's famous Philharmonic Hall, Liverpool's home of music, vanished in a roar of flame. And the city had scarcely recovered from the shock of losing what was said to be the finest concert hall in Europe, when another devastating blow descended. The famous old Royal Court, the city's oldest existing theatre, was also wrecked by fire. It was a double disaster of the first magnitude for concert and theatre lovers. No one knew the cause of either. No one cared very much about causes. All they felt was a deep and cruel loss—two harsh setbacks to the cultural life of the city in just over two months.

The fire at the Phil was one of the fiercest and fastest the city had ever known. Within a few short hours all that had been the home of Merseyside music for 84 years was nothing but a smouldering wreck. Gone, as it seemed, in a flash, was the spacious, lofty, beautifully proportioned building that had known the great in the world of music. Gone was the wide, imposing entrance hall, the stairways with their wrought-iron railings cast in symbolic lyres, the little salon, the artistes' Green Room with its gently tinkling crystal chandelier, and the little cottage piano in the corner. Gone was the fine new £2,000 organ, and the boxes with their plush-covered chairs and hangings. Gone was all that reflected the best in Victorian tradition. Gone for ever was Liverpool's Covent Garden. The next day, concert lovers looked saddened at the soaked, still smouldering carnage. Some wept.

Many valuable instruments were lost, and a loss felt deeply, too, was the autograph album containing signatures of the world's most famous artistes. A new concert hall could be built, but that precious album was irreplaceable. Among the few things salvaged from the blaze was the plaque to the memory of the musicians who were lost in the grim Titanic disaster. The blaze was so fierce that the heat was felt in the surrounding streets—an intense heat felt also by passengers in the trams passing by before being diverted. Crowds gathered from all parts of the city. They had to be kept well back by a strong barrier of police. The following day all that was left of the old Philharmonic Hall was a gaunt, blackened shell.

It was Saturday night, September 23rd, 1933, that the Royal Court Theatre went up in flames. And that, ironically, was the night that the old theatre had seated its biggest audience since the recent change to variety. At 11.30 p.m., the managing director and other officials left the building, well pleased with their success. Twenty five minutes later, Miss Norah Bird, employed at the Victoria Hotel, which used to stand opposite, was getting ready for bed when she noticed the red glare of fire above the theatre roof. She immediately gave the alarm, but it was too late. A few minutes later, the roof of the auditorium fell, burying most of the stalls, circle and gallery. The theatre became a shambles— twisted girders, shattered masonry, flames, seared timber, and rivers of water. The fire brigade could do nothing to save it.

Turning to happier events, Liverpudlian Walter Kay was one of a two-man team who achieved a remarkable feat in the early 30s by crossing Europe and Africa in a tiny Morris Eight. The 13,370-mile adventure took Walter and co-driver Alan Gilg, from Liverpool to Cape Town in four months. Walter, of Channel Beach, Blundellsands, recorded the trail-blazing trip on film which was unearthed after 45 years and used for a television documentary. This pioneering duo had to detour from a tribal uprising, traversed the Sahara Desert and the jungle, warding off elephants, locusts and forest fires. What a marvellous achievement in such a tiny car!

The 30s were the years when speed brought national prestige. On sea, land, and in the air, men strained every nerve to break records. Men like Henry Seagrave, Kaye Don, and Malcolm Campbell did marvels for Britain on land and on water, and broke world records galore. The Queen Mary and Queen Elizabeth won glory by winning the Blue Riband of the Atlantic. The prestigious Schneider Trophy of the air was won outright for Britain.

But my story is about Merseyside and Merseysiders. And about a certain locomotive named 'Hector'. It begins in Manchester. On September 18th, 1932, an express train steamed out of Manchester at its normal time and reached Euston Station, in London, in 189 minutes. That was six minutes ahead of schedule and it won for Britain the European non-stop record for distances over 150 miles.

As has always been the case, what Manchester could do Liverpool felt that it could do even better. It was decided that a Liverpool express on the London run would have a crack at the record. The train chosen was the 5.25 p.m. from Lime Street drawn by the locomotive 'Hector'. Its crew, Driver J. Farrell and Fireman J. Pritchard, were under no illusions as to the difficulty of their task. It was no hit or miss effort. Everything had to be carefully planned. With regard to the speed, Farrell realised that the record could only be broken in a succession of stages—each stage to be reached within a strict timetable. Pritchard knew that, in about three hours, he had to feed 'Hector's' fire with four and a half tons of coal—not just heaving it on frenziedly but by placing the fuel accurately and scientifically.

The plan worked perfectly. At 8.28 p.m., the train steamed triumphantly into Willesden. With a long blast of 'Hector's' whistle, a beaming driver and a sweating fireman signalled that they'd captured for Liverpool the non-stop European record. Six minutes ahead of time, they'd covered the 152 miles from Crewe in 136 minutes, averaging 67 m.p.h. It was a sweet triumph. What was just as sweet was that Liverpool had scored over Manchester.

I'm always amazed and saddened these days when I see healthy, robust youngsters taking the bus in order to travel one or two stops to school, or to the local disco. Back in the 30s, we thought nothing of walking the ten miles to Anfield or Goodison Park and back. We walked everywhere—there was no money for tram fares. Our youthful shanks would willingly have taken us twice as far to watch our favourite team.

To get in the Boys' Pen we paid the princely sum of fourpence. Boys indeed! Many of the 'boys' chins had that bluish tinge that comes from years of shaving—the officials always went by your size and not by your appearance, so that you had the ridiculous situation of hefty lads of thirteen refused admission while tiny youths of seventeen or eighteen admitted without question.

Those were the primitive days of the 'change board', on which were chalked the last-minute team changes. The man who carried the small board walked right round the ground, and a loud groan on the other side of the ground was a sure indication that one of the stars was injured and that some 'stiff' from the reserves was deputising.

My favourite local cricket team as a boy was Sefton. What glorious Saturday afternoons I enjoyed at Sefton Park in my youth watching a team that was full of real characters. There were Mel Coomer, a fine batsman and brilliant fielder, a swashbuckling batsman named Tompkinson, the Reverend J. M. Swift, Jenner, Stevenson, Killikelly, a marvellous little wicket keeper named Trill, and the professional fast bowler, Lewis, who, I seem to recall, was 'mine host' at the Brook Hotel just opposite Sefton Park in Smithdown Road. It was a side of real class and quality. Where have all the 'characters' gone? There are few of them around the local cricket scene nowadays.

Cricket was easily my favourite game, and I followed the fortunes of Lancashire C.C. with eager enthusiasm. The county had some truly great players in my youth—the Tyldesley brothers, Ernest and Dick, Charlie Hallows, Frank Watson, Harry Makepeace, Len Hopwood, Jack Iddon, Frank Sibbles, Ted MacDonald and Eddie Paynter. Lancashire had a formidable team in those halcyon years, and rarely lost a match. How are the mighty fallen!

Before the war, many children would wend their way down to Princes Parade at the Pier Head on Sunday mornings and wait for the ships from Canada or Ireland to land their livestock. They'd help the drovers to drive the cattle on the long trail through Leeds Street, Alexander Pope Street, Richmond Row, Soho Street, Stafford Street, St. Andrew Street, and on to the abattoir. That was Liverpool's famous cattle trail. If any householder in, say, Alexander Pope Street, forgot to close his front door it would be no surprise to find a cow in his kitchen. The state of the streets after hundreds of cows, sheep and pigs had passed through can well be imagined. They had to be hosed down at night.

The sight of herds of cattle being driven along the Liverpool streets was a common occurrence, and the resultant chaos to traffic can be imagined. Some cows would break off down a side street and cause quite a commotion before they were rounded up. We often followed the cows to the slaughter house, and it was possible to see them being killed. Not a pretty sight, and I feel very strongly that they should have taken the necessary precautions to prevent young children witnessing the rather gruesome proceedings. In fairness to ourselves, however, we didn't go there with the express intention of watching the slaughter, but merely to obtain a bladder which we used as a kind of football.

Shopping in the city was a real pleasure in the 30s. Outside of London, Liverpool, arguably, had the best shopping centre in England. It was something of a shoppers' paradise with so many high-class stores and quality grocers that you were stuck for choice. Nowadays, there isn't a great deal of noise apart from the sound of traffic—not even that in the pedestrianised walkways. But the city had a voice in the 30s—the Mary Ellens outside the old St. John's Market with their cries of 'sage-a-mint-a-parsley!', the flower girls outside Central Station—'Bunch of flowers, lady!', the many street vendors outside the big stores shouting their wares of matches, balloons, jigsaw puzzles and cheap toys and games of every description, and the newspaper boys with their shrill cries of 'Echo or Exie!' Yes indeed, the city centre had a voice, and it was a homely voice.

Liverpool Airport has enjoyed a chequered career, and it will continue to do so until the City Fathers make up their minds one way or another. Whenever the city is in serious financial straits the cry goes up: 'Close the airport!' Many people still argue that the close proximity of Manchester's international airport makes Speke's prospects of a rosy future decidedly bleak. It ain't necessarily so!

Liverpool owes much to the enthusiasm and enterprise of Sir Alan Cobham. But for him, Speke Airport might now still be a grass strip. For it was Sir Alan, in the early 30s, who persuaded the City Fathers that commercial flying had a brilliant future, and that Liverpool could share in the coming prosperity. And he backed up his sales talk with thrilling flying exhibitions over the Speke farmland and on fields near Maghull. Practical demonstrations were followed by a comprehensive development plan complete with sketches, and sent to the Town Clerk. He brought a Giant Moth aircraft to the city, and gave the Lord Mayor and councillors a taste of what flying was like. Then he did the same for members of the general public. He brought his famous Flying Circus to Liverpool giving displays of stunt flying, mock bombing and joy rides.

Once the decision to build an airport had been taken, progress was remarkably swift. Imperial Airways made their first 'show the flag' flight from Speke on June 18th, 1930. At the controls of the machine was the bearded figure of O. P Jones, veteran of 700,000 miles of flying. The first control office and airport headquarters were all in a converted old farmhouse. It was a memorable day in the history of Liverpool when the airport was officially opened in July, 1933, by the Marquess of Londonderry with a spectacular display. It was the greatest display outside Hendon, and 100,000 visitors arrived to see the 246 aircraft taking part. All the latest aircraft were demonstrated—the Percival Gull, the Spartan Clipper, the Monospar, the Miles Hawk, the De Havilland Dragon and the B.A.C. Drone, which droned around at just 50 m.p.h. There must be many people on Merseyside who indulged themselves in a joy ride at that magnificent display.

The first regular non-subsidised service from Speke was operated by Blackpool and West Coast Air Services, which carried passengers from Liverpool to Blackpool for eighteen shillings a head. Later, a service linking Liverpool to the Isle of Man was introduced. The future prosperity of the airport seemed assured, as more and more airlines began to use Speke, and in 1936 the 611 (County of Lancaster) Hawker Hart Bomber Squadron of the Auxiliary Air Force was based there. Then, in 1937, the late Lord Derby opened the new control tower.

During the 30s, many famous aviators visited Speke, including Jim Mollison, the Atlantic record breaker, who was formerly an instructor at R.A.F. Sealand, his wife, Amy Johnson—'wonderful Amy', whose heroic exploits had thrilled the nation and made her the darling of the British public, and the great Charles Lindbergh. But when Lindbergh flew in on July 7th, 1937, he almost went un-noticed. He was charged the usual shilling landing fee, and when he came again two days later he was charged a similar fee. This time he was spotted. The Echo reported: 'Colonel Lindbergh sprang a surprise on Liverpool Airport by arriving this afternoon. He arrived in his own plane, a Miles Mohawk—a racy looking machine in red and blue'.

And Speke was ideal for the hundreds of famous people who came to see the Grand National in the 30s—famous actors and actresses, statesmen and politicians, the rich and the titled, and jockeys and their owners and trainers. But not everyone was impressed. One day in August, 1934, the Deputy Stipendiary, who was meting out justice at Liverpool Stipendiary Magistrates Court, was very annoyed when a low-flying plane interrupted the proceedings. Turning to the police prosecutor, he remarked, testily, 'I think somebody whose duty it is to observe the rules might attend to that'. I wonder what he'd have said many years later if a Concorde or a Jumbo Jet had flown over!

Not all the flying memories of Liverpool Airport are of success. There were crashes, too. Perhaps that which caused the greatest sensation was the collision between an R.A.F. light bomber and a racing monoplane which cost the life of Captain T. Campbell Black, the famous British aviator and winner of the England to Australia air race in 1934.

The date was Saturday, September 19th, 1936. Hundreds of spectators had assembled at Speke to watch Campbell Black give a display in the £3,000 Percival Mew Gull racing plane presented to the city by Mr. John Moores for the England to South Africa air race. Named 'Miss Liverpool I', the tiny Mew Gull, with its long nose containing a racing engine which partly obscured the pilot's forward view, was taxi-ing out for take-off with a member of the ground-staff at each wing tip.

Campbell Black gave the signal for the men to let go, and it was then that the spectators noticed the Hawker Hart biplane coming in from the river. There was nothing anyone could do to prevent the imminent disaster. Shouts could not be heard above the roar of the engines, and before the horrified eyes of the watchers the Air Force machine, which was travelling slowly along the ground, ran into the small Gull, killing Campbell Black.

I like the story of Speke in the mid-30s when pilots were forbidden to land near a patch of grass about four inches in diameter. It lay directly in the path of K.L.M.'s giant airliner, 'Lapwing', but each evening the pilot would swerve to avoid it. The reason was that a skylark was busy raising chicks there and, according to all reports, they passed out and flew solo, to everyone's satisfaction.

There was great excitement in 1936 when Harry Richman, that celebrated New York night club owner and entertainer, and ace airline pilot, Dick Merrill, announced that they'd take off from Speke in an effort to break the Atlantic record. Speke seemed ideal, as their heavily-laden monoplane, 'Lady Peace', needed a clear run of 1,500 yards with no obstacles to surmount as it became airborne. However, they changed their minds a few days before take-off, and decided to go from Birkdale shore, carrying a huge number of table-tennis balls to give the aircraft buoyancy in the event of ditching.

After running out of fuel they were forced down in a Newfoundland bog. But they were more than six hours ahead of the record. Later they travelled to New York where they presented Mayor La Guardia with copies of the Liverpool Daily Post and a message from the Lord Mayor of Liverpool.

Dick Merrill was back on Merseyside just a year later with a new partner, Jack Lambie. The Atlantic record was again their aim. They also hoped to carry a film of the Coronation to America. Once again it was their intention to take off from Speke, but once again they changed their minds and decided on Birkdale. When eventually they did take off in their streamlined Lockheed monoplane they had to go without the Coronation films which had been delayed by bad weather. There were no hitches this time, and they landed at New York 24 hours and 22 minutes later, having broken three records on the flight. It was the fastest trip ever, and it was also the first time one aviator had completed two round trips.

Chapter Fifteen
So Many Memories

The Grand Nationals of the 30's never lacked drama—and shocks. Two great horses dominated the famous steeplechase in those years—Reynoldstown, who won twice in successive years, 1935 and 1936, and the immortal Golden Miller who triumphed in 1934 and had also won the Gold Cup at Cheltenham five years in a row. It was little wonder that, the following year, he became the hottest favourite in the glorious history of the race. He could have been the greatest horse of all time. The bookies stood to lose a fortune.

Spectators numbered a quarter of a million, and the Prince of Wales joined Lord Sefton's party in the special stand close to Valentine's Brook. The Prince was to witness one of the greatest shocks in the history of racing.

For, as the magnificent Miller came to the ditch after Valentine's the first time round, he refused to jump and shot his rider, Gerry Wilson, off his back. Sensation! Few of the crowd knew what had happened, and there were gasps of astonishment when they realised that Golden Miller was not among the horses still running. The bookies were jubilant as Reynoldstown, jumping faultlessly, came in a clear winner.

There was a great deal of controversy and speculation over the downfall of this marvellous horse, and it still continues to this day. Shrewd judges were of the opinion that it wasn't a case of the Miller not being good enough, but that he was too intelligent. After a hard season he found himself back at the toughest four and a half miles in steeplechasing—and he remembered it. After taking nine fences he decided he'd had enough and just refused to go any further. The truth will never be known, but it seems significant that in 1936 and 1937, with different trainers and riders, Golden Miller refused again—on each occasion at the same fence that had been his downfall in the 1935 race. If only horses could talk?

Reynoldstown proved to be a worthy winner of the 1935 National and proved his brilliance by winning again the following year, to become the most famous horse in the history of the

National, only to be overshadowed by the legendary Red Rum many years later.

The 100th running of the Grand National was honoured by the presence of King George VI and Queen Elizabeth in 1937, so it was natural that the punters looked down the long list of runners to try to pick out one with even the remotest connection with Royalty. Their obvious choice was Royal Mail, who duly obliged them by winning.

'Jump Sunday' was a magnificent occasion in the 30's, when hundreds of thousands of people treated it as a holiday and walked round the course and inspected the towering fences the horses had to jump. They were much more difficult in those days. The tipsters did a roaring trade, of course, and one of the most picturesque characters there was Prince Monolulu, dressed in magnificent robes and feathered head-dress, and with his famous cry which will never be forgotten as long as the race is run: 'I gotta horse!' When folk discuss the most famous steeplechase in the world they still talk about Prince Monolulu who always added that extra little bit of colour to an already colourful occasion.

Local owners enjoyed mixed fortunes in the Grand National in the 30's. The decade started off well when Shaun Goilin won by a neck in a thrilling finish for the Liverpool cotton broker, Mr. W. H. Midwood. The good fortune continued the following year when Grakle won for Liverpool business man, Mr. Cecil Taylor. Then there was a lapse of several years when, in 1939, with the shadow of war overhanging the nation, Liverpool owner Sir Alex Maguire had the thrill of seeing his horse, Workman, cantering home first. It was a fitting climax to the 30's

Most people enjoy a good ghost story, especially if it's true. The local papers related the experience of a Brownlow Hill book-seller named Collins in 1934. Mr. Collins bought a big old house in Liverpool and moved in with his family and his elderly mother. For some reason he also took in a lodger named Griffiths, who was allotted a room on the top floor.

Uncanny things started to happen on the very first night, when the lodger heard sinister, sibilant whispering which seemed to come from the trap-door in the ceiling, and the mysterious voices were followed by eerie footsteps. The same thing happened every night for a week. Mr Griffiths might have put up with this, but he became really alarmed when he felt an icy wind blowing across his bed, and something tugging at his blankets.

Most certainly it was not just imagination as Mr. Collins, apparently, had experienced the same weird 'goings on' in his room below. These eerie manifestations became even more terrifying as the week went on. Then, to Mr Griffiths' horror, he saw the shadowy figure of a man emerge from his wardrobe, float across to the closed window and vanish. This, added to similar experiences by the rest of the occupants, was too much of a good thing. They packed up and left. The moral seems to be that, before you switch off the light at night you should take a peep into your wardrobe. Of course, it could have been Mr. Griffiths' bank manager!

Merseysiders, no matter what class, creed or colour have always been intensely loyal to the monarchy. So they were thrilled and delighted at what was unquestionably the romance of the year when the popular Prince George of Kent wed the charming and beautiful Princess Marina of Greece at Westminster Abbey on November 29th, 1934. It was an immensely popular marriage. Princess Marina had for some time been the leader of London fashion, and women started wearing 'Marina Green'.

They were equally delighted when, on October 9th, 1935, the now Duchess of Kent gave birth to a boy. It seems very unlikely that the Duke and Duchess of York, who'd been blessed with two beautiful daughters, but no son, felt the slightest bit jealous, but I'd read somewhere that a rather witty reporter wrote at the time: *'I wanted a gent', said the Duchess of Kent. 'Drat that old stork', said the Duchess of York.*

And it seemed to be perfect planning when the Duke and Duchess of Kent's second baby, the present Princess Alexandra, was born early on Christmas morning, 1936. A Christmas baby! It appealed to people's imagination. Princess Alexandra has always been one of the most popular members of the Royal Family. Could it be because she was so strikingly like her mother?

The previous year, in 1935, there was a joyous occasion—the Silver Jubilee of King George V, and I think that even the anti-royalists on Merseyside and elsewhere were willing to pay fitting tribute to a dedicated and popular monarch. Derek Whale, the Liverpool Echo journalist, described it so very nicely when he wrote, in the 70's:-

'One is almost tempted to say that 'they were poor but they were happy' in looking back on the Merseysiders who celebrated the Silver Jubilee of King George V in 1935. For, although 29.9 per cent of Liverpool's insured population were unemployed, the

City Council poured £10,000 into the carnival kitty to eclipse all the city's former royal jubilee celebrations and to lift the depression for a few days at least.

'The city raised about £30,000 towards the King's Jubilee Fund, and a richly-decorated, colourful vellum scroll of loyal greetings was sent to the King. Tramcars did a roaring trade with special sixpenny 'all-day' travel tickets, and, on the last Saturday a record number of 920,000 passengers was recorded. Pubs stayed open from 11.30 a.m. until 10.30 p.m.—quite a bonus for the strict 30's.

'The city went *en fete* on Jubilee Day, May 6th, which was warm and sunny, although it snowed on May 14th, and about ten o'clock that night, a nationwide chain of bonfires was lit. Local fires, manned by boy scouts, were lit at Mossley Hill, Birkenhead, Wallasey, Warrington, Hightown, Formby, and on the established beacon sites like Ashurst and Parbold. The fire on Snaefell could be seen from Blackpool.

'The parks were particularly lovely at night, with colourful lights set among the foliage. Statues like that of Peter Pan, and the Palmhouse at Sefton Park were also floodlit. Some public buildings were floodlit, too, and Liverpool's illuminated tramcar, with upperdeck band, moved tunefully along the major routes of the city. The first of 25 trees, which form part of Calderstone Park's Jubilee Avenue, were planted.

'A thousand local schoolchildren took part in the city's biggest pageant, 'Silver Trumpets', which performed daily at venues like Walton Hall and Princes Parks, Wavertree Playground, and on the city's Exchange Flags. Some 440 schoolteachers also assisted with this mammoth pageant, which illustrated in mime, song and dance, major events in the King's reign, and also included some notable Liverpool events, like the opening of Gladstone Dock and the Queensway Tunnel.

'Souvenir jigsaw puzzles were distributed among 142,000 schoolchildren, and tea parties at school and in the streets were the order of the day. Street decorations alone were a sight for the tourist, and humble homes, pavements, lamp-posts, and even the roadways were given the loyal treatment with paint, chalk, coloured paper, silver and gold paper, bunting, flags, streamers and balloons.

'The Pitt Street tenements of Liverpool's Chinatown had the most magnificent display in gold and crimson. Kids galore, and old folks too, sat outside in the closed streets at trestle tables, to eat mountains of sandwiches, cakes, fruit, jellies, and drink pop and tea. Everybody swung into the party mood. Doors and windows opened, and wireless sets were turned up for the strains of Henry Hall's and Jack Payne's music to float into the street.

'Special dance programmes were arranged at nearly all the regular dance halls from the city to the suburbs. London exhibition dancers, Ferrata and Tania, gave a display at the Adelphi Hotel, where folk danced from 8 p.m. until 2 a.m. on Jubilee night. And over at the State Restaurant, Dale Street, where Juan and his Band were playing, a midnight cabaret was produced by Mr. Tom Clarke of Birkenhead's Argyle Theatre. Among the artists were Liverpool soprano, Nancy Evans, making her debut, and Ellis Rimmer, who shot the winning goals at the Wembley Cup Final, and who was also a talented pianist.

'Blackbirds of 1935' was the Empire Theatre's show that Jubilee week. 'Too young to marry' was being performed at the Playhouse. There was 'Love on the Dole' at Bootle's Metropole, Frank Randle at the Argyle, and Wilson, Kepell and Betty were sand dancing at Southport's Garrick Theatre. Greta Garbo, Herbert Marshall and George Brent were appearing in the drama 'The Painted Veil' at the Majestic Cinema, and Bing Crosby in 'Here is my Heart' at the Paramount. A marionette show from Munich was presented at the David Lewis Theatre, and, of course, there was the traditional holiday circus - Bertram Mills' at Wavertree Playground - and funfairs at other open spaces. And four thousand Territorial soldiers took part in a military pageant at Sefton Park's parade ground on Jubilee Day, when the ceremonial Trooping of the Colour was performed by the 7th Battalion, Kings Regiment, Liverpool. Lord Derby took the salute.'

Yes, Derek described it all perfectly there, and not for many years had Merseyside enjoyed such a festive and magnificent occasion. The city, and the whole country seemed to explode in a massive demonstration of loyalty and affection. King George V was moved to say: 'I never knew they cared for me so much'.

Just over a year later, the Blackshirts marched through the streets of Liverpool on their way to a rally at the Stadium in October, 1936. The police had their hands full trying to deal with continual disturbances, and the Blackshirts' leader, Sir Oswald Mosley, was prevented from taking the salute in Lime Street as he had intended. He returned exactly a year later to give a speech to ten thousand people on a piece of waste land in Queens Drive,

Walton. There was bitter opposition, and as he stood on the roof of his van, missiles of every description began to rain on him. A brick hit him on the head. Unconscious, and bleeding profusely, he was rushed to Walton Hospital where he was detained for several days.

That was one of the grimmer episodes in Liverpool's history. But there was plenty of humour as well, and grown-ups didn't have the monopoly in quick-fire repartee—youngsters could hold their own. The story goes that one day in the mid-30s a small boy was kicking a paper ball along a shabby Liverpool street. The vicar came along and spoke to him. He said: 'My good little fellow, don't waste your time kicking that ball about. Go home and study instead. If you do that you might grow up to be a famous man. Why, you might even become Bishop of Liverpool'. The boy looked him over carefully, then glanced down lovingly at the paper ball, gave it an affectionate flick with his toe and replied : 'Thank you very much, sir, but I'd much rather be Dixie Dean of Everton'. Exit vicar, completely deflated!

It was claimed by someone, I forget who, that the construction of the Mersey Tunnel was the most uplifting event for Merseyside morale that occurred in the 30s. I wonder whether the army of unemployed and desperately hard-up people would agree with that. I have my doubts. At least it was considered important enough for the King and Queen to come to Liverpool to open it.

We were only allowed to walk through the completed tunnel on two occasions. I remember the first occasion very well, as I was one of the 35,000 people who plodded through from Liverpool to Birkenhead. We took the ferry back. That was on December 18th, 1933, and we paid sixpence for the privilege, which went to the Liverpool Echo Goodfellow Fund. It was quite an experience, but some people expressed disappointment at not finding portholes along the length of the tunnel through which they could see the fishes.

The following Easter, the public were allowed through again, two months before it was officially opened, and once again the proceeds went to local charities. Then there was an unofficial trial opening when, at six o'clock one morning, a fleet of vehicles of all kinds—lorries, vans, taxis, and private cars descended on the tunnel in one mass. This was a sort of dress rehearsal to test the ventilation system. To make it as authentic as they possibly could it was arranged that the drivers paid with cardboard money, and received similar change. All went quite smoothly.

The official opening took place on July 18th, 1934, by King George V with Queen Mary before tens of thousands of spectators. The only thing to mar the occasion was the passage overhead of an advertising plane whose engines drowned the official speeches, much to the annoyance of all the civic dignitaries. The firm responsible later apologised and asked the Lord Mayor to accept £5000 for charities to atone in some measure for the unfortunate incident. All was forgiven.

In spite of its historical importance to Merseyside, it seemed of little importance to me at the time, and, instead of milling with the throng trying to catch a glimpse of their Majesties, a pal and I decided to get out our old bikes and take a trip to Camp Hill, in Woolton, where we preferred to sunbathe all day. Long official speeches never appealed to me. When we arrived home, all the excitement was over.

There were scenes similar to those in a Mack Sennett comedy when the tunnel was opened to the traffic. Motorists seemed to go crazy in a wild scramble to be first through. I'm convinced there must be dozens of people who, with tongue in cheek, claim: 'I was the very first to drive through the Mersey Tunnel'. One motorist wrote to the newspapers claiming that, although he was only the fifth to pay, he was actually the first through because he drove past the other four between the booths and the tunnel entrance. This led to quite a lengthy correspondence, as the others reported that if he'd done this he must have driven eighty miles an hour in the wrong lane!

The opening of the Tunnel had a big effect on the Woodside luggage boats, which ferried vehicles across the Mersey, and on the Rock Ferry passenger ferry boats. Heavy losses were incurred and the luggage ferries reduced sailings to one boat to run as required, and then finally stopped altogether. So, too, did the Rock Ferry service. In contrast, the new tunnel prospered. During its first year more than three million vehicles drove through it, and its revenue was £250,000.

But after the initial burst of enthusiasm for this undoubted major engineering achievement, custom dropped off alarmingly, and there was a time in the 30s when customers were so few and far between that the authorities were compelled to advertise for them. They took full page advertisements in the newspapers— 'Use the world's largest underwater highway and travel from Liverpool to Birkenhead in 6½ minutes'.

Merseyside, in common with the rest of the country, mourned

the passing of King George V in 1936. It seemed so very soon after the pomp and splendour of the Silver Jubilee celebrations the previous year. But the popular King had been ailing for some considerable time, so the news, though sad, was not entirely unexpected.

So we had a new, young King, popular in the extreme, and of whom great things were expected. But a very strange thing happened at King George V's funeral. As King Edward VIII walked sorrowfully behind the coffin on its sombre way from King's Cross to Westminster, the ball of diamonds and the cross became detached from the State Imperial Crown, which rested on a velvet cushion on the royal coffin.

As the gun-carriage crossed the tramlines, the cross fell to the ground. The Grenadier Guards formed the bearer party, and one of the guardsmen swiftly picked up the jewel, slipped it into his pocket and carried on as if nothing unusual had happened. King Edward was apparently unperturbed at the incident, but he was seen later to turn and speak to his brother, the Duke of York. Some of the onlookers regarded it as an omen.

Perhaps it was, for the reign of the King who was never to be crowned was brief and controversial. The details of his infatuation for Mrs. Simpson are too well known for me to repeat them here, but I remember buying an Echo one dreary December evening in 1936 and reading the enormous headline—'King Abdicates'. I felt very sad, for I admired the man enormously. I suppose his broadcast to the nation on December 11th, 1936, renouncing his Throne will always be the most dramatic in the history of the B.B.C.

Some superstitious people remembered the crown incident at his father's funeral. Others were reminded of the prophecy of Gypsy Rose Lee, the Romany Queen. Before she died in February, 1933, she warned that the grandson of King Edward VII would come to the throne but would never be crowned. That Christmas, many children, unaware of the deep sense of tragedy overhanging the nation, were singing: 'Hark the herald angels sing, Mrs Simpson's pinched our King'.

It was decided that the coronation of the new king, George VI, would take place on the date originally fixed for his brother. This made good sense, as preparations were in a very advanced state. Once they'd got over the shock of the abdication the British people began to look forward with great eagerness to the great day. They hadn't enjoyed a coronation since 1911, so they were in a mood to celebrate in a big way. The Duke and Duchess of York had always been enormously popular, and everyone thought the world of the two little princesses. Perhaps, after all, things had turned out for the best.

'Nowhere throughout the provinces has the crowning of the King been celebrated with greater fervour than on Merseyside'. That was what one reporter wrote during that Coronation week. For Merseyside exploded in another riot of gaiety and pageantry unequalled anywhere outside London. The lavish celebrations surpassed even those for King George V's Silver Jubilee.

Coronation Day itself started off at 9 a.m. with the ringing of bells at many municipal buildings and churches, and flights over the city by the 611th Company of the Lancashire Bomber Squadron of the Auxiliary Air Force. From 10 a.m. until midnight there was a great mercantile marine display in the Mersey, in which the ships were decorated with flags and illuminated at night. At 10.30 a.m., the Civic Procession from St. George's Hall to the Cathedral set off, led by the band of the 2nd Battalion of the King's Regiment, and, half an hour later, the public were invited to listen on Exchange Flags, St John's Gardens, and the Rupert's Lane and St. Martin's Recreation Grounds to the relay of the Coronation Service from Westminster Abbey.

Then, at 11.30 a.m., the State Service at the Cathedral and at the Founders Plot in St. James's Road began. There was the Acclamation, the greeting of the King's Loyalty, and the Challenge. At noon a Royal Salute of 31 guns was fired by the batteries of the Royal Field Artillery of the 55th (West Lancashire) Division at Long Lane Recreation Ground, Garston, Sefton Park, Calderstone's Park, Newsham Park, Stanley Park and Walton Hall Park. In the afternoon, at 2.30, band performances were enjoyed at eleven local parks and recreation grounds. At three o'clock came the parade and march past of H.M. Forces. Or, if you preferred it, you could have watched the performance of the magnificent pageant play, 'The Early Birds', at the Stadium. At four o'clock there was a distribution of gifts to the men in the Crosby, Formby, and Bar lightships.

There were more band performances in the parks during the evening, another performance of the 'Early Birds', a massed gymnastic display called 'Rhythm and Beauty' in Walton Hall Park, the procession and pageant 'Drums and Bells' through Richard Kelly Drive to Walton Hall Park. At 7.50 we listened to his Majesty's broadcast speech, and then followed another pageant play in Walton Hall Park, a grand display of fireworks, and a searchlight display by the 38th King's Regiment, Royal Engineers. There were more firework displays at Long Lane Recreation Ground, Garston, and Fazakerley Hall Recreation Ground. If you enjoyed the fun of the fair there were funfairs at Sefton, Stanley and Sheil Parks. The Illuminated Tramcar made its way through the streets of the city, and at eleven o'clock there was another searchlight display and illuminations.

Many people will remember the beautiful and elaborate floral carts in the great procession during Coronation Week, each one drawn by four magnificent Shire horses. The floats were a sheer delight, and represented Westminster Abbey, H.M.S. Victory, the Coronation Regalia, 'Drums and Bells', 'Fairyland', and, by no means the least attractive, a wonderful model of the Mersey Docks and Harbour Building.

The pageant play, 'The Early Birds', was a mime fantasy of Liverpool, in which was enacted the story of Liverpool at the beginning of its history. It included a really charming ballet, starting with the Ballet of the Golden Trumpets, followed by the Ballet of Pre-historic Liverpool, the Ballet of the Sacrificial Stones, the Ballet of the Golden Eggs, which included the Dance of the Seagulls, the Dance of the Baby Seagulls, and the Liver Family and the Stork. Then came the Sailors Hornpipe, the Ballet of the Old Everton Toffee Shop, the Ballet of the Departure from the Station, the Ballet of the Golden Liver Bird, and the Grand Finale. It was a truly memorable performance, and the cast was drawn from Dancing Schools and Dramatic Societies from all over the city.

The procession and the pageant, 'Drums and Bells', was led by the Knight Challenger (mounted), the Band of the 2nd Bn. King's Regiment, the Crown Choir of Heralds (1st Group), and followed by the Lord Mayor and Lady Mayoress in their State Coach, the Crown Choir of Heralds (2nd Group), the Changing of the Guard, the floral car 'Westminster Abbey', The Challenge, The Car of Empire with Britannia, the Crown Choir of Heralds (3rd Group), the Band of the Blue Coat Hospital, the Yeoman of the Guard, the floral car 'Coronation Regalia', the Band of St. Edward's Orphanage, and finally another floral car, 'The Mersey Docks and Harbour Board'. This impressive procession was followed by the pageant itself—the presentation of a unique collection of customs of various counties of the United Kingdom, entitled, 'This Happy Country'.

The non-stop celebrations went on day and night for a week. As with the Silver Jubilee Celebrations, one of the most colourful areas during the festivities was Pitt Street, in the heart of Liverpool's Chinatown . A reporter recalled: 'With silver paper covering iron railings, lanterns, lights, flags, flowers, and bunting, the residents turned their humble tenements into a fairyland. Throughout Coronation Week people flocked from far and wide to see this brilliant spectacle'.

This was Merseyside at its brightest and best. Since then, of course, we've had equally joyous celebrations for Queen Elizabeth's Coronation, her Silver Jubilee, and the fairy-tale wedding of Prince Charles and Lady Diana. But must we wait another 25 years or so to let our hair down again and enjoy another week of festivities? Surely there are occasions in these drab times when we could celebrate in style and provide us with the uplift in morale that most people need. For instance, what about a special holiday on the Queen's birthday every year? And let's make it a day of rejoicing.

I think there are many people on Merseyside who remember Al Harris's Air Circus in the 30s. It consisted of two or three World War 1 biplanes. The pilots were Captains Roxburgh, Jones, and Rimmer, who put the aircraft through their paces— aerobatics, flour bombing, and the usual air flips for the public. Al Harris was the parachutist—a small man, round faced, and with dark, curly hair. Around 1937 they came to Rainford—to a Mr. Blackburn's farm, with their planes, giving joy rides to the public for 5/- and 7/6d. On one occasion Al invited two men to accompany him on a flight, and asked them to push him off the wing to parachute safely down. We heard so much about Alan Cobham's Air Circus. Al Harris deserves a mention, as he gave a lot of pleasure.

All this is a hotch-potch of memories as they come to me, and mention of the bands taking part in Liverpool's coronation celebrations in 1937 reminds me of a much more humble band which many Liverpudlians from the Dingle area will remember with affection. This was the Toxteth Temperance Band which played on Sunday afternoons on the corner of Park Street and Park Road. This was popularly known as 'Tom Hughes's Band', as it came from the workmen's mission in Mill Street, where Tom Hughes was the popular pastor. The band used to go to the Isle of Man at Eastertide to give concerts, and collect large sums of money for the poor children's holiday home known as the

Liverpool Cottage, in Balfessen, Port Erin.

They were the days when the newspapers offered readers free gifts in their struggle for circulation—pens, cameras, teasets, cutlery, clothing, including silk stockings, classical volumes and encyclopaedias. The Daily Express once sent out ten thousand pairs of silk stockings to their delighted women readers. To qualify for these gifts readers had to undertake to take a certain newspaper for an agreed period of time. Competition was intense. One paper gave away an article, and another would try to go one better and offer something even more worthwhile. I can remember getting a box camera and a useful set of twelve books on almost every subject under the sun from these offers. I still have them.

They weren't always free. Sometimes you had to pay a nominal sum. For instance, the Daily Herald stole a bit of thunder by offering registered readers sixteen volumes of Charles Dickens' novels—worth, I suppose about five pounds at the time, for eleven shillings. They were quite handsome books, so the offer was quickly taken up. Whereupon other newspapers went one better and offered similar sets of Dickens for ten shillings. It was cut and thrust. It must have been very costly for the newspapers, but the readers didn't mind. For many of them, one paper was pretty much the same as any other, so they took full advantage and always went for the best offer.

The first official visit of King George VI and Queen Elizabeth to Liverpool was made on May 19th, 1938, when they lunched with the Lord Mayor and then proceeded to Goodison Park to present new colours to the Liverpool Scottish, of whom the King was colonel-in-chief. He also presented colours to the 5th King's Battalion, who were receiving colours for the first time on ceasing to be a rifle battalion. It was a great day for the city and for these two famous Territorial Army battalions.

This was an unforgettable day for me, personally, as I was parading that day as a piper in the Liverpool Scottish band, which contained such fine characters as Pipe-Major Angus McLeod, Drum Major Smith, Sergeant Alexander and Corporal Bill Gardner. At that time the battalion was commanded by Lieut-Colonel McGuinness, and the adjutant was Captain Myers from the Queens Own Cameron Highlanders. I still treasure the photograph that was taken of the Pipe Band on the steps of Goodison Park when the colourful ceremony was over. Then the Liverpool Scottish marched all the way from Goodison Park to their barracks in Fraser Street, with bayonets fixed. That was probably the highlight of my years with the Liverpool Scottish.

Motorists travelling from Liverpool to Southport and back in the 30s didn't enjoy having to drive through Formby, with its many twists and bends. So it was a welcome occasion for them when the new road which by-passed Formby was opened on Saturday, December 10th, 1938, by Lord Derby. It only saved a matter of about ten minutes on the journey, but it cut out all those tortuous bends. The cost was around £200,000—a lot of money in the 30s, but it was money well spent. With Adolf Hitler and the ominous events taking place in Europe in mind, no doubt, Lord Derby wished that they could straighten out all the crooked things in the world as well as they'd straightened out that road. A very worthy sentiment.

'Crazy weather—why can't we get together?' That's a line from a popular song of the 30s, and during that decade, Merseyside saw some weather at its craziest. The first year, after quite a severe winter with skating on Sefton Meadows and other places, the summer turned out to be sunny and warm. There were all night queues for the Isle of Man steamer at August Bank Holiday week-end. They didn't mind waiting as the nights were warm and everything augured well for an enjoyable holiday. Just nine days later, Arctic conditions descended on Merseyside, bringing snow, sleet and ice, and a very unwelcome early winter. Holidaymakers in their thousands cut short their holidays and came home.

In 1935 we had a heavy snow storm as late as May 17th, just when everyone was looking forward to a lovely summer. Children built snowmen, while at Birkdale, play in a big golf tournament had to be abandoned as conditions became so atrocious that a caddie collapsed from the intense cold. But we had the sunniest August since 1914, although this was followed by another hard winter.

1936 came in with a roaring gale of 92 mph on January 10th, when sailors reported the worst night at sea they'd ever experienced in 35 years. Merseyside was scattered with fallen slates and uprooted trees. February was far worse, and ice-breaking tugs had to be used on the Leeds and Liverpool canal while, at Southport, even the sea was frozen.

Then, in March, 1937, when folk were saying 'goodbye winter' and anticipating a pleasant spring, we had to endure gales and blizzards which imperilled ships, snapped off radio masts in

Caernarvonshire, and cut off electricity supplies from large areas of North Wales.

Perhaps 1938 brought the craziest weather of all. The Echo described the auroral display of January 26th as looking like a vast, translucent cinema curtain waving in the Northern sky— and it caused a radio black-out on the short waves and interfered with railway signalling so that many trains were delayed. It brought thousands of Merseysiders out of doors, spending the evening staring up at the sky. That was 45 years ago, and I haven't seen anything like it since.

The Queen Mary had to fight her majestic way against waves a hundred feet high in the Atlantic during April of that same year, while 'flaming' June brought an 80 m.p.h. gale which stranded Fleetwood trawlers. Then in August, freak storms brought hailstones which shattered roof slates, and torrential rain which flooded streets, hotels and houses, and caused thousands of holidaymakers to abandon their cars on the roads.

So, when we complain about the vagaries of the British climate nowadays, and there's a lot to complain about, let's not forget that we endured plenty of freak weather in the 30s when, during the Siberian August of 1930, one Liverpool store offered consolation by advertising itself as a holiday resort!

In June 1939, an item of news burst like a thunderbolt—news that filled all Merseysiders in particular with shock and dismay. It was announced that the Thetis, Britain's newest submarine, built at Cammell Lairds, was missing in 132 feet of water, during her sea trials in Liverpool Bay.

The fact that it was so near to us made us all feel all the more helpless, and the tension of waiting for news of the trapped men was almost unbearable. On June 2nd, it was reported that marker buoys, released from the stricken submarine, had been located. Hopes were raised. Those of us who remember the disaster will never forget the strain and the desperate anxiety we all felt as we awaited news, hoping for the best but fearing the worst.

Then, on the 5th, all hope had gone, and the whole of Britain mourned the loss of 99 men. Only four managed to escape, and the last remaining survivor, Mr. Frank Shaw, of Wirral, died in January, 1981. I said the news burst like a thunderbolt. Ironically, when, later on, the Thetis was raised and reconditioned, she was renamed Thunderbolt, and went into service against the enemy.

Although war had been declared three months earlier, this had nothing to do with the wreck off Ainsdale which claimed 23 lives.

At 3.30 a.m. on November 26th, 1939, during a severe storm and in complete darkness, Liverpool Pilot Boat No. 1, the Charles F. Livingstone, was driven ashore by a fierce gale and remorselessly struck by heavy seas for hours until the tide receded.

Six survivors were rescued by the Blackpool lifeboat. They'd clung to the mast riggings for eight hours and had watched helplessly as their colleagues were swept off the deck and superstructure by huge waves. It was all the more tragic that they were only 500 yards from the shore on which their ship would be high and dry within a few hours. Southport had no lifeboat to launch and, because of a dreadful misunderstanding, the New Brighton, Hoylake, and Rhyl lifeboats were sent on fools errands, and didn't even sight the stricken vessel, having been told that she was somewhere between the Bar Lightship and the Great Orme. At the subsequent inquiry, it was revealed that this incorrect information came from the Charles F. Livingstone herself, when her crew believed they were somewhere off the North Wales coast. Darkness and the storm had confused them.

This tragedy, as I've said, happened nearly three months after we'd gone to war with Germany. But this was the so called 'phoney war', when little seemed to be happening, although Merseyside had felt the horror of war at its most beastly when the liner Athenia was torpedoed almost immediately after war was declared, with enormous loss of innocent life. It was obvious that the enemy U-Boat had been lying in wait even before Chamberlain made his fateful announcement on Sunday morning, September 3rd, 1939.

But the war is not part of my story. The phoney war continued throughout the winter, and people were not too badly inconvenienced. A mood of cautious optimism prevailed and there was talk of the war being over within a few months. When the balloon finally went up in the spring of 1940 with the blitzkrieg on the Low Countries and France, followed by the epic of Dunkirk, it was the end of Merseyside as we knew and loved it. It was never to return to its former glories.

Chapter Sixteen
'This Is Station 6LV Calling'

'This is BBC Radio Merseyside broadcasting on 202 metres medium wave, and V.H.F.—your friendly station!' As we sit back today and enjoy the top class entertainment BBC Radio Merseyside provides us with, many of us can be excused for looking back with a certain amount of understandable nostalgia to quite a different message—'This is the Liverpool station 6LV calling!' Anyone today who can remember hearing those words as they came over the air amid the hiss and crackle of atmospherics some fifty years ago will recall the pleasure they brought.

For those were the days when Liverpool had its first very own radio station, on the medium wavelength, with the result that it came in at great strength on almost any kind of receiver. Families sat tethered to the table by headphones and leads—and the primitive wireless equipment they used to bring those programmes into their homes—crystal sets with delicately poised 'cats whiskers', and early valve receivers that lit up the room. And tuners that operated with swinging coils and huge dials. The hiss and crackle of atmospherics did nothing to spoil the pleasure those early broadcasts brought.'

You reached the 6LV studio by taking the large lift just inside the old Arcade in Lord Street. You'd probaly pass Davis's Music Arcade with its shooting gallery etc., and the old Edinburgh Cafe. You might have been tempted into buying some of those delicious Cottle's Eccles cakes, which were claimed to be the finest tasting in Liverpool. The studio was above Reeces' cafe, and it was just like entering a padded cell with its thickly carpeted floor and heavy draped curtains all round the room which contained some easy chairs and two pianos—an upright and a grand. The director was Mr. H. C. Pearson, and Muriel Levy was the station accompanist. She must have played for many now famous people. But, by 1932, 6LV had closed down, and Liverpool had lost its own radio station. A great many years were to elapse before BBC Radio Merseyside came on the air for the first time.

Those first 'Heath Robinson' wireless sets were weird and wonderful. The 'cats whiskers' on the crystal sets meant an interruption if anyone banged the door. The set of one West Derby man was made from old cocoa tins, discarded razor blades, tinfoil, and a coil wound round an empty bottle. Somewhere in the set and essential to its working were a clothes peg and a cigarette rubbed with graphite. He tuned it by sliding one cocoa tin inside the another, which brought music from stations all over the country.

Listening on a crystal set was far different from listening as we know it now. The listener sat tethered by his headphones, noiseless himself and completely shut off from the noises of ordinary life. Unless you, too, had headphones, you couldn't guess what he was listening to. With a crystal set you took your listening very seriously indeed, and you couldn't impose it on anyone else.

Crystal sets and headphones could be bought for a few shillings. In the 1920's you could buy them complete for 7/6d, headphones for 2/- and aerials for 1/8d. These were the cheapest possible, but for a few pounds you could get an outfit good enough to make listening even more of a pleasure. From the earliest days schoolboys and wireless enthusiasts were buying endless components—valves, batteries, coils, loudspeaker units,—and building them into weird and wonderful assemblies plentifully festooned with wire. How well I remember making my own crystal set in the science laboratory of my school in Anfield. I found it a tricky job, but succeeded in the end, although the unsatisfactorily reception didn't justify all the work I'd put into it.

If you weren't careful your crystal set would turn into a transmitter and emit the frenzied howls and whoops known as oscillation, which was the bugbear of primitive radio. The BBC campaigned ceaselessly against this offence, broadcasting requests to guilty areas, such as: 'Will residents in West Derby Road, Liverpool, look to their sets, as they are causing severe interference to their neighbours'. As late as 1928 they were still receiving 15,000 complaints of oscillation in a year, and a cartoonist named H. M. Bateman, as well as drawing 'The man who boasts he can get Timbuctoo on one valve', drew another cartoon of men shunning a fellow commutor on a suburban railway platform above the caption: 'Suspected Frigidity on the 9.15'. But they were great, exciting days, and we enjoyed every minute of them.

Many people will remember those old accumulators, which were the cause of some of the choicest language ever uttered. They were glass-jarred low-tension batteries that had to be detached from your primitive wireless set and taken to a shop to be re-charged once a week, in exchange for a fully-charged one. The shop we used charged fourpence a week. We carried the accursed accumulators home very carefully indeed, so as not to disturb them too much for fear of spilling the acid. When you took it in for re-charging they gave you half a ticket—the other half was attached to one of the terminals so that they could identify yours in a week's time. And those accumulators had a horrid habit of running out at the most awkward moment—very often late at night when you'd settled down to enjoy some late night dance music by Harry Roy, Bert Ambrose, or Roy Fox. Then the bad language began!

It was round about the mid-30s that we acquired an 'all mains' wireless so, at long last, those maddening accumulators could be discarded. But if you still used a High Tension battery—Exide mainly, weren't they, or Siemens?—they too caused a lot of annoyance, although they weren't anywhere near as bad as accumulators. They gradually lost their power over several weeks, as all batteries do, so they did at least warn you that it was time to buy a new one, but they cost around seven or eight shillings, which wasn't exactly peanuts in the 30s. There was the story that if you put the battery in the oven for a while it would regain some of its power, but in my experience this little device never worked. When the new battery arrived, the necessary connections were made and suddenly a most glorious sound came booming out of the set with a volume you'd forgotten existed. It was a great relief when we went 'all electric' and those batteries were consigned to the dustbin.

I count myself exceedingly fortunate that I grew up with the BBC, so to speak. When I was an infant the BBC was in its infancy, and I became a wireless addict at a very early age and, as I grew up, I was able to witness the 'growing up' of the BBC ever since those wonderfully exciting pioneering days of 2LO—Savoy Hill. It seems like only yesterday that I heard the welcome announcement 'This is 2LO calling'. And those marvellous early broadcasts which I remember to this day.

How clearly I remember the cheery voice of Jack Payne introducing his BBC Dance Orchestra from Savoy Hill, and the voices of those early announcers such as Rex Palmer, John Snagge and Stuart Hibberd. The late night dance music broadcasts captivated me from the very beginning—played immaculately by the Savoy Havana Band and the Savoy Orpheans, Jack Payne as I've mentioned, and later Henry Hall, who took over from Jack as leader of the BBC Dance Orchestra.

Of course, it was the BBC who made these bands famous throughout the land and, thanks to their broadcasts, the bandleaders themselves became idols—Roy Fox, Lew Stone, Billy Cotton, Harry Roy, Carroll Gibbons, Jack Harris, Bert Ambrose, Maurice Winnick, Jack Jackson, Joe Loss, Sydney Lipton, Geraldo, Jack Hylton, and many others. From 10.30 until midnight we sat back and enjoyed British dance music at its brightest and best from the top clubs, hotels and restaurants in London, and also from the studio. And again, thanks to the BBC, the bands' gramophone records sold in their hundreds of thousands.

There were some very fine band vocalists, too, whom we first heard on radio. Roy Fox had Al Bowlly, Denny Dennis, Jack Plant, Peggy Dell and Mary Lee. Lew Stone had Al Bowlly, Alan Kane and Sam Costa. Henry Hall boasted several well-known singers—Val Rosing, Les Allen, Dan Donovan, George Elrick, Leslie Douglas, Bob Mallin, Kitty Masters and Phyllis Robins. Sam Browne, Elsie Carlisle, Jack Cooper and Evelyn Dall sang with Ambrose and his Orchestra. Jack Payne had Billy Scott Coomber, Ralph Sylvester and Ronnie Genarder. Through-out the 30s many vocalists sang with Jack Hylton's Band—Jack Plant, Leslie Sarony, Ennis Parkes who became Mrs. Jack Hylton, Dolly Elsie, Eve Becke, Sam Browne, Bert Yarlett , and the one who was with him right through the decade—Pat O' Malley.

The popular Billy Cotton had the ever faithful Alan Breeze or 'Breezy', as he was affectionately known. Carroll Gibbons had Anne Lenner, George Melachrino and Eric Whitley. Monte Rey will always be associated with Geraldo's Gaucho Tango Orchestra, and the main singer with Joe Loss during the 30s was the estimable Chick Henderson. I should emphasise that Al Bowlly and Sam Browne sang with dozens of different bands but mainly with those I've mentioned.

Other famous broadcasting bands were Billy Merrin, Victor Silvester, Oscar Rabin, Lou Preagar, Charlie Kunz, Harry Bidgood, the Blues Lyres, Eddie Carroll, Nat Gonella, Teddy Joyce, Debroy Somers, Sidney Kyte, Harry Leader, Louis Levy, Mantovani, Bram Martin, Sid Phillips, Jack White and Billy Thorburn, and to add to the popular singers I've mentioned there were also George Barclay, Vera Lynn, Doreen Stephens, Bill Currie, Dorothy Carless, Shirley Lenner, Ann Shirley, Brian Lawrence, Cyril Grantham, Hughie Diamond, Gene Crowley, Janet Lind, Chips Chippendall, Celia Lipton, Ken Crossley, Beryl Davis and Doreen Lundy.

The BBC gave us some wonderful programmes during that golden decade, and it would take a whole book to mention them all, so I'll content myself with mentioning just a few of my own favourites. Top of my list would be the charming 'Out with Romany', which delighted children and their parents alike. 'Children's Hour', with Derek McCulloch (Uncle Mac) was a constant delight and ran for many years and became almost an institution. There was the popular 'In Town Tonight', the cleverly contrived 'Cafe Collette', the pleasantly soothing 'Soft Lights and Sweet Music', the eagerly awaited 'Monday Night at Seven', the ever popular 'Music Hall', John Watt's famous 'Songs from the Shows', and Louis Levy's 'Music from the Movies'. A must for many listeners was Doris Arnold's 'These you have loved', as was the songs and comedy of 'The Kentucky Minstrels'.

Eric Maschwitz produced the famous 'Scrapbook' series, each programme of which took us back to the most important events of one particular year. We enjoyed the Rev. Dick Sheppard's brilliant sermons from the pulpit of St. Martins-in-the-Field, London, Henry Hall's memorable 'Guest Nights', and, towards the end of the decade, Arthur Askey and Richard (Stinker) Murdoch in 'Bandwagon', which took 'Big Hearted Arthur' to the very summit of stardom, and what was almost certainly the most famous radio series of them all—Tommy Handley's I.T.M.A.

George Orwell once wrote of 'the queer spectacle of modern electrical science showering miracles upon people with empty bellies. Twenty million people are underfed but literally everyone in England has access to a radio'. A rather cynical comment to which I have only one answer. Would he have made things even more miserable by denying us the pleasure of listening to the radio when it was at its brightest and best? Things would have been much worse with empty bellies and *no* radio.

I've tried in this chapter to remind readers of the lighter side of radio broadcasting in those early days. I would say the 1920s were the pioneering days of radio, the 1930s the golden days. But in the 1940s, in wartime, the BBC enjoyed its finest hour. Not only did it provide war weary Britons with the entertainment

159

that was so vital, but it also gave comfort and hope to the millions of enslaved people in Europe. When they were desperate, and hope nearly gone, they tuned into the *verboten* BBC at great risk to themselves, and what they heard enabled them to carry on with renewed hope and fortitude. While they could still hear the BBC all was not lost. All in all, BBC radio has done a magnificent job. Take a bow, 'Auntie Beeb'!

Chapter Seventeen
The Great Little Ships

One of the saddest aspects of Merseyside since the fabulous 30s has been the rapid decline as one of the world's greatest seaports. There was a time when majestic liners queued up for a berth at the Landing Stage—a time when the Mersey was full of big ships and little ships of every description. Those were the days when Liverpool seemed to be the centre of the world. The names of the great liners that graced the Landing Stage are well known to readers of my generation, and much has been written about them. My story is about the little ships.

To speed along the movement of the passenger liners which thronged the Mersey in the golden years, a lot of work was done by tender. Canadian Pacific ran three tenders—Bison, Moose and Wapiti. White Star had the Magnetic, and Cunard the Skirmisher. Also for ferrying passengers there were the Mersey Docks and Harbour Board's Flying Breeze, and the Egerton, owned by the Alexandra Towing Company.

The only ships allowed to remain at the Landing Stage overnight were the troopers—that was when we had an Empire—the Anchor Line's California and Tuscania, carrying troops and their families to and from India. On arrival in the Mersey, baggage would be discharged overnight and the passengers landed in the morning. After embarking passengers at Glasgow, the Donaldson Line's Athenia and Letitia would come to Liverpool for the remainder of their passengers. These would be carried over to them, waiting in the river, by the Skirmisher. On return from the voyage there would be the same manoeuvre. Yeoward Line had five ships sailing to the Canaries, and passengers for these would also embark and disembark by tender.

In the early 1920s, Flying Breeze took thousands of adults and children on two-hour cruises from Princes Landing Stage to Crosby and back for 1/- and 3d respectively. But her main function, of course, was as a tender. She had a magnificent lounge, upholstered in red, and a wide staircase. Captain Johns was the master of Flying Breeze, and at Christmas time she would sail out to the Bar Lightship with seasonal fare for the crew on behalf of the Mersey Mission to Seamen. Captain Johns was

Father Christmas for this happy occasion. This busy little tender, whose long career included attendances at the launchings of the Queen Mary and Queen Elizabeth, was scrapped in 1962.

In 1932, the Alexandra Towing Company bought the former White Star tender, Magnetic, which had been built in 1891. She was renamed 'Ryde' and, during the summer of 1934, with her hull painted black, with green booting and a yellow funnel, she was based at Llandudno as a pleasure steamer, giving pleasure to hundreds of holidaymakers.

One of my radio listeners told me that his first recollection of Flying Breeze goes back over fifty years when, as a boy, he joined the annual trip to the Bar Lightship on Christmas Eve. Many years later, he made the same trip, taking along a party of young people from North Wales, and on that particular occasion he was invited to join several members of the clergy who were also making the trip, for drinks in the saloon. Alas, by the time he arrived in the saloon the clergy had dealt most effectively with the spirits and he had to make do with lemonade!

For nearly a hundred years the principal towing company on the Mersey has been the Alexandra Towing Co. Ltd., founded in 1887. In 1935 they operated a fleet of 34 tugs, most of which were based at Liverpool. Most of them were named after Liverpool docks, like Gladstone, Huskisson and so on. Today the company has only about eighteen tugs on the Mersey, but has spread its operations and now operates on the Thames, and at Southampton, Felixstowe and Harwich. Coastal and overseas towage also now feature in its operations.

The Rea Towing Company had its origins in the coal industry towards the end of the last century. The business was first known as the Rea Transport Company, but in 1922 the Rea Towing Company was formed to develop ship towage operations at Liverpool. By 1935 they had ten tugs working on the Mersey, handling shipping, and three smaller ones for barge and lighterage traffic. All bore 'garth' names—Poolgarth, Yorkgarth, Minegarth, etc. The company still exists today as a subsidiary of the Ocean Transport and Trading Group, better remembered as the Blue Funnel Line.

The Liverpool Screw Towing Company which owned the well-remembered 'Cock' tug fleet, was founded in 1877 by Mr. William Becket Hill. In 1935 they owned eleven steam tugs on the Mersey—Fighting Cock, Holm Cock, Thistle Cock, etc. Readers will probably remember that they all carried a weather cock at the masthead. For many years they handled all the towage work for Cammell Lairds, attending launches and trial trips. In 1966 the company was taken over by the Alexandra Towing Company and its tugs merged with their fleet.

J. H. Lamey Limited was formed in 1916, when Mr. J. H. Lamey bought the tug Hero. By the mid-30s five Lamey tugs were working on the Mersey, among them the famous paddle tug Troon (what memories that brings back), which the company bought in 1934 and operated until 1948, when she was broken up on Tranmere Beach. Troon had been built in 1902, originally for the Glasgow and South Western Railway Company.

The Mersey Towing Co. Ltd. was a subsidiary of Canadian Pacific and, during the 30s, had the passenger tender Bison, which also doubled as a tug, and the two steam tugs Moose and Wapiti working with Canadian Pacific liners on the Mersey. After the war, the Bison was sold to Greek owners, while the Moose and Wapiti passed to the Liverpool Screw Towing Co. and became part of the 'Cock' fleet. The Mersey Towing Co. Ltd. was then wound up.

The Furness Withy group of companies had their own tug fleet on the Mersey for many years. It had its origin in 1896, when the former Johnston Line had the tug Amore built to attend to docking and undocking of their ships at Liverpool. In 1916 the Johnston Line was taken over by Furness Withy and in 1929-30 the Amore was joined by three more tugs—Beemore, Ceemore and Deemore, all built by Cammell Lairds. The Amore was sold soon afterwards. The three other tugs lasted until 1958, when they were sold to the Alexandra Towing Co. Ltd. and sent to work at Swansea.

There were numerous small barge and lighterage tugs working on the Mersey during the 20s and 30s for companies like Richard Abel and Sons, Ltd., William Cooper and Sons Ltd., the Grain Elevating and Automatic Weighing Co., Liverpool Lighterage Co. Ltd., W. Bate and Co. The river would be alive with them around the time of high water. All have gone today.

The Cunard passenger tender Skirmisher could also act as a tug when required. She was built as long ago as 1884, and lasted until 1946, when she was dismantled to a hulk in Langton Branch Dock, Liverpool. The hulk was subsequently towed to Garston beach in 1947, where it was finally demolished. The White Star tender Magnetic was built at Belfast in 1891. In 1933 they sold her to the Alexandra Towing Co. Ltd. who, as I've already mentioned, renamed her Ryde for tender work, and spent the summer of 1934 based at Llandudno, making excursions along the North Wales coast from the pier. The following year she was sold for breaking up at Port Glasgow.

And then there were the pilot boats. During the 20s and 30s, the Mersey Docks and Harbour Board owned four steam pilot boats—the Walter J. Chambers, built in 1917, the ill-fated Charles Livingstone, built in 1921, the James H. Beazley, built in 1921, and the David Fernie, built in 1898. The David Fernie was sold in 1937 to Norwegian owners and was replaced by the William M. Clarke, built in 1937. They maintained station at the Bar and off Port Lynas, putting pilots on board inward bound vessels and taking them off outward bound ones.

Inevitably, the Mersey ferry boats were called up for service during World War II—and after the part played by Wallasey steamers Iris and Daffodil at Zeebrugge in the Great War, they had quite an example to follow. Royal Daffodil II, built in 1934 by Cammell Lairds, was pressed into action early on, and one of her jobs was to stand by troopships during blitzes, to take men off the ships if they were bombed.

Unfortunately, during one heavy raid on Liverpool on May 8th, 1941, she was hit on the starboard side of the engine room, and she sank. Luckily, no one was injured, but one man, blown out of the engine-room, lost his false teeth. Three attempts were made to refloat the ferry before success was achieved thirteen months after she sank. When she floated to the surface she was a sorry sight—no funnel, no mast, and smothered in marine growth, and with three hundred or more tons of mud and silt aboard. Because the Admiralty required two Wallasey ferries for secret duties, she was quickly repaired and back on duty on June 2nd, 1943.

And that's part of the story of the Mersey's little ships. There must be many now retired men on Merseyside who served with distinction on one or more of the ships I've mentioned, and who, I'm quite sure, have many a good story to tell.

Chapter Eighteen
'I Say You Fellows'

'I say you fellows, I've been disappointed about a postal order!' How many readers, I, wonder, remember that famous utterance and its origin?

Well, it was spoken on thousands of occasions by Billy Bunter, the fat boy at Greyfriars School in the pages of that famous twopenny weekly periodical, the Magnet. Bunter, of course, was on the cadge, as usual.

In the 20s and 30s, our pocket money was regularly spent on those joyous weekly papers such as the Magnet and the Gem. They were full of good, wholesome reading, and written by a prolific author named Charles Hamilton, who poured out hundreds of thousands of words week after week, year after year, to the delight of thousands of young readers. His pen-name for the Magnet was Frank Richards, for the Gem, Martin Clifford, and for the Popular, Owen Conquest.

Charles Hamilton's output was truly phenomenal. The Magnet contained long stories of the mythical Greyfriars School and the Famous Five—Harry Wharton, Bob Cherry, Frank Nugent, Johnny Bull, and the Indian boy, Hurree Jamset Ram Singh— 'Inky' for short. Perhaps the most amusing and popular character for readers of the Magnet was the fat, greedy, gregarious 'Owl of the Remove'—the legendary Billy Bunter, whose antics were truly hilarious.

The Gem related the adventures of the boys of St. James's School, or 'St. Jim's'—Tom Merry, Harry Manners, Monty Lowther, Jack Blake, and the aristocratic Arthur Augustus D'Arcy, popularly known as 'Gussy'. There was a fat boy at each of Charles Hamilton's public school creations and, at St. Jim's, Billy Bunter's counterpart was Baggy Trimble. At Rookwood School, which was featured in the Popular, the heroes were Jimmy Silver and his pals—the fat boy there being Tubby Muffin. Of course, there were also the 'cads' at each school—Skinner Snoop and Stott at Greyfriars, Racke and Crooke at St. Jim's, and Cecil Ponsonby at Rookwood.

Hamilton had a remarkable gift for characterisation, and over the years he painstakingly painted a portrait of each and every one of the many boys he featured in his yarns, with the result that they became very real to us, and we became associated with them. In fact, so realistic and plausible did he build up his characters that there were many boys of my age who believed these schools actually existed.

There was a high moral tone to Hamilton's school stories which many people today would regard as 'old hat'. He emphasised the virtues of truth, loyalty, courage, and honesty in all things. His heroes never smoked, never told lies, never gambled. The 'cads' of his schools did all these things and were roundly condemned by the decent boys and severely punished by their masters. And such was the extent of Charles Hamilton's reading public that there's little doubt that his immensely interesting yarns must have had some influence for good among his youthful readers.

Some might claim that his most famous creation—apart from Billy Bunter, was Herbert Vernon Smith of Greyfriars—a complex character who loved to kick over the traces from time to time to indulge in a quiet smoke or a little flutter on the three o'clock at Plumpton, much to the disgust of his loyal pal, the reliable Tom Redwing who was always trying to keep him on the straight and narrow. Vernon Smith, consequently, was known as the Bounder. In this rather wayward character, Charles Hamilton was emphasising that not everything in the world is entirely black or white. In between there's a shade of grey.

The decent boys always came out top in the end. The cads received their just reward—which was usually six of the best administered on the seat of their trousers by the headmaster. So honesty, truth and loyalty was vindicated. All of which would probably be sneered at nowadays by our trendy, vociferous, so-called progressives, who have much to answer for.

And if I've evoked some happy memories for some people who used to revel in those wonderful stories, let me remind them of some more of Hamilton's characters. At Greyfriars there was also Horace Coker, the aggressive, bumbling, self-opinionated youth of the Fifth Form; Henry Samuel Quelch, the stern but just master of the Remove, whose steely eyes bore like gimlets into any boy with a guilty conscience; Paul Pontifex Prout, the pompous master of the Fifth; George Wingate, the popular school captain; Fisher T. Fish, the avaricious American boy; Percy Bolsover, the bully of the Remove (every school had its bully as well); Peter Todd, William Wibley, Mrs. Mimble, the dame at the school tuckshop, and Gosling the cantankerous old school porter whose greatest joy in life was slamming the heavy school gates shut on the faces of late-coming boys as the old school clock chimed seven o'clock.

Other characters at St. Jim's were Herries, Digby, Talbot, Figgins, Skimpole, Fatty Wynn, Percy Mellish, Kildare, the school captain, Mr. Railton, the master of the Shell form, and the revered headmaster, Dr. Holmes. At Rookwood we enjoyed the exploits of Jimmy Silver, Kit Errol, Teddy Grace, Arthur Lovell, Valentine Mornington, George Raby, Tommy Dodd, and Clarence Cuffy. They were all great fun and every year, if we were lucky at Christmas time, we were able to read of all these schools in a bumper book called 'The Holiday Annual'.

Another popular weekly school periodical was the 'Nelson Lee'. Nelson Lee had been a famous private detective but had decided to retire from the sleuth business to the more serene and tranquil surroundings of a public school named St. Francis's—St. Frank's for short, where he became the highly respected master of the Remove form. The St. Frank's yarns were written by a talented and imaginative author named Edwy Searles Brooks, and many of the characters he created during the long years of writing for the Nelson Lee are still remembered today—his loyal assistant and captain of the Remove, Dick Hamilton, otherwise known as 'Nipper', the aggressive head-strong Edward Oswald Handforth and his long suffering chums, Walter Church and Arnold McClure, and a host of others such as Archie Glenthorne, Reggie Pitt, Ralph Fulwood, Vivian Travers, Claude Gore-Pearce, the 'cad' of the Remove, Teddy Long, Enoch Snipe (there's a name for a wrong 'un) and Edgar Fenton, the school captain.

Public schools were never like Greyfriars, St. Jim's, Rookwood or St. Frank's. The boys seemed to spend an interminably long time on holiday, travelling all over the world and finding themselves in all sorts of predicaments. But for the boys of my generation and background it was all glorious escapism from the drab conditions and surroundings of depressed Merseyside in the years before the war. We shared those schoolboy adventures— we identified—and we wished we were fortunate enough to attend a school like one of those.

I remember having a Magnet confiscated by one of my schoolmasters when he spotted me reading it under cover of the desk lid. It gave us great amusement for the remainder of the lesson observing him reading it from cover to cover behind his high desk. The net result was that he returned it to me at the end of the afternoon, together with twopence for next week's edition—no, not for me, but for himself. I felt I'd gained an important convert, as he was no less than the English master!

I always devoured the Sherlock Holmes novels, and when I'd read most of Conan Doyle's famous stories I turned to another well-known detective, Sexton Blake, whose thrilling cases were related in the pages of another twopenny weekly called the Union Jack. How we revelled in the adventures of Sexton Blake and his boy assistant, Tinker, as they pitted their wits against some remarkable villains such as the sinister Doctor Satira and Doctor Reece, the resourceful 'Jim the Penman' and 'Waldo the Wonderman'!

We could also enjoy Sexton Blake in the monthly 'Sexton Blake Magazine' which cost fourpence and worth every penny. There was also the 'Thriller' and the 'Detective Weekly', which contained stories written by such eminent writers as Edgar Wallace and John Creasey. They continued to churn out detective stories of the highest quality.

Many boys favoured the 'Boys Magazine', which was a miscellany of yarns. Glancing at one dated September 14th, 1929, I notice the stories were: 'The Range of Riddles—featuring the Cowboy Detective of the Golden West, The Ranger Ace', 'Wiggles the Wizard'—all about 'the aristocratic freak of Africa'; a thrilling scouting series entitled 'the Scout Treasure Seekers'; a school yarn about the boys of St. Gideon's, or 'St Giddy's, as the boys called it—'The Famous St. Giddy's Sports Meeting'; another detective yarn about Falcon Swift, the 'sporting detective', called 'Prepared for Peril'; and 'Our thrilling wonder serial—'The Land of Marvels'. Blood and Thunder? Not a bit of it. They were all well-written stories, and I know for a fact that they helped some of the more retarded boys in their reading.

There was an excellent twopenny weekly called 'The Modern Boy' in the mid-30s, and this catered for boys who were scientifically minded, and which also contained some tip-top stories written by such people as George E. Rochester, John Brearley, Percy F. Westerman, and Flying Officer W. E. Johns, who wrote about that popular hero, Biggles of the Royal Flying Squad. These were all famous authors, and their stories weren't an insult to our intelligence as is much of the rubbish written for boys nowadays.

And many readers will look back with considerable nostalgia

to such weekly papers as 'The Boys' Friend', 'The Boys' Realm', 'The Scout', 'The Triumph', 'The Champion', 'The Bullseye', 'The Marvel', and 'The Schoolboys' Own', not to mention that 'famous four' of boys periodicals, Adventure, Rover, Wizard and Hotspur.'

One of the fascinating characters in the latter four papers was 'The Smasher'—a steel robot which left a trail of destruction in its wake. Another creation, human this time, was a character called 'The Black Sapper', who operated a kind of land submarine with a diamond-tipped revolving head which burrowed underground. Then we had a fellow with huge suckers on his hands and knees, who used to crawl up the tallest buildings. There was the strongest man in the world, 'Morgyn the Mighty' and that marvellous goalkeeper who put Elisha Scott in the shade—'Cast Iron Bill', who in all his playing days never had a goal scored against him. I wonder how many millions he'd be worth now!

These stories weren't comic strips. They were full length yarns—a complete story every week, and the writing was of a very high quality, which leads me to suspect that some of our leading authors weren't averse to making a bob or two by scribbling out stories for those magazines of our boyhood days. Some of them continued after the war, but Hitler effectively put an end to those great fictional schools—Greyfriars, St. Jim's, St. Frank's and Rookwood. It seemed a pity that such characters, built up so carefully over many years, had to disappear for ever.

I'm always amused whenever I glance at some of the strange adverts in those old weekly papers. This one from 1935, for instance,—'Be Strong! I promise you robust health, doubled strength, stamina, and dashing energy in thirty days, or money back. My amazing course adds 10 to 25 inches to your muscular development. Brings iron will, self control, and virile manhood. Complete course 5/-' And this one: 'Blushing. Free to all sufferers, particulars of proved home treatment that quickly removes all embarrassment, and permanently cures blushing and flushing of the face and neck. Just enclose a stamp'. And what about this one: 'Have you a red nose? Send a stamp and you will learn to rid yourself of such a terrible affliction free of charge!' And: 'Don't be bullied. Some splendid illustrated lessons in ju-jitsu. Articles and full particulars free. Better than Boxing. Learn to fear no man! Send 2d stamp for postage'. Is it any wonder we won the war?

More gems—'Height increased in 14 days or money back. Be

tall! Three to five inches rapidly gained. Amazing complete course sent for 5/-' 'Stop stammering! Cure yourself as I did. Particulars free'. 'Handsome men are sunburnt—'Sunbronze'—1/9d and 3/-. Remarkably improves appearance. Send stamp'. 'Smoking habit positively cured in a few days. Complete treatment 2/9d'. 'Ventriloquists Double Throat. Fits roof of mouth. Astonishes and mystifies. Sing like a canary, whine like a puppy, and imitate birds and beasts'. 'Are you happy? Bright and Cheerful? It is impossible to be so if you suffer from nervous fears, awkwardness in company, nervous depression, blushing, timidity, sleeplessness, lack of will power or mind concentration. You can absolutely overcome all nervous troubles if you use the Mento-Nerve Strengthening Treatment. Guaranteed cure or money refunded'. All I can say is we must have had some marvellous amateur doctors in those days!

And then there were the comics of our childhood days. They made us laugh then but collectors today take them very seriously indeed. I'm told that the most popular of all are the early issues of 'Dandy' and 'Beano'. The first issue of the 'Dandy' came out on December 4th, 1937, and collectors are always on the look-out for copies of this, especially if they still contain the tin whistle that was given free with that first number. Collectors are always optimistic.

But that was comparatively recent. In the 20s my favourite comic was the 'Rainbow', which came out every week, and whose star attraction was Tiger Tim and the Bruin Boys. I also enjoyed 'Bubbles' and 'Tiny Tim's Weekly'. Not so long ago I read about a man in London who owned the world's greatest collection of comics—more than 20,000 stacked from floor to ceiling in almost every room in his house. Now that must have been a real fire hazard. I wonder what his wife thought about it all?

In that massive collection I'm quite sure there'll be many copies of all those other ha'penny and penny comics we used to enjoy so much when we were children—Jester, Comic Cuts, Funny Wonder, Butterfly, Chips, Merry and Bright, Film Fun, Kinema Comic, to mention those that come readily to mind.

The Comic World had a language of its own. None of the characters spoke normally. Instead, they tootled, chortled, wuffled, twittered, or warbled, except for the villain who, resplendent in morning suit, shiny topper, and waxed moustache, forever gnashing his teeth, expressed himself with a continuous flow of hisses. The words they wuffled, twittered or warbled were enclosed in a balloon emanating from the speakers' mouths.

We soon became familiar with the comic slang. Trousers were known as reach-me-downs, shoes were tootsies or corn-cases, while a single shoe was an offside trotter-case. One's head was referred to as marble top, memoriser, or idea cabinet, bad eggs were called tired hen fruit, and fishing was known as worm dangling. The rich man didn't smoke a choice cigar—he smoked a Flor de Cabbage or a Havabanana, while the tramp had to content himself with a gasper.

And while we chortled over our comics, our mothers read 'Red Star Weekly', 'Home Companion', 'Woman's World', 'Passing Show' and 'Peg's Paper', while our fathers, when not engrossed in the racing paper, read 'Answers' and 'John Bull'. The latter was a sober and serious paper which contained a popular competition called 'Bullets'.

Chapter Nineteen
Those Wonderful Theatres

In the so-called Turbulent 30s, long before the intrusion of television into almost every home, a night out at least once a week was traditional. Nowadays, many folk never budge from their chairs and settees in front of the 'box'. Their week's entertainment comes entirely from the T.V. programmes, and it's little wonder that cinemas and theatres closed down in their thousands.

It seems rather surprising now that by the end of the 30s there were close on a hundred cinemas on Merseyside, and in all of them films were showing to capacity audiences. I recall that if we wished to go to the cinema on a Saturday night it wasn't unusual to stand in a long queue and hope for the best. Going back even further—to the 20s, I notice that Merseyside boasted as many as 43 theatres and hundreds of cinemas. Nowadays, bingo has claimed most of the cinemas and the few remaining theatres are hard put to keep going.

Fortunately, the Empire Theatre now appears to have a very bright future, while the Royal Court staggers from one crisis to another. The present Liverpool Empire was opened on March 9th, 1925, and was built on the site of the old Royal Alexandra Theatre, originally called the New Prince of Wales Theatre and Opera House. Its seating capacity is enormous, and it's still the largest provincial theatre and bigger than the London Palladium. It was modelled on a New York theatre, and as the design was copied at the time of America's prohibition, no bars were provided. But it boasted fourteen of the first ever theatre dressing-room showers—a luxury about which that great dance band musician, Tiny Winters, was quick to comment on when he was a guest on my radio programme. I've little doubt that some readers of this book were present at the opening of the Empire in 1925, and that they'll remember the stars of that first show— Maisie Gay, Stanley Lupino, Ruth French and Anatole Wiltzac. It must have been quite a spectacle as one of the audience lost his eye-glass there.

That first show was Julian Wylie's production of the swinging review 'Better Days'. Thousands of people, not only from Merseyside, but from all over Britain, tried to book for the opening performance, but had their cheques and postal orders returned as the theatre was fully booked several weeks in advance. It was to prove one óf the most popular theatres in the country, and with its extravagant shows, brilliant pantomimes, and its host of glittering star performers, it enjoyed a long period of success unequalled by nearly every other theatre in the country. During the golden era of British dance bands nearly every top orchestra in the country played at the Empire. Having heard those big bands on radio I never missed the opportunity of going to see them in the flesh, even if it only meant a humble seat in the 'gods' for sixpence.

One show I was determined not to miss at the Empire was the one Sophie Tucker appeared in during the week commencing July 16th, 1934. I remember standing in a long queue at the box-office hoping against hope that the tickets wouldn't run out before it was my turn. I was lucky. The programmes said: 'Sophie has not long arrived back in England, three years having elapsed since her last visit to this country. Needless to say, she is as bright, breezy and refreshingly cute as ever, and when she opened her tour a few weeks ago in London, she was received with the same warmth and riotous enthusiasm that marked her previous visits. Sophie Tucker, who is called 'the last of the red-hot mommas', mixes her material with delightful artistry, switching rapidly from grave to gay, and in her renderings of old and new favourites it is obvious she has not lost a particle of her old dash and vigour. This visit of hers will always remain deeply engraved in her memory , for she had only just arrived in this country when she heard the news that she was to appear before their Majesties the King and Queen in the Royal Command Performance at the London Palladium. A great honour and a great thrill for her'. And Sophie entirely lived up to her reputation the night I saw her. She was one of the greatest artists I've ever seen.

And how well I remember seeing Leslie Hutchinson—the great 'Hutch' at the Empire one night in the 30s. He was always one of the most welcome visitors to Merseyside. Always elegantly dressed, with a red carnation in his buttonhole, and a highly polished shoe tapping away under the great black piano, he always gave us full value for money. The audience made gentle fun of that white handkerchief tucked delicately in his sleeve, and brought out at the end of each number to be patted lightly over his forehead.

Bandleader Henry Hall said that it was in 1930 at the Empire that he saw what was probably the most sparkling play and the most sparkling cast anywhere in the world at that time—Gertrude Lawrence, Noel Coward, Laurence Olivier and Adrienne Allen in 'Private Lives'. What a cast! Some years later, the 'Private Lives' show was in a way reversed. Gertrude Lawrence sat in that same theatre, the Empire, and saw a show of Henry's called 'Something in the Air'. She was appearing at the Royal Court in what was to be her last show in Britain—'September Tide'. Afterwards they met at her supper table and Henry introduced her to Ted Ray, who was in Henry's show. All three of them had had one spell on the variety halls years before, and what put them into sentimental, reflective mood was an unusual cigarette lighter inscribed simply: 'To Henry Hall from his girls in 'Something in the Air'. Miss Lawrence was as enthralled with this charming gesture as Henry was.

When I interviewed that popular singer, Monte Rey, some time ago, he told me he wished he had a 'fiver' for every time he topped the bill at the Empire, where he once had an embarrassing but rather amusing experience. His signature tune was 'Donkey Serenade', and he was asked to sing this so often that he became known as Monte (Donkey Serenade) Rey. Said Monte: 'One memorable night at the Empire, just before singing 'Donkey Serenade', I announced that I had sung it six thousand times. And, right in the middle of the song, which I knew backwards, I completely forgot my words. I was going along merrily when, suddenly, my mind went completely blank and I had to stop. There was an embarrassing silence. I had to explain that, although I had sung it thousands of times, I had forgotten the words. The Liverpool audience really enjoyed that, and some three thousand people who were there will still remember that night. How they laughed and applauded! I got a bigger laugh than any of the great comics who were there on that particular bill'.

But the visits of those marvellous big bands were undoubtedly the highlights of the 30s. Through their late night broadcasts they'd made themselves household names, and there was such a glamour about them that nearly everyone wanted to see them in the flesh. The bandleaders had become the great stars of radio, and many people knew every single musician in the bands and what instruments they played. There was a charisma about them, and the chance to see them was far too good to be missed.

So, topping the bill at the Empire at regular intervals were the bands of Jack Hylton, Jack Payne, Lew Stone, Roy Fox, Henry

Hall, Joe Loss, Bert Ambrose, Jack Harris, Sydney Lipton, and so many others, including the irrepressible Harry Roy, whose show was always a riot. The first part of the show would be taken up with various variety acts which were an appetiser for what was to come. After the interval the curtain would rise to the strains of the famous signature tune, and as the lights went up there, before our very eyes, was the band we'd heard so many times on the radio but had never actually seen. In those days the musicians were always dressed immaculately, most of them in white tie and tails, and Roy Fox, in particular, was the epitome of sartorial splendour. They were moments to savour.

Then the band would play through its repertoire of popular songs, and the glamorous singers such as Denny Dennis, Sam Browne, Al Bowlly, Chick Henderson, Elsie Carlisle, Dan Donovan, Phyllis Robins and Evelyn Dall would come to the microphone and captivate their admirers. Most of the bands played it straight, with just a little comedy, which was what I and many others preferred, but Billy Cotton and Harry Roy, in particular would include all kinds of zany behaviour and the show would become a riotous hour of glorious fun. For the people who enjoyed this sort of show, Harry Roy's visits to the Empire were the most popular of all. They were never-to-be-forgotten days when the visit of a famous band always meant standing room only.

There was an unusual case in 1932 when the Stipendiary Magistrate of Liverpool fined the producer of a revue at the Empire £25 for putting on a sketch which was considered to be vulgar and distasteful. The high code of standards was so strict in those days that when I explain how completely innocuous it all was, readers will be surprised. It was merely a variation on a scene which had already been passed by the Lord Chamberlain.

The offending sketch was part of a review called 'Restez la Nuit', and involved a husband, a doctor and a lodger. The husband says: 'The time has arrived. A little stranger is about to come to town'. To which the lodger replies: 'I knew that would happen one of these days', and the doctor enters with the baby under his arm. Both men shout, simultaneously: 'Hurrah!' The doctor then asks the lodger who he is, and he replies: 'I'm the man from the Prudential', and the curtain comes down. However in the offending version at the Empire, the doctor holds out his hand to congratulate the father, and both the husband and the lodger step forward. The counsel for the defence was a young lawyer named Selwyn Lloyd, but, despite his eloquence, the fine was still £25.

Five years after the disastrous fire which completely gutted Liverpool's famous Royal Court Theatre, the handsome new theatre opened on October 17th, 1938. The first show was given by Jack Hulbert and Cicely Courtneidge in their new musical comedy, 'Under your Hat'. The final rehearsals were fraught with difficulties, as the limited size of the stage necessitated many adaptations, especially as an aeroplane figured in the show. The problems were surmounted, however, and the show was a big success.

Going back into the dim and distant past, I wonder how many people remember Liverpool's old Adelphi Theatre? Apparently, it was once a circus, until the interior was beautifully rebuilt and the building re-opened as 'The Theatre Royal Adelphi'. It was situated in Christian Street, and inevitably with 'scousers', who couldn't resist cutting a name down to size, it soon became the 'Delly'.

It was quite an impressive place, as the interior was spacious and boasted the largest stage in the city. The 'Delly' began life on quite a high standard with some excellent shows but then gradually deteriorated until in the end, it became distinctly scruffy, both in appearance and in the quality of its shows. That was the time when you could get into the gallery for a penny. It was twopence in the pit, threepence or fourpence in the dress circle, and if you wanted luxury you paid sixpence for the 'box'. The size of the stage is best illustrated by the fact that when Fergus Hume's famous melodrama, 'The Mystery of the Hansom Cab' was produced at the theatre, there was ample space for a real hansom cab, with horse and driver, to run up and down—brought in, incidentally, from the nearest cab rank. But that, as I say, was a long, long time ago.

Many Liverpool people have affectionate memories of the Westminster Music Hall, or the 'Wessie', in Kirkdale, which opened its doors for the first time on April 11th, 1887, and was the venue for many of the top artists of many years ago. One Walton man told me that he clearly remembers seeing George Hackenschmidt, The World's Strongest Man' at this popular hall. 'To see him bending iron bars and lifting girders of terrific weight was a sight you never forget', he said. Among those who appeared at the 'Wessie' were Marie Lloyd and Robb Wilton. But it was still third-rate as a variety theatre compared with the Empire, the Hippodrome and the Olympia. They often held talent concerts there, and people came considerable distances to compete. They must have had hearts of lions because the audiences were quite unmerciful.

The Westminster Theatre, after lying idle for some years, was refurbished and became the Doric Cinema. Across the road from the theatre stood the more modern Garrick Cinema, considered the 'posher' of the two but, nevertheless, catering for those Saturday afternoon children's matinees which showed cliff-hanging serials—'to be continued next week'—each performance preceded by the doorman bawling: 'Penny you stand in the queue—twopence you walk right in!' The Doric was destroyed in the 1941 blitz when an oil-storage yard next door was hit by incendiaries. But people still remember it as the 'Wessie'.

In its palmy days, the Rotunda, named because of its round appearance, was one of the happiest, funniest, jolliest music halls in Britain. It was almost as lively outside as it was inside, with the neighbouring shops ablaze with light until midnight, and the cheerful, good natured Mary Ellens in shawls selling fruit from large baskets outside its doors. It invariably played to packed houses, and there were some wonderful shows there in pre-war days, including such stars as Ted Ray, Bud Flanagan, Issy Bonn, Lucan and McShane, Kitty Gillow, Peter Rennie, Tubby Turner, Wally Wood, the Four Paradise Girls, and Harry Castelli's Accordeon Band. To keep the queues happy outside there were the inevitable buskers.

Ted Ray had very happy memories of the 'Roundy', as it was the very first theatre he ever played in. This was in a show called 'On the Panel' with Tubby Turner, and he was so impressed with the atmosphere of the place that he appeared there many times after. Ted had a very soft spot for the audience. If you were good they were the friendliest, most appreciative people in the world. If you were bad they soon let you know it. He said that the Rotunda was in a very tough district, where the police walked in threes, so it was a great experience, and London was a piece of cake after playing at the 'Roundy'. Ted recalled one comedian who wasn't doing too well in a show with him. Someone threw a rotten tomato at him which hit him on the chest. Obviously a good comedian, he shouted to the offender: 'Thanks for taking it out of the can!'

Sandy Powell also performed at the Rotunda, and the day when he celebrated his 21st birthday there in between shows was recalled fairly recently by a former Tiller girl who played many times at the 'Roundy'. This girl was Kitty McShane, of Lucan and McShane fame, who was only a girl of 20 when she was a member of a dancing troupe appearing there. 'They were the finest and most appreciative audience I ever played before—even if they did shy the odd tomato on occasions', she said. 'They seemed to radiate a tremendous warmth of feeling, and you always knew when you had got them. But the time I remember best is when we were playing 'Cinderella' pantomime with Sandy Powell in the cast. Somehow we got to know that it was his 21st birthday, and someone in the show bought him a ring as a present. Then we all had a drink in the wings. And that was all. It was a case of back on stage again because we were giving three shows a day—a matinee and two evening shows'.

Kitty went on to say that Sandy's mother was also in that Cinderella pantomime,—'She was a beautiful lady and had a splendid voice, and the song she used to sing was, 'I'm trying so hard to forget you'. Even now, when I sing that song to the old-age pensioners, my mind is back in the Rotunda Theatre and those happy days'. Kitty, who also played with George Formby at Liverpool's Olympia Cinema, said she was born behind her father's grocery shop at the corner of Athol Street and Latimer Street. 'Times were so hard for the people of that time', she said, 'that some used to go to a great deal of trouble to pinch a bit of bacon. It was the grocer's habit in those days to spread the bacon on the counter, in small piles, ready for quick weighing. The trick was to put a bottomless basket on the counter, cover it momentarily with a shawl and remove a bit of bacon'.

Bud Flanagan's real name was Reuben Weintrop. When he played at the Rotunda in his early days he was told that accommodation had been booked for him with a motherly little Irish woman near Scotland Road. He arrived the day before the show was due to open, and was greeted with great warmth by the woman who was absolutely delighted to have an 'Irishman' with the name of Flanagan lodging with her. She went out of her way to make him as cosy and comfortable as possible, even to the extent of putting a statue of the Virgin Mary, a picture of the Pope, and a Rosary in his bedroom.

Bud, of course, was Jewish, and he was so touched by her hospitality that he didn't have the heart to tell her she'd got it all wrong. She took it all for granted that he'd want to go to early Mass every morning, so on his first morning there she woke him up with a cup of tea and told him that a good breakfast would be waiting for him when he arrived back from church. Bud was in a spot. He had no wish to disillusion such a kindly little woman, so every morning, at the crack of dawn, he got up, washed and shaved, and took himself for a long walk down to the Landing Stage, arriving back in time for breakfast. She was so obviously pleased to have staying with her such a devout catholic as Mr Flanagan. Polite to the end, Bud took his leave on the Saturday. She hugged and kissed him, and then, to his astonishment, she pushed the rosary in his hand as a parting gift.

Bud once played at the Tivoli, New Brighton, where business was so bad that on the Thursday all the acts were told to be at the theatre early to do fly-posting—sticking up bills—and also to give out handbills for a special performance.

Bud had met, at the Queens Park Hippodrome, Manchester, the top of the bill—a magician calling himself 'The Great Magnet', who offered him a job to help him with his conjuring. So they dished the bills out round Birkenhead and other places. Each bill was headed—'Cannibalism in the 20th Century', and went on to say: 'I, the Great Magnet, will positively eat a man at both houses of Friday night at the Tivoli, New Brighton. If I fail to do this, or leave a morsel for the cat or dog, I will give 500 guineas to the Wallasey Maternity Hospital. Signed—The Great Magnet'.

Of course, the challenge spread like a prairie fire, especially through the shipyards of Cammell Lairds, where the workers were always game for something different.

The first house on Friday was packed, and the audience waited in nervous suspense and impatient expectation. At last the curtains parted to reveal a huge streamer emblazoned with the word 'Cannibalism', an operating table with knives and other instruments, and a surgical trolley.

The Great Magnet entered impressively in a surgeon's full rig-out. He called for a volunteer. 'Any Gentleman, please, to be eaten by me!' There was a buzz in the auditorium. No takers! He then announced that he had a volunteer for the second house.

When this opened they were practically hanging from the chandeliers. The volunteer was a youth of 19. The nurse started to strip him to the waist and Magnet held up a document which he read out slowly and solemnly. 'I, John Rigby, swear that I am over eighteen years of age, and that I enter into this knowing that whatever happens to me I do not hold the Great Magnet responsible.'

Then a clause from the 'contract'. 'I, The Great Magnet, will in the event of John Rigby's death, pay to his parents for the rest of their natural life, the sum of £5 a week.' Deafening applause from the audience.

A pen was held out by the nurse and John Rigby was now slightly less confident. He signed with a shaky hand. He then lay down on the operating table while Magnet started his preparations. John was rather alarmed by then, and more so when Magnet picked up a wicked-looking scalpel and tested it for sharpness. He advanced slowly on John who by now was in a bit of a panic.

On the trolley by the side of the operating table stood a bowl. The magician did a bit of byplay with the knife, seized John's left arm and made a slight incision about an inch long, drawing blood. John screamed, leapt off the table, jumped over the orchestra rail and vanished. The Great Magnet walked to the front, shrugged and said cheerfully, 'Can I have another volunteer?' Nobody accepted the invitation and the curtain came down.

Wallasey Maternity Hospital, needless to say, did not benefit to the extent of 500 guineas.

Some will remember the Fortescue Players who used to put on two plays a week at the Rotunda. They were the famous old melodramas which appealed to so many of the older generation, and they always played to full houses. One week they decided to perform the most bloodthirsty of them all—'Jack the Ripper', and, to make things more realistic and menacing, they decided to place the Ripper and a young actress in the middle of the audience before the curtain went up.

Suddenly there were screams of terror from the girl as the Ripper was seen to stab her. Then he ran up the aisle with a knife in one hand and a gruesome piece of flesh in the other. This, of course, was going too far, and many of the audience were panic stricken and jumped from their seats in horror. Not even the staff had been told about this decision, so it isn't surprising that many people objected to it strongly. When the police heard about it they quickly put a stop to it, as it could easily have led to a stampede and one or two cases of heart failure. It was quite a novel idea, but it was taking realism just a little too far.

Many top artists had, and still have, fond memories of the old

'Roundy'. Arthur Askey recalled passing the theatre on his way to watch Everton play at Goodison Park, and he enjoyed many great shows there. Comedian Issy Bonn remembered that in his early days at the theatre his friendly Scotland Road landlady promised to meet him at the stage door and escort him home if the audience gave the 'thumbs down' to his act.

That well-remembered Bootle-born male impersonator, Kitty Gillow, made her first appearance there when she was only fourteen, the first of many appearances. Kitty summed it up nicely when she said: 'I loved playing the Roundy because there was a terrific audience. They came to be entertained, and if they liked the show they certainly let you know it. They were wonderful shows. We used to do three a day then and think nothing of it. We were at the theatre from noon until midnight. That was really show business. In those days you couldn't just make a record and become a star overnight. You did it the hard way. I was there the week before it was bombed. We just got out in time. The manager said we'd better close down and not take any more chances. A week later it was bombed'.

It was when Liverpool suffered its worst blitz in 1941 that the Rotunda, along with many other famous buildings, was completely destroyed. But even the German Luftwaffe never succeeded in wiping this famous landmark from the memories of Liverpudlians. For many years after it disappeared the corporation buses were still using the name 'Rotunda' on their destination indicators, and for even longer, passengers would ask to be put off 'at the Rotunda'. Perhaps they still do.

For those who enjoyed their bloodthirsty melodramas there were one or two Liverpool music halls which catered for just that, showing such lurid tales as 'The Drunkard', 'The Gamester of the Metz', 'The Silver King', 'The Face at the Window', 'The Strangler of Paris', 'Secrets of the Harem', 'Blood for Blood', 'The Dumb Man of Manchester', 'Maria Marten', 'Driven from Home', 'Hoodman Blind', 'The 10.30 Down Express', 'Claudian' and 'The Grip of Iron'. They were blood and thunder melodramas and you needed a strong stomach for them. The stage 'ran with blood'. But the audiences loved them.

The Royal Hippodrome, or to give it its proper title, The Royal Hippodrome of Varieties, had been a variety hall since 1876. It was an enormous theatre, with a seating capacity of 4,500. The circle alone held well over a thousand. It was originally built for the Dane, Charles Hengler, who, with his sons, John and Edward, ran a circus there for 25 years. The huge stage was eighty feet wide and forty feet deep. The ceiling was a work of art, having been painted by the famous artist, Secard. It was one of the most popular theatres in the land, and it did wonderful business.

Some of the most spectacular shows in the country were presented there, and many of the most famous old time stars such as escapologist Harry Houdini, Charlie Chaplin, Little Titch, the Russian wrestler Hackenscmidt, Florrie Forde, George Robey, Robb Wilton, G. H. Elliott, Harry Champion, Vesta Victoria, Vesta Tilley, and illusionist Lafayette had trodden its boards. Needless to say, it was never the Royal Hippodrome to the locals. It was always the 'Hippy'.

But then, one day in 1931, there were genuine tears of sadness. The theatre was packed to the doors, and dozens of people were content to stand at the back as there wasn't a seat available. The huge crowd had turned up not merely to applaud the artists— Harry Champion with his rollicking choruses, and the delightful Vesta Victoria with her 'Waiting at the Church', supported by many more top stars of the period.

They'd come to say a sad farewell to their beloved theatre which was closing down as a variety theatre, and this was the final performance before the curtain came down on the last music hall act so that it could go over to talking films. It was the end of an era—a glorious era, and, reluctantly, the management had decided they could no longer compete with the talkies. Only the previous month the Forum Cinema in Lime Street had opened with organist Reginald Foort on the Compton organ as the star attraction. When the Hippodrome opened as a cinema that same year, the first talkie show was 'Dracula', which played to an audience of 30,000 in one week. Few people will ever forget the old 'Hippy'.

Not far from the Hippodrome was the Olympia, built in 1905 on an island site in Boaler Street. The site was formerly occupied by an asylum, and the wags of the district said that Moss was 'barmy' himself to build another music hall there. Be that as it may, the Olympia was twice as big as the London Hippodrome, seating 3,750 people. In its heyday the music hall glittered in scarlet, gold, green and purple, and seats could be had for 2d, 4d and 6d. Beneath the stage there was a solid brick and concrete pit which stabled elephants, horses, etc., of the bygone circus days. In the darkness beneath the stage there was also a lions cage. A tunnel leading from the pit was the animals' entrance from West Derby Road.

At one time, at the flick of a switch, the vast stage would sink within twenty seconds to reveal an enormous 80,000-gallon lake which was used for the spectacular aquatic displays. One night, actress Ruth Maitland, tied to a stake by a villain in the melodrama 'Sands o' Dee', nearly drowned in this lake when the water rose higher than anticipated. She was rescued, gasping for breath, in the nick of time. And the Olympia even had a ghost, in the form of a phantom of a woman violinist who was said to haunt the back-stage dressing-room area.

In March, 1925, the Olympia closed as a music hall, to re-open as a cinema, and the very first film shown was 'The Thief Of Bagdad', starring Douglas Fairbanks. There have been many arguments over the very first talking film ever to be shown in Liverpool, and whether it was at the Olympia or the Hippodrome. First in the field, in fact, was the Olympia, which was actually Liverpool's first cinema and the fourth outside London to be wired for sound. So it was there on January 23rd, 1929, that Liverpool heard its first all-talking film, 'The Singing Fool', featuring Al Jolson.

What glorious memories the Argyle Theatre in Birkenhead evokes. It was one of the very few local theatres I never once set foot in, and yet it was probably the most famous music hall in the provinces. It was very small, with a tiny stage, and yet practically every star of variety played there during its long existence. They may not have been stars when they first appeared at the Argyle, and very often their names were in small type at the bottom of the bill, but the vast majority of them went on to much greater things and to become some of the most famous acts in the land.

They were very demanding audiences at the Argyle, and they demanded only the best. A poor act was very quickly given 'the raspberry' by this knowledgable audience, so artists had to be absolutely on their toes. During the 30s Liverpool's own Robb Wilton received £70 for a week's engagement there, and Flanagan and Allen were paid £45—but this was before their Crazy Gang act which was to provide so much fun and hilarity.

The BBC soon cottoned on to the popularity of this great little theatre, and it was radio that made the Argyle a household name all over the country with its broadcasts which gave listeners their very first taste of music hall on the air. The very first of a weekly series of variety broadcasts were transmitted over the old BBC North Regional Station on April 14th, 1931—the first of many, and compered by Richard North. Among the famous artists who got their first start at the Argyle were George Formby Senior, G. H. Elliott—the 'chocolate coloured coon', and Donald Peers, who sang 'Babbling Brook' for the first time on the air from there. Everyone seemed to listen to the popular 'Saturday Night at the Argyle' broadcasts. Gertie Gitana sang there when she was only ten years old.

It was a black day in British music hall history when fire bombs put an end to the Argyle. Penetrating the roof they set fire to the auditorium, balcony and dressing rooms, and very soon it was a smouldering ruin. This was on the night of September 26th, 1940. Next morning, Birkenhead folk lamented the loss of their beloved music hall as they viewed the wrecked building with the Union Jack still fluttering over its ruins. Practically the only part that survived was the office, its walls still displaying playbills of seventy years before, and its walls adorned with pictures of old-time artists. If it was any consolation to the people of Birkenhead, an income-tax office had been hit at the same time and all its records destroyed.

Just as the Hippodrome became the 'Hippy', the Westminster Theatre the 'Wessy' and the Rotunda the 'Roundy', so the old Pavilion Theatre in Lodge Lane became known to Liverpool people as the 'Pivvy'. It still holds many happy memories for Liverpool's older generation, many of whom still remember its owner, William Henry Broadhead, who built and was the owner of many theatres throughout the north-west. He not only owned the theatres, but very often, as in the case of the Pavilion, he bought up neighbouring houses so that the staff could live there. He was a very popular character and when he died, in 1931, a special train took more than 400 mourners from Liverpool to his funeral in Blackpool.

I always found the 'Pivvy' to be a cosy little theatre, and I have happy memories of some really good shows there. Perhaps because it was my last visit there before war broke out I clearly remember the show on March 23rd, 1939. The main artists were that successful comedy duo, Jewell and Warris, that fine Canadian singer Les Allen, who had once been Henry Hall's lead singer, and Harold Ramsey playing on his mighty theatre organ.

That splendid actor, Tod Slaughter, found great success in the 30s with his famous old melodramas, always popular on

Merseyside, and I can remember some of them performed quite brilliantly at the Pavilion. My own particular favourite was 'The Face at the Window', the story of a citizen involved in a grisly series of murders in Paris in the late 19th century. Fortunately, I never suffered from nightmares. Tod Slaughter also performed 'Maria Marten' at the 'Pivvy'. It was spectacular entertainment—if you liked that sort of thing

If the Pavilion was cosy, that wonderful little theatre in Fraser Street, the Shakespeare, was even more so. I spent some marvellous evenings there in the 30s. It was a typical Victorian theatre, ornate, with glitter and gold, and decorated with beautiful murals and mirrors. As with the Argyle, nearly all the great stars of variety played the 'Shaky', and, as it was such a small theatre, you had to queue for ages to get a seat for the more popular shows. Those queues, I recall, stretched right along Fraser Street and round the corner into London Road.

Many folk will remember the Shakespeare as a great pantomime theatre. It was, in fact, the first theatre in Liverpool to bring a Drury Lane panto there. One of the great principal boys of those days was a Liverpool girl named Maggie Duggan, and she played alongside such stars as George Robey. Robert Courtneidge also played in pantomime there when Zena Dare was Cinderella, and Phyllis Dare the fairy godmother. This was a magnificent star-studded cast and it was the first time that the role of Dandini was played by a man—John A. Warden.

Bootle and Seaforth theatre-goers had many an enjoyable night out at the Old Metropole Theatre in Stanley Road. This was yet another cosy, attractive theatre, and many leading music hall artists appeared there. Many will remember seeing Jan Van Albert, the Dutch giant, when he appeared at the Metropole in 1927. His height was given as an amazing 9ft 3½ inches, but it's possible that, for publicity purposes, the height given for these theatre giants was often exaggerated. According to reference books and well-informed text books, no man has ever attained nine feet. Apparently, the tallest man ever known was Robert Pershing Wadlow, of Illinois, who was 8ft 11 inches. When Holland was overrun by the Germans in 1940, Jan Van Albert was sent to a prison camp because he was a patriotic Dutchman and refused to entertain German Troops.

The Lyric Theatre, in Everton Valley, was very popular in its day, and is still talked about by some folk who write to me with their memories. It was there that Ted Ray gave his first performance in 1927 for the handsome fee of £7. His real name, of course, was Charlie Olden, so Ted decided to reverse the letters of his surname and call himself 'Nedlo—the Gypsy Violinist'. He was discovered by E. C. Jedson, of the agents Jazon and Montgomery, of Lime Street. And 'Nedlo' was no mean violinist. Later on he appeared at the Clubmoor Cinema and the Olympia, as well as the Rotunda, of course. When he played the Lyric, Nedlo shared a dressing room with that other famous comedian, Ben Warris, who was then doing a black-face act. Ben Warris went on to much greater things while Ted Ray became one of the best-loved comedians in the land.

Ted served his apprenticeship in the rough, tough music halls and, as he became more successful, he was able to adapt his style to radio. He was one of the many top comics who derived much of his humour from the grim but often amusing conditions prevailing on Merseyside in the 20s and 30s. Actually, he was Wigan born, but most people looked on him as a Liverpudlian. When the family moved to Oakfield Road, Anfield, under the shadow of the famous Spion Kop, it was perhaps inevitable that he became a staunch supporter of Liverpool F.C. He was a talented footballer, playing regularly for Ainsdale F.C. and then for Liverpool Reserves. He was such a good violinist that he played in several well-known dance bands, and might well have become one of the country's leading dance band musicians had he not decided that his special forte was comedy.

Liverpool's famous Playhouse Theatre has always been the training ground for actors and actresses who went on to make great names for themselves in films, in the theatre, and in broadcasting. Early Playhouse bills include the names of such noted people as Miles Malleson, Diana Wynyard, Judy Campbell, Jane Baxter, Cecil Parker, Richard Bird, Percy Marmont, Milton Rosmer, Geoffrey Toone, Rachel Gurney, Cyril Luckham, William Mervyn, Wyndham Goldie, Godfrey Winn, Deryck Guyler, Alfie Bass, Peggy Mount, Sebastian Shaw and Robert Donat. Now there's a brilliant galaxy of stars for you. And there were many more.

Is it any wonder that up-and-coming young actors and actresses loved to appear at the Playhouse? The theatre was also responsible for some real life romances—notably those of Michael Redgrave and Rachel Kempson, Robert Flemyng and Carmen Sugars, and William Lucas and Rowena Ingram. Perhaps the most famous, however was that of Arnold Bennett and Dorothy Cheston

Bennett, Arnold's biographer, when they met at the Playhouse in the early 20s.

In its heyday the other Empire Theatre—the one in James Street, off St. Mary's Road, Garston, was quite a good little theatre, and many famous stars performed there. In 1916, Archie Pitt wrote a revue called 'It's a Bargain', which ran for more than two years up and down the country, but then struck a very bad patch, and after a poor week in a small Durham town, they were stranded without sufficient money to pay their fares to their next destination, which was the Garston Empire.

The managing director of this theatre was a Mr. Arthur Williams, who forwarded a cash advance, and all was well, as their show at the Empire brought good attendances. Gracie Fields, who later married Archie Pitt, had a supporting role in the play and was earning £5 a week, which was good money in those days. One year later, Archie wrote the review 'Mr Tower Of London', which ran for over seven years and made Gracie a household name. I wonder what might have been had not Arthur Williams been sympathetic and taken a chance by forwarding that money?

The legions of Merseysiders who recall, with affection, Jackson Earle's 'Melody Inn' show at the Floral Pavilion, New Brighton, may also remember Frank Terry's show in the 30s. Frank's 'Pleasure on Parade' revue was a landmark in the history of the Floral Pavilion. A poll, conducted by a national newspaper, voted it the best concert party in Britain. That was praise indeed. 'Pleasure on Parade' ran throughout the first half of the 30s. The BBC broadcast it on a hundred occasions and several million people who'd never been to New Brighton listened in to the Floral Pavilion.

Chapter Twenty
'To Be Continued Next Week!'

And what of Merseyside's cinemas? The silent films are often referred to as the golden era of cinema, but it was during the 30s that movie-making enjoyed its halcyon years. I've already said that by the end of the decade there were close on a hundred cinemas on Merseyside and all doing wonderful business. When an outstanding film was being shown it was almost impossible to walk right in. On most nights of the week, and especially Saturday, it meant taking your turn in a long queue. But it was all worth while, and in those days we were privileged to see, not only the glamorous stars like Greta Garbo, Marlene Deitrich, Rosalind Russell, Constance Bennett, Bette Davis, Clark Gable, Ronald Coleman, Robert Taylor, Spencer Tracy and Humphrey Bogart, but also the curly-headed, dimple-cheeked Shirley Temple, who sang and danced her way into the hearts of thousands of Merseysiders.

We enjoyed the marvellous dance routines of Fred Astaire and Ginger Rogers, the hilarious comedy of Laurel and Hardy, who had Merseyside audiences rolling in the aisles, and the more zany antics of the Marx Brothers. We had the stupendous Busby Berkeley musical extravaganzas, usually starring the singing and dancing of Ruby Keeler, Joan Blondell and Dick Powell, and we were always gripped to our seats watching the cold-eyed, black-coated gangsters like Edward G. Robinson, James Cagney and George Raft as they mercilessly gunned down their rivals. And we had the outrageous Mae West. In short, we in the 30s witnessed the silver screen at its zenith.

There were several different types of picture palaces. There was the so-called luxury cinema with its plush, comfortable seats and air of splendour and opulence; the 'dump', as many people called the average run-of-the-mill cinema, and at the bottom of the list there was the 'bug hutch' and the 'fleapit', where admission was to be had for a few coppers. I never got to know whether the bug hutch was slightly superior to the flea-pit, or vice-versa. But we had many of these on Merseyside.

The Trocadero, in Camden Street, was probably Liverpool's finest cinema in the late 20s. As with many picture-houses at that time it had a first-class orchestra. Not only that, it had a splendid Wurlitzer organ and an equally splendid organist in Sydney Gustard. This proved to be extremely popular, as Gustard was an organist of the highest class, had great personal appeal, and his choice of programmes could not have been bettered. The special musical half-hour on Friday evenings was often one of his well-remembered organ recitals.

The Troc used it's gimmicks, too, and for the screening of the film, 'Strictly Confidential' in 1935, the management hit on the idea of introducing that well known hunter, 'Old Bill', accompanied by his owner in full hunting kit, and also a vet who was there to make a note of the horse's reactions in front of a large, enthusiastic audience. This was a most successful gimmick, as it brought the crowds in droves, and two policemen were needed to hold them back. All traffic was blocked in Camden Street, and the rumour quickly got about that the horse was none other than the famous winner of that year's Grand National—Reynoldstown.

Naturally, we all had our favourite cinemas, but sometimes, if we went into town, it was a case of deciding which was the shortest queue and settling for that. The Scala, in Lime Street, was very popular and, like most other places, often used gimmicks to advertise a certain film. There was one occasion, in the early 30's when they engaged a man to stand outside the cinema and portray the character in the leading role—this time an officer of the French Foreign Legion, resplendent in uniform and carrying a glittering sword. There was a placard affixed to his back stating the times of the performances and the price of admission.

Suddenly the comparative peace of Lime Street was shattered by the terrified screams of a woman. At the same time, the heroic-looking officer of the Foreign Legion forgot his dignity, turned tail, and flew. A frightful looking brute was approaching in menacing fashion, its little piggy eyes staring ahead, and its long, outstretched hairy arms apparently reaching out for a victim. The people in Lime Street took one look and ran for their lives, hotly pursued by a most fearsome-looking gorilla. There was panic. Suddenly, a small van screeched to a halt, and a man jumped out and approached the now frantic animal. He produced an article from his pocket, seized hold of the gorilla, made a quick movement, and a gorilla skin fell to the ground revealing a very frightened, perspiring and embarrassed human being.

There was relief mixed with anger on the part of the pedestrians.

Full of apologies, a film manager explained what had happened. Apparently, another cinema in Lime Street was showing the film 'King Kong' that same week and, not to be outdone, had also hired an 'extra' to patrol the streets and advertise the film. All would have been well if the placard pinned to his back had stayed in place. Alas, it had become unfixed and lost. The unfortunate man had been imprisoned in his gorilla skin by means of a padlock and, far from wishing to attack the panic-stricken people, he was merely making frantic appeals for them to try to release him.

The splendid Forum cinema in Lime Street opened its doors for the first time in May, 1931, and at once became the favourite haunt of hundreds of cinema-goers. Designed by Liverpool architect, Ernest Shennan, who became Lord Mayor of Liverpool, this 1500-seater picture palace was one of the finest in the country. Certainly it was one of the most luxurious. The opening was quite an occasion and one of the features was a film about Liverpool narrated by the then Lord Mayor, Alderman Edwin Thompson. The main film was 'Almost a Honeymoon'.

The first real hint of the golden days of the 30s had, however, come the previous August in Birkenhead with the opening of the Plaza—the largest cinema on Merseyside with 2,298 seats, under manager Jack McAree. Readers who were there will remember that the first film to be shown was 'The Last of Mrs. Cheyney', starring Norma Shearer. Jack's pride and joy was the orchestra lift. At a touch of a button a platform rose from the pit, bringing the whole of the orchestra into view and to the level of the stage. It was a large orchestra of 22 talented musicians and conducted by Louis Cohen, and they gave a 20-minute performance at the first and second houses. The Plaza also boasted the Compton organ, the first in any Merseyside cinema. These shows were not only warmly welcomed by the cinema-goers, but perhaps even more so by the musicians themselves, as the arrival of the talkies had thrown many of them out of work.

However, the talkies had come to stay, and more and more cinemas were being built—many of them in the super class. One such luxury cinema was the Paramount, later to become the Odeon, in London Road, which opened on October 15th, 1934, and seated 2,200 people. As was usually the case they chose a spectacular film as the 'opener', and huge crowds queued up to see Claudette Colbert and Frederic March in 'Cleopatra'.

The Paramount, too, presented some outstanding stage shows, and on that opening night it was Teddy Joyce and his Band, together with a performance on the Compton organ. This was the sort of thing to draw the crowds. But there was almost a calamity. At the end of the opening night's celebrations, an executive inadvertently turned on the sprinkler stop valve system on the stage, and there was water everywhere. The console of the beautiful organ was saturated and there were no further organ interludes for two weeks while technicians rewired it.

One week they showed that magnificent film, 'The Lives of a Bengal Lancer', with a tremendous cast including Gary Cooper, Richard Cromwell, Franchot Tone, and C. Aubrey Smith. Flushed with the enthusiasm and patriotism of youth, and a shilling in my pocket, I went to see it on the Monday night. I thought it was such a wonderful film and I was so thrilled that I saw it again on the Wednesday and again on the Friday. I was repaying the borrowed money for several weeks afterwards. I can't remember the exact date, but I know it was some time in 1935.

It was another great day for Birkenhead cinema-lovers when the famous Ritz Cinema first opened its doors to the public on Monday, October 4th, 1937. Robert Taylor was to have opened it when he was over here making 'A Yank at Oxford', but he was mobbed so much by the adoring girls that he had to go home. So that honour fell to Gracie Fields, and who could possibly have done it better? The film was 'The Man in Possession', starring Robert Taylor and Jean Harlow.

The Ritz rightly called itself 'The Showplace of the North', for not only did it show the very latest and best films, but it also presented first class stage shows. The show on that first night included Jan Ralfini and his Band and the Dagenham Girl Pipers, to say nothing of Reginald Foort who gave the very finest performance on the big 4-manual Compton organ. What a show!

Subsequently, many of Britain's top dance bands performed there, and many of the leading broadcasting organists such as Reginald Dixon, Robinson Cleaver and Reginald New. You could enjoy a marvellous three-hour entertainment for as little as sixpence in the front stalls. It was without doubt the best value-for-money entertainment in the whole of Merseyside, perhaps even in the whole of the north of England. Bill Boht, the manager, insisted on only the very best, and he proudly presented such top-line artists as Elsie and Doris Waters, Anona Winn, the Beverly Sisters, George Formby, the portly xylophone player Teddy Brown, and even Gregory Peck, Richard Todd and Michael

Redgrave. They got 20,000 people at the Ritz every week.

If Bill Boht remembered the Ritz with pride, he also recalled the demanding silent film days of 1927 when he had the musical control of thirteen cinemas, not only on Merseyside but also the Capitol in St. Helens. He used to direct the orchestra at the Coliseum in City Road, Walton, but one night a week he'd put a deputy in charge and would go round the other cinemas to see how they were doing. Each Monday morning he'd send to every orchestra a bundle of music which he'd prepared in advance, after seeing the films scheduled for their cinema. It was a big and arduous task, and they had a special theme for the hero, one for the heroine, and, of course, 'villainous' music for the villain. I wonder what Bill chose as 'villainous' music! But it's to men like Bill Boht that we owe so many hours of grand entertainment in the 20s and 30s. Those Ritz shows were super.

Incidentally, while on the subject of cinemas in their heyday, I've a mental picture of the manager standing at the entrance for the evening performance, all spruced up, carnation in buttonhole, and smoking a huge cigar as he beamed at the customers. A colleague of mine was once a pre-war picture palace manager, and I remarked once on the extravagance of those cigars. To my astonishment he explained that they were only permitted a couple of drags at each performance, and that one cigar had to last them a whole week. He may have been having me on, but he seemed sincere enough, and I can well believe it.

It really was extremely difficult to introduce a little bit of realism to those silent films. Apart from having to play appropriate music to suit the particular scene, it was also necessary to provide suitable sound effects. Realising the need for this, two Liverpool brothers named Linaker used to hire themselves out to provide such sounds. They fired pistols for cowboy films and used tins containing stones for rain scenes. No doubt, also, coconut shells knocked together for galloping hooves. Special girls with reasonable voices were engaged to sing songs like 'Smiling Through' while the film of that name was being shown.

Another enterprising local man named John Darlington, who spent half a century in the business, once told about the wind and wave machine he designed. It resembled an old-fashioned washing mangle, but its rollers were made of metal instead of wood, and were long and hollow. Inside he put sea shells. 'When you turned it on you got the sound of rain', John said. 'A canvas sheet was pulled over the drums for wind effects. The quicker you turned the wheel the fiercer the wind howled'. John and his boss, Mr. R. H. Godfrey, used to go behind the transparent screen at Runcorn to synchronise with the films. 'It was great fun', John added. 'One film where we used this machine to great effect was 'The Ten Commandments'.

Even though times were so hard and money so scarce in the 20s and the 30s, people usually managed to find the necessary few coppers to take them to their local cinema at least once a week. Each district of Merseyside boasted its own group of picture palaces, and the poorer areas seemed to have more than others. Take the south-end of Liverpool for example, where you had your choice of the 'Jamie' (the St. James's Cinema) in St. James's Place, the Warwick, the Granby, the Park Palace in Mill Street, the Beresford in Park Road, and the Rivoli in Aigburth Road. Some of them were 'fleapits'. Or were they 'bug houses'? Later in the 30s, the Rialto, which also housed an excellent ballroom, opened and, of course, this became the 'posh' picture house of the district.

There was another old cinema called the Park Royal, in Park Road, which some older readers will remember. I'm told that the entrance to this squalid little cinema with the imposing name was little more than a large hole in the wall. A beery-looking commissionaire stood at the entrance in a uniform which, my informant suspected, came from the Battle of Waterloo. You walked along the passage and pushed open the entrance door to find yourself in a long, narrow room furnished with wooden forms. 'It was like a scene from a Dickens novel', he told me. 'Children ran about playing 'tag', while orange peel and screwed-up paper bags flew through the air. Women breast-fed their babies. Young lovers shyly kissed under the dim light, while old ladies continually chattered into each others ears. All was good humour and conviviality, and there was no violence at all. Not many people will remember the Park Royal, but I will—always!' He omitted to mention what the entertainment was like.

A plush new cinema in Dingle was opened on March 29th, 1937. This was the Gaumont, and it was built on the site of the old Dingle Picture House a hundred yards or so from the Overhead Railway terminus in Park Road. It was a notable addition to Liverpool's luxury cinemas. The opening programme included a cartoon in colour, 'Birds in Love', and an Edgar Kennedy comedy, 'Vocalising', the Gaumont British News, William Whittle at the Wurlitzer organ, and the main feature film, 'My Man

Godfrey', starring William Powell and Carole Lombard. Prices were: front stalls 6d, back stalls, 9d, back circle 1/- and front circle 1/3d. The Gaumont is still there, but these days, it's devoted, like most others that have survived, to the noble art of bingo.

Many readers will remember, with affection, the Rivoli Cinema. It was formerly called the Aigburth Assembly Picturedrome, and before that the Sefton Park Assembly Rooms, but more popularly known as 'Pa Scott's Opera House'. But that's going back a long way—long before my time. I understand it became a repertory theatre in 1925, but was then bought by Gaumont British and became the Rivoli Cinema.

It's always fascinating to read the old handbills, and one of them reads: 'The Aigburth Assembly Picturedrome, Aigburth Road—Exclusive animated pictures of all the finest subjects of the day, including Filmacolour—Complete change of pictures Mondays and Thursdays—Special matinee for children every Saturday at three o'clock—Only approved pictures shown—Prices 1/-, 9d, 6d, and 3d'. Only approved pictures! I wonder what they'd have thought of some of the permissive material shown today?

Crosby had its share of fine cinemas. There were the Regent and the Corona in Crosby itself. Waterloo had the Queens and the Winter Gardens, and Seaforth boasted the Stella and the Palladium. A monthly programme for the Regent of 1929 shows that on Monday, February 11th, for three days, you'd have been able to see John Gilbert and Greta Garbo in what was described as 'the screen's most passionate drama'—Flesh and the Devil'.

The programme changed on Thursday to 'The Love Mart', featuring Billy Dove, Gilbert Roland and Noah Berry. 'Billy Dove, more beautiful than ever', said the programme, 'as the slave sold on the auction block—then given the freedom she did not want. The most colourful and romantic period of old Louisiana, with its slave runners, buccaneers and Creole dandies'. Other films advertised for the Regent later that month were 'The Cohens and the Kellys in Hollywood', 'Two White Arms', 'But the Flesh is Weak', George Arliss in 'The Silent Voice' and another Greta Garbo film, but this time starring Ramon Novarro, Lionel Barrymore and Lewis Stone in 'Mata Hari'.

Harry Proctor of Crosby must surely have been the longest-serving cinema projectionist on Merseyside. He served the Regent, Crosby, in this capacity for 41 years, starting in the silent era in 1926, and retiring in 1967. Harry had a spell at the Playhouse Theatre in the 20s, and he knew some of the young, aspiring actors who later became famous—men like Hugh Williams, Rex Harrison and Robert Donat. And Harry said it was former Playhouse actor, Wilfred E. Shine, who appeared in the first talking film shown at the Regent in 1930—'Under the Greenwood Tree'.

A luxurious new cinema, the Plaza, was first opened in Crosby on September 2nd, 1939, and the following day war was declared, so it was closed again and remained closed for a fortnight or so. There was a notice over the entrance carrying the message: 'World Record—Opened and closed the same day!' The resident organist was George Dawson, who was there from the beginning in 1939 until 1943. The beautiful Compton organ was removed from the cinema, then called the Classic, in 1974, having been bought by a private individual and re-installed in his residence somewhere in Cheshire. Happily this fine cinema is still going strong.

The curtain came down for the last time at the Abbey Cinema, Wavertree, on Saturday night, August 4th, 1979. It had enjoyed a good innings, compared to many, and it first opened on March 4th, 1939, by the Regal Cinema Company, Liverpool, at a cost of £50,000—a great deal of money in 1939. It was unique in that it was the last city cinema to be opened before the war, and many readers will recall the first film, 'Joy of Living', in which that delightful actress, Irene Dunne, starred. A special feature of that opening night was the appearance of Mrs. Wilf Hamer and her Band from the Grafton Rooms.

Runcorn readers may remember a go-ahead Scottish actor named Godfrey, who adopted the stage name of Bob Hamilton. For years, Bob had shown ten-minute films during his variety shows at the Public Hall before he developed the Empress Cinema. The pianist, Albert Sproston, will always be associated with the music at the Empress. He'd been discharged from the army suffering from wounds received at the Dardanelles. Mr. R. H. Godfrey, the elder son of the founder, and joint managing director of Cheshire County Cinemas, claimed that Albert could provide music for every conceivable situation. Nothing beat him—that is, nothing until the advent of the talkies. He was a very handy man to have around.

Allerton boasted a particularly pleasant cinema, the Classic, which first opened in 1928 as the Plaza. It was always well patronized and showed some excellent films in its time. One of the unusual features of the Classic was its goldfish pond with brass handrails. Unfortunately, it eventually disappeared to make way for a smaller cinema and shopping centre.

And there was a cinema called 'The Swan' in Mill Lane, where Arthur Lucan and Kitty McShane once appeared in person as Old Mother Riley and Daughter, long before they made the characters famous. The footlights at the Swan were encased in old biscuit tins.

In the 1920s, cinemas took quite big advertisements in the local press. Take one week in June, 1926, for instance. The Prince of Wales Cinema was showing the 'Queen of Sheba'. The advertisement read: 'The beautiful Betty Blythe in 'Queen of Sheba'—the story of a love sacrifice that is without parallel in the world's history. A picture too good to miss, with special musical settings by Kieran and his Orchestra'. They knew how to put it over even in those days. And: 'Betty Blythe, supported by a cast of 10,000—showing at 2.0, 4.03, 6.26, and 8.56. Matinee prices as usual—stalls 6d, balcony 1/-'.

And that very same week at the Palais de Luxe: 'A stirring romance of the Life-Saving Service—Lois Wilson and Wallace Beery in 'Rugged Water'—a drama that begins with a terrific storm wherein brave hearts and strong bodies clash for love and duty, and a man is rescued in such spectacular circumstances that he became a hero whilst his rescuer is forgotten'. Also at the same cinema that week: 'Special engagement of Miss Clara Collier, the renowned Liverpool soprano—direct from her provincial success. 700 afternoon stall seats at 6d'. Well, it pays to advertise and those films played to packed houses. The Trocadero was advertising that week: 'The picture that draws aside the veil on 'Satan's Smart Set'—'Hell's Four Hundred'. Strangely enough, it failed to mention the names of the actors.

1930 saw the end of the never-to-be-forgotten silent serials— gripping instalments that captured the imagination of pre-war generations, or perhaps I should say post-Great War generations. Cliff hanging adventures that kept us all coming back for the next thrilling episode. When the episode reached its cliff-hanging climax there'd be groans of frustration as the caption, 'To be continued next week', was flashed on the screen. Much the same thing happens on television nowadays—even in such soap operas as 'Coronation Street'! But millions eagerly followed those silent serials, hissing and booing the villains, and cheering loudly when the forces of right and justice triumphed over evil.

I suppose the most famous silent serial of all time was 'The Perils of Pauline', starring Pearl White, but that was way back before my time. The classics I remember well were 'The Indians are Coming', which starred that dashing cowboy hero, Tim McCoy, 'The Fatal Warning', 'The House without a Key', 'The Mark of the Frog', and 'The Chinatown Mystery'—serials so exciting that they had us youngsters jumping out of our wooden seats. To miss an instalment was stark tragedy.

And just to give a couple of examples of some of the lurid instalment titles, take 'The Indians are Coming'. The episode titles were: 'Pals in Buckskin', 'A Call to Arms', 'A Furnace of Fear', 'The Red Terror', 'The Circle of Death', 'Hate's Harvest', 'Hostages of Fear', 'The Dagger Duel', 'The Blast of Death', 'Redskins Vengeance', 'Frontiers Aflame' and 'The Trail's End'. And the chapters of 'The Fatal Warning' were: 'The Phantom Flyer', 'The Crash of Doom', 'The Pit of Death', 'Menacing Fingers', 'Into Thin Air', 'The House of Horror', 'Fatal Fumes', 'By Whose Hand?', and 'Unmasked'. With titles like that, how on earth did our parents expect us to keep our twopences in our pockets every week?

There was one period during the halcyon years of the silver screen when fierce competition between the various cinemas developed, and it became so cut-throat that the idea of serving refreshments during the interval was introduced. If one cinema served tea and biscuits another would go one better and give the customers tea and cakes. This was fine and dandy for the patrons, but it did no good at all for the cinemas' finances. In the end a halt was called and at the request of the exhibitors, the Liverpool authorities placed a ban on such inducements. A great pity, but it was great while it lasted. Had it continued we might possibly have enjoyed a three-course dinner!

No account of the glorious days of the cinema on Merseyside would be complete without further mention of the interval when the spotlight would focus on the figure in full evening dress, seated at the cinema organ as it rose from the depths of the orchestra pit. Some illustrious organists played in Merseyside cinemas— I've already mentioned Sydney Gustard, but there were also Charles Smitton, Frank Gordon, Horace Finch, Reginald Foort, Ian Hamilton, Jess Yates, David Vaughan Williams, Bill Hopper, Howard Jennings, Cyril Busfield, and many more.

Charles Smitton went straight from Liverpool College at the age of 15½ to become resident organist at the Curzon, Old Swan.

He was at the time the youngest professional cinema organist in the country and, at 18, he became the youngest to broadcast—a record which stood for 21 years. Running him close for the record are Ian Hamilton, who started on the old Paramount circuit at the age of 16, and David Vaughan Williams, who began part-time as a boy.

Bill Hopper began his career before the First World War, playing for silent films. Charlie Chaplin's 'Shoulder Arms' was one, and it was a sensation, he recalled. When Bill first came to Merseyside he was pianist in an orchestra at the Scala Cinema in Lime Street. At one time, the famous band leader, Geraldo, played in the Scala orchestra. Bill recalled there was a big orchestra for the evenings and a relief orchestra for the afternoon. Musicians were cheap—a typical wage for an orchestra player was £2.50 a week, with £5 for a conductor unless you were lucky enough to get into a city cinema where a violinist could get £7 and a conductor £10.

Round about 1931 or 1932, Sydney Gustard was playing the delightful two-manual Wurlitzer organ at the Trocadero. He then moved to the Gaumont, Chester, and when he left there in 1937 Bill Hopper took over from him on the Compton and stayed there until he went to the Odeon in Southport in 1939.

Jess Yates started at the Odeon, Llandudno, and came to Liverpool as manager of the Odeon Cinema in 1944 only a few weeks after coming out of the army. Jess is remembered in Liverpool principally as an organist, and for the lavish shows he put on at the Odeon. He formed the Littlewoods Girls Choir and featured them in his stage shows for a week at a time. He travelled round the circuit, playing at the Odeon, Crosby, among other cinemas, and also gave a recital at the Philharmonic Hall.

Turning to other forms of entertainment we used to enjoy on Merseyside, Lewis's store always did us proud in the 30s. There was always a top band to provide entertainment while we were enjoying our lunch or dinner. But they excelled themselves for the Royal Week celebrations from July 17th to the 21st, 1937. The poster for that week says: 'Ronald Frankau, Olive Groves and George Baker, Flotsam of Flotsam and Jetsam fame, Eve Becke, Children's Talkie Films a wide variety—Lewis's Wonder Miniature Zoo. A working model of the Mersey Tunnel—a scale model showing detailed construction of the world's engineering masterpiece. 'Travel through the Ages'—an amusing working model showing the History of Transport, and 'Mannequins Parade of Beachwear'.

That 'Wonder Miniature Zoo', as they called it, was a tremendous attraction for children in the 30s. It was situated on the roof, and there were leopards, wolves, bears, lions, goats, kangaroos, penguins, storks, cranes, pelicans, flamingoes, a wallaby and baby, monkeys, snakes, eagles and ponies. And whenever a family went shopping at Lewis's the children always came out with a monster balloon.

There was some fine entertainment in many of Merseyside's public parks in the 30s—mainly military bands but quite often dance bands and light orchestras. Right up to the outbreak of war, all the crack military bands performed at Vale Park, New Brighton, on Saturdays and Sundays. Some of these contained regimental dance bands which played during the interval. Possibly the best dance band of them all was that of the King's Royal Rifles. Dancing on the grass wasn't as easy as dancing on a polished ballroom floor, but hundreds tried it and enjoyed it.

One Sunday, around the mid-20s, hundreds flocked to Vale Park to listen to the music of Don Pedro and his Mexican Band. They played some beautiful, gentle music for a while, and then, suddenly, they had the temerity to start swinging it up with 'Valencia', one of the popular songs of the day. And that kind of thing on a Sunday afternoon in the 20s was considered sacrilege. Many of the audience got up and walked away. The Sabbath had been desecrated.

Looking back to the 20s and 30s, life was certainly no bed of roses for us less well-off folk. Very often it was more like a bed of nails. But it was a very colourful period. We had our entertainment, and there were many moments of pleasure and happiness—moments to savour, and memories to treasure.

Chapter 21

The Dancing Years

Outside London, the great ballroom dancing era made the most lasting impact on Merseyside, where the locals thronged the dance halls, large and small, to dance dull care away. For Merseyside boasted some of the finest ballrooms in the country, dozens of highly-talented orchestras, and many of the best dancers in the land.

Going back many, many years, I'm sure that many of our senior citizens will remember the Palais de Danse in Knowsley Road, Bootle, which opened on Easter Monday, 1922, and which had been converted from a cinema into a cosy, attractive ballroom. There were dances every evening, and also on Wednesday and Saturday afternoons. One of Merseyside's first dance bands played there—Delmonte's Jazz Band, and later, Johnny Collins' Harmony Four.

Thursday nights at the Bootle Palais de Danse became a rendezvous for many of the best dancers on Merseyside. The standard of ballroom dancing was extremely high, and the frequent demonstrations, together with cabaret and burlesque, made it a very popular place indeed. It also had what was probably the best children's class in Liverpool. Malcolm Munro, that well-remembered pioneer of Liverpool ballroom dancing, was the pianist for the twice-weekly classes, and the children were put through their paces by Mary Cheshire and Topsy Steele.

That first Christmas party for the youngsters in 1922 was also a huge success, and one of the mothers brought along her small son, Harold—in later years to become the well-known 'Chips' Chippendall, of broadcasting fame, and who sang with Mrs. Wilf Hamer's Band at the Grafton Rooms, and with Sidney Lipton's Orchestra at the Grosvenor House Hotel, in London. A critic in the Liverpool Evening Express described the Palais as 'a cosy little ballroom, with soft lighting, and a beautiful, springy, maple-floor, with an assembly of smartly-dressed young ladies and gentlemen dancing in the modern style—and a young gentleman M.C., who possessed the heaven-sent gift of tact'.

That same year, 1922, regular dances were being held at the New Brighton Assembly Rooms, which were more popularly known as the 'Pic O' Dances' or the 'Pico Ballroom', and this, too, attracted many of Merseyside's best dancers. Arthur Williams ran two dances a week, and Arthur was the first to introduce big-name bands there from other parts of the country, such as Spinelly's Dance Band, and another famous combination, the London Celebrity Band with Johnny Stein at the piano and Mick Burberry on saxophone.

The opening of the Embassy Rooms in Mount Pleasant, Liverpool, on January 29th, 1923, was a grand and glittering affair, befitting such a magnificent ballroom. Malcolm Munro became the first Master of Ceremonies, and the opening night was a brilliant success, with the cream of society there. The orchestra, comprising twelve musicians, was led by Arthur Davies. On the following night, the pianist was none other than a youngster named Gerald Bright, who later went on to fame as Geraldo and led one of the finest dance bands in the country.

There was also a small relief band of four—Mary Daley, who later became Mrs. Wilf Hamer, as pianist leader, Jack Cheshire on drums, Harold Ormian on violin, and Malcolm Munro's younger brother, Wilf, on the banjo. Wilf, using 'Hamer' as a professional name, was then only 15. There were many fabulous dancing occasions at the Embassy Rooms, not least being the first Spanish Fiesta ever held in Liverpool, and attended by almost the entire Spanish colony in their beautiful costumes. A special feature of the Fiesta was the tango, which made Liverpool really tango conscious. There was also a Derby Night Floral Carnival and a Japanese Fete. Arthur Davies's Orchestra was subsequently succeeded by Mick Burberry and his Celebrity Band, which came from the Pico Ballroom in New Brighton.

The Embassy Rooms was destined to become the leader of dance fashions outside London. Dance teachers came from all over the country—not only to view the glorious suite of rooms, but also to take lessons in an atmosphere unrivalled for ballroom dancing. The Embassy formed its own orchestra for the winter season of 1923. They re-formed the small relief band they'd used at the opening of the Rooms earlier that year, with Mary Daley on piano, Harold Ormian violin, Alex Matthews drums, and young Wilf Hamer on banjo.

Gerald Bright, who was playing for Arthur Davies's Band at the Blackpool Tower Ballroom, wanted to return to the Embassy Rooms. It was Malcolm Munro's original intention to have Gerald as pianist-leader of the orchestra, with Mary Daley as relief solo pianist, and Gerald Bright asked for a salary of £10 a week. When Munro put his application before the managing director, that worthy blew his top. 'Ten pounds a week!' he exploded, 'why, I wouldn't pay that to any musician!' So Gerald Bright, who was later to earn £1000 a week as Geraldo, was turned down flat, and Mary Daley got the job as leader for £5 a week.

They'd been thinking of adding a saxophone player to the small orchestra, and a young man named Brown was interested in the job. He admitted he could play only one tune on the saxophone, but was confident he'd be able to play anything by the time he was due to start. There's confidence for you. He gave an audition with the band and played his solitary tune—the Gershwin number, 'I'll build a stairway to Paradise'. He got the job, and to give Mr. Brown his due, he was able to play all they required when he joined the orchestra, which they christened 'The Embassy Bohemians'. Jacques Brown, on his tenor saxophone, made a special feature of such famous 1920s tunes as 'Chicago', 'Running Wild' and 'I'm just wild about Harry'. Subsequently, Mr. Brown went on to earn fame in another direction as Jacques Brown, the well-known BBC producer.

The first anniversary Ball at the Embassy Rooms on January 28th, 1924, was a glittering success, the forerunner of many brilliant functions there. Many of the pantomime stars from local theatres came to the Anniversary Ball, including Dorothy Ward and Shaun Glenville. The souvenir programme read: 'Exhibition Dances by Malcolm Munro and Mary Daley—Malcolm Munro, Topsy Steele and Clarice in 'Reminiscences of the Wellington Rooms' (that, of course, had been the name of this magnificent suite of rooms before it became the Embassy), and, 'The Embassy Bohemians Orchestra, leader Mary Daley, solo pianist, Jimmy Hands'.

Jack Hylton's famous band came to Liverpool to play at the Embassy on Grand National Eve, 1925. His contract stated he was to supply an eight-piece orchestra, and the managing director informed the board of directors that he'd engaged an orchestra of 'eight pieces'. This was greeted with great amusement, but apparently, the phrase became the origin of 'Harry Gold and his Pieces of Eight'—a famous band of later years.

When the Jack Hylton Band was first mooted for the Embassy, it was intended that Jack was to front his own band but, in the meantime, he'd become very successful, and he backed down on this point. In the event, when the band arrived, it wasn't the one they expected, but another—Jack Hylton's Florida Band from Bognor. However, after hearing them play a few special arrangements, Malcolm Munro came to the conclusion that it was a much better outfit than the one they'd negotiated for. The Florida Band included many musicians who were destined for fame—Joe Crossman, that brilliant saxophone player, Jackie Greenwood, a dynamic little drummer, and Guido, a noted banjo player. Under the leadership of Bert Zeimar, it was the finest band ever heard in Liverpool.

At this stage, it might be appropriate to mention something of Malcolm Munro, whom many readers will remember so well. He started in show business just before World War 1 and was, in fact, booked to go to Australia with 'The Girl in the Taxi' as assistant manager to the producer, Reggie Hunt Firth, when war broke out.

He volunteered for the Liverpool Scottish, served throughout the war, and when he returned to civvy street his interest turned to ballroom dancing. He'd always been fond of music and enjoyed the Jazz Age that followed the war. But he soon became interested in the teaching and the technical side. He joined first the National Association of Teachers of Dancing, and then the British Association. He opened a ballroom for assemblies in 1920, and in 1921 attended one of Belle Harding's teaching weeks at the Merrick Rooms, Kensington, in London.

This converted him to ballroom dancing so completely that he was to devote the rest of his life to serving the profession and, in particular, to spreading the 'gospel' in the north-west of England. Malcolm made constant trips to London and knew all the leading dancers of the day. When, in 1922, he was offered the position of manager of the new Palais de Danse in Bootle at a salary of £4 a week, he was able to invite dancers north, and to promote local competitions. In May, 1922, he was at the Blackpool Festival, partnered by Mary Daley, and they came second with a number called 'Chin Chin' in the one-step section.

Malcolm's big opportunity came in 1923 when he was offered the job of M.C. and manager at the Embassy Rooms in Liverpool. This elegant ballroom with its beautiful chandeliers, now in the British Embassy in Ottawa, was more suitable for what he wished to promote, and the directors gave him good financial backing. He staged World Championship Heats for Camille de Rhynal, brought Cynthia and Cyril Horrocks from London for cabaret, invited P.J.S. Richardson to judge competitions, and brought

Monsieur Pierre and Meredith Owen to Liverpool. The first ballroom dancers were Alex Moore, then 16 years of age, dancing with his sister, Avis, who had just won the Blues championship. The band leaders who were with him at the time were Mr. and Mrs. Wilf Hamer, Tommy Kinsman, and Jacques Brown.

Josephine Bradley and Wellesley Smith demonstrated for him in 1926. It was their very first visit to Liverpool, and Munro always maintained that they gave the finest ballroom demonstration of all time. They were the best dressed and most stylish couple in the West End, so it was quite a scoop to get them to come to the Embassy.

In 1927, Munro opened the Bath Assembly Rooms in Leamington Spa. Later that same year he joined Liverpool's famous Grafton Rooms in West Derby Road as manager. When he accepted the job he didn't realise that he was in fact saddling himself with an overdraft of £12,000, but by working tirelessly on a shoestring budget he overcame all the financial difficulties and made the Grafton world famous. He brought all the best demonstrators, sometimes paying part of the generous fees out of his own pocket. He promoted Thursday night dances for over two decades, and even during World War II he brought top class bands from London and featured competitions for every grade of dancing. He was responsible for the revival of old-time dances in the north-west.

In the mid-20s, Liverpool was rapidly becoming recognised as one of the leading centres of ballroom dancing outside London, and the city was firmly placed on the map of the dancing world when it was decided to hold the first heats of the World Ballroom Championship in Liverpool—the first time ever in the provinces. That was in November, 1924. It was organised by Camille de Rhynal and 'The Dancing Times', and took a full week at the Embassy Rooms, with the final on the Saturday.

This event created enormous interest. In addition to the 300 couples dancing in the various competitions, there were record crowds of spectators during the week. The competitions were the world's professional, amateur, and mixed Ballroom Championships, and the adjudicators were Belle Harding, Monsieur Pierre and Camille de Rhynal. Tremendous excitement was aroused on the final night from a packed house, which included the Birkenhead Park and Belfast Rugby Teams, particularly when the professional section was being danced with two well-known local couples ranking favourites for the provincial title. Camille was a great showman, very astute, and certainly one of the leading personalities of the dancing world in the 20s. In a witty and characteristic speech he summed up the whole week by declaring: 'Liverpool dances with its heart as well as its feet'.

The major dancing event of 1925 was the coming of the Charleston. Robert Sielle and Annette Mills introduced the dance into England. Fresh from a trip to the United States they presented the first ballroom version of it to a large gathering of teachers in London in July, 1925. It didn't create any great stir at the time, but gradually it caught on, and the Charleston legend began. At the height of the craze, an enormous Charleston Ball was staged at the Royal Albert Hall. The uninhibited gyrations of the dancers inflicted so much physical damage that the slogan 'p.c.q.' (please Charleston quietly) had to be introduced.

Following the London premiere of the ballroom Charleston by Robert Sielle and Annette Mills, Malcolm Munro is believed to be the first to introduce the new dance to the provinces. This was at the Embassy Rooms in Liverpool on August Bank Holiday, 1925. Malcolm was partnered by Vi Thomas, a well-known amateur champion of the time. The Embassy dance orchestra on that occasion was augmented by several members of the Chez Henri Club Orchestra, who were on a visit to Liverpool. This band was later to be directed by the one and only Charlie Kunz.

The new dance created only a mild sensation at first. Most of the dance teachers ridiculed it, many people condemned it as being cheap and vulgar, and many dance halls actually banned it. As Malcolm Munro once said: 'The surest way for a dance to become popular is to ban it', So gradually it made its presence felt and it became one of the most popular dances of the generation. After all, the Prince of Wales was seen to enjoy doing it, so it became acceptable.

Malcolm Munro enthused over the Charleston. But his enthusiasm failed to impress the critics. Their comment was: 'The solo Charleston will never catch on in this country'. The honours went to the Embassy Rooms in presenting the first solo Charleston competition to be held in England—on August Bank Holiday, 1926—twelve months after the ballroom version was introduced. It was demonstrated by Leon Cassel-Gerard, and there were more than a hundred competitors. Proving the critics wrong, it was an instantaneous success, and after spreading all over the country it culminated in a Grand Charleston Ball at the Royal Albert Hall, organised by C.B. Cochran. Second, third and sixth places went to Merseyside competitors.

During the same year in which Malcolm Munro took over at the Grafton Rooms, Billy Cotton's Band joined the new Rialto Ballroom in Liverpool. That, was 1927. It was in 1925 that Bill and his London Savannah Band came to the Southport Palais, and it's said that the building was so new that the paint on the walls was hardly dry. It was a top-class band—three saxophones, three brass, sousaphone, piano, and Billy himself on drums. Later, the band was augmented by Sydney Lipton on violin, Joe Ferrie on trombone and Clem Bernard on piano, and the Palais drew hundreds of enthusiastic dancers, not only to dance, but also to listen to the best band in the north-west. In fact it became so popular that special trains were put on called 'Dance Expresses' to take the dancers to Southport.

This was the time that Bill Cotton became so interested in motor-racing. He was a versatile character and even piloted his own plane. He wasn't averse to any challenge. At Southport they used to hold the sand racing championship, with a hundred guineas in cash and a hundred guinea gold cup for the winner. Bill entered into it with a will and I think he always regretted the fact that all he ever won was a silver cup. It was while he was at Southport that he drove Sir Henry Seagrave's famous 'Sunbeam'. He proved to be one of the top racing drivers in the country, and long after the band had left Southport, he used to go back there regularly to race on the sand.

In 1927, a smallpox outbreak hit Southport, and people were advised not to go to crowded places such as theatres, cinemas and ballrooms. Naturally this hit the ballrooms badly, especially the enormously popular Palais, and the attendances were very poor. The General Theatre Corporation had built a palatial new cinema and ballroom in Liverpool, the Rialto, and when Billy Cotton was invited to take his band there he readily accepted. And so, with a magnificent new ballroom, one of the best bands in the country, and hundreds of enthusiastic dancers, the Rialto became one of the best-known places on Merseyside. Bill always retained fond memories of Liverpool and Southport, and many readers will remember dancing to his popular band at the Rialto and at the Southport Palais.

At that time, tea dances were proving to be very popular indeed, and dancing the afternoon away to the accompaniment of a good band, and cream cakes and a pot of tea thrown in, made a nice little break for many folk. Some readers will recall that it was also in the late 20s that another palatial ballroom was opened—the Casino, in Kensington, and this, too, proved an enormous attraction.

The band playing at the Grafton Rooms in October, 1928, was Monty Wilson's Commanders—they'd been resident there for a year. Then Monty accepted an offer to play at a brand-new Palais de Danse in Bolton. The result was that the Grafton commissioned young Wilf Hamer, then playing first alto in Billy Page's Band at the Palais-de-Danse in Douglas, Isle of Man. Hurriedly, he formed an orchestra of eight players under the title of 'Wilf Hamer's Atlanta Dance Orchestra'. This famous combination continued with few changes of personnel from October, 1928, to January, 1956, except for a season at Tony's Ballroom in Birmingham, a season at the Nottingham Palais, five summer seasons at the Queens Dance Hall, Rhyl, and one summer season at Payne's Majestic, Llandudno.

Some of the finest floor shows ever presented in a ballroom were seen at the Grafton, under the title 'Cavalcade', including 'The Bridge of Athlone' on St. Patrick's Night, and 'The Grand March Lancers' on Armistice Night. There were Hallowe'en nights, with ghosts, gnomes, witches, goblins and hob-goblins, and the ballroom succeeded in creating a hilarious atmosphere. Then they had 'Flora Dora' nights, with the lovely melodies of Leslie Stuart, Gaiety Galas, Nautical Nights and Spanish Fiestas. They were truly great days for the Grafton.

Camille de Rhynal visited the Grafton in 1932 and brought with him the world's professional champion dancers of that year from Paris. They showed a new version of the rumba—the 'Beguine', which came from Martinique, in the French West Indies, and also a vigorous and exciting paso doble—the best yet seen in England.

At the end of the year, the first recognised championship for amateur dancers in the North of England was staged. It was won by the well-known Merseyside couple, Billy Martin and Dolly Nolan. Then, early in 1933, the musical publication 'Rhythm' sponsored a dance band championship, adjudicated by Julien Vedey and the famous dance band musician, George Scott Wood. The winning band was Harold Dobbs and his Orchestra from Bangor, North Wales, whose first alto and clarinet player was a young man named Harry Parry, who went on to become the famous jazz musician and band leader. With his swinging sextet he made hundreds of broadcasts. Harry, alas, died in his late twenties.

1933 was 'a year of great attractions' at the Grafton. Duke Ellington and his legendary band stopped the traffic in West Derby Road, and the fans besieged the band platform. This was the second time a top American band had appeared in a Liverpool ballroom—the previous occasion was when Paul Whiteman played at the Adelphi Hotel on a Grand National Eve. Geraldo and his Gaucho Tango Orchestra made their first appearance in a Liverpool ballroom—the Grafton, of course, in August, 1933. A lot of water had flown down the Mersey since Geraldo, then a youngster named Gerald Bright, had played at the Embassy Rooms in 1923—ten years before.

Then, in September, Jack Hylton's Band came—still the greatest big band attraction in the country—and the familiar 'Jack's Back' poster was displayed on the hoardings.

1934 was a memorable year at the Grafton for the number of famous big band attractions. Lew Stone broke every attendance record on his first visit on April 12th. The famous Monseigneur Restaurant combination included the legendary Al Bowlly, as well as ace musicians Joe Crossman, Nat Gonella, Alfie Noakes, Tiny Winters, Joe Ferrie and Monia Liter. They were followed by Syd Seymour and his Mad Hatters, Roy Fox and his Band with Denny Dennis and Peggy Dell, Billy Cotton, Debroy Somers, Mrs Jack Hylton, Teddy Joyce, and Jack Hylton again.

1935 was Royal Jubilee Year. The Grafton arranged a cavalcade of modern ballroom dancing on Easter Bank Holiday Monday, and the leading professional and amateur dancers on Merseyside co-operated in the most ambitious floor show ever seen in a Liverpool ballroom, culminating in a formation team display—the first yet to be seen in the North of England. There were some famous dancing personalities, and the celebrations continued the following evening with a cavalcade of old time music and dancing.

The first broadcast of Wilf Hamer and his Band took place on May 15th, 1935, on the North Regional wave-band. Then Wilf and the boys went off to Rhyl for a summer season on the North Wales coast. That celebrated Liverpool bandleader, Jack Gordon, took over at the Grafton, and it's interesting to recall that the second alto and vocalist in his band was Robert Dorning, who later made his mark in ballet dancing, and then became a very successful actor. And, of course, that tip-top vocalist, Eric Whitley, was with Jack Gordon's Band for a time, but that was at the Pico Ballroom in New Brighton and, as Eric ruefully recalls, the Pico burnt down just after he was engaged by Jack.

A magnificent floor show was presented at the Grafton in October, 1935, with the excruciatingly funny Barry Lupino, Mona Vivian the pantomime star, and Jan Ralfini's Band. Just as funny was the annual Hallow'een Carnival on the 31st, with Wilf Hamer dressed as Mephistopholes, with property fire and everything, and the boys of the band as naughty gnomes, weird witches, ghostly goblins, and naughty hob-goblins. The huge assembly included Santos Casani and Charlie Kunz as spectators.

The first broadcast of Hamer's 'Melodious Memories', comprising fifty tunes in half an hour of old-time dancing, was a huge success on December 12th, 1935. The Radio Pictorial of February 7th, 1936, after taking a poll of 'what listeners like', concluded: 'Old-fashioned dance music at least hold its own with modern jazz'. Geraldo's 'Dancing Through' and Wilf Hamer's 'Melodious Memories' had three times as many votes as Ambrose, Henry Hall and Jack Payne. Which was a remarkable tribute to the popularity of Wilf Hamer, although the magazine's reference to the music of Ambrose, Henry Hall and Jack Payne as 'modern jazz' is extraordinary.

One of Merseyside's most popular amateur dancers, Billy Martin, joined the staff of the Grafton Rooms in September, 1935, and proved himself a real asset—not only to the executive part of the business, but also to the professional side of ballroom dancing, and due to his wide experience as a juvenile performer of cabaret items, he helped to make the Grafton floor shows the envy of other ballrooms in Britain. And it's good to know that Billy's still very active with his well-known School of Dancing in Liverpool.

Wilf Hamer's Band began their second season in Rhyl on Whit Saturday, 1936, with a broadcast on the Welsh Region, so Jack Gordon's Band filled the breach once again. Roy Fox brought his band back, together with his popular singers, Denny Dennis, Mary Lee and Bobby Joy. Ambrose came again in June with all his superb musicians, and a newcomer—Vera Lynn. Other bands included Liverpool's own Jack White from the Astoria Ballroom, London, Sydney Lipton from the Grosvenor House Hotel, Geraldo, and the scintillating Harry Roy.

And then, suddenly, in July of that year, tragedy struck. After a very short illness, the popular Wilf Hamer died. This was a cruel blow, not only for the Grafton and the people who loved to dance to his music, but most of all for his wife, Mary. With admirable fortitude and determination, Mary, who'd had some experience as the bandleader at the Embassy Rooms years before, took over Wilf's baton in Rhyl, and carried on. When they returned to the Grafton, Mrs. Wilf Hamer and her band, as it now was, broadcast on the North Region on November 30th, 1936, and again on New Year's Eve. Obviously, with Mary as leader, the band had lost nothing of their ability and popularity.

Joe Loss and his Orchestra made their first appearance in a Liverpool ballroom at the Grafton in April, 1937,—Coronation Year. Joe had achieved fame as the 'perfect tempo band', and with their feature 'Dancing Time for Dancers', few bands rocketed into the limelight as quickly as this sparkling combination of expert musicians and singers. The personnel of the band included two Liverpool boys—Clem Stevens and Bill Boland, as well as Danny Miller, the young drummer, Jackie Greenwood, who'd played at the Embassy Rooms with Jack Hylton's Florida Band in the 20s, and that fine singer, Chick Henderson, who was later killed in the war while serving in the Royal Navy.

Mrs. Wilf Hamer proved to be a very capable and popular leader, and the band went from strength to strength. When entertainment began again during the 'phoney war', after a temporary lull in 1939, the Grafton was an oasis in the black-out, where people, young and old, came in their thousands. 'House Full' notices went up as the ballroom filled nightly. The Grafton was one of the few ballrooms in the country to create good ballroom dancing as a major wartime event. But the Grafton in wartime is another story, and I haven't the space to relate it here. Suffice to say that, for Mrs. Wilf Hamer, it was probably her 'finest hour'.

I can't possibly leave the Grafton without mention of the wonderful dances BBC Radio Merseyside have put on in the famous ballroom during the past twelve years. For the dancers who were privileged to attend, they provided a nostalgic return to the Grafton when it was at its brightest and best. The guest appearances of top singers like Denny Dennis, Eric Whitley and Eve Lombard enhanced the occasions. Most of all, on each occasion, Mary Hamer returned to the scene of her former glory to play some of her delightful piano medleys. It was just like old times. Mary was as sweet, charming and gracious as ever. If these dances brought happy memories flowing back to her, then the dancers who saw her and danced once again to her music most certainly had even happier memories. For the name of Mrs. Wilf Hamer will always be synonymous with the Grafton Rooms.

Jack White was a very popular Liverpool bandleader, and thousands of customers danced to his perfect rhythm music in the State Restaurant in Dale Street fifty years ago. The band was known as Jack White and his Collegians.

Jack's band originally started at the Albion Street Conservative Rooms in Liverpool, and consisted of piano, violin, and Jack on the concertina. A man who was a drummer in the army had just been demobbed, and he asked Jack's father if he might join the band. He didn't want any payment—all he wanted was to practise playing dance music. He stayed with them for about six weeks but, as there were very few drummers in the whole of Liverpool, and everyone was screaming for them, he was soon away. Jack said: 'To us the band sounded awful without the drums, so my mother, bless her, bought me a set of drums, and I said a fond farewell to the concertina. That was about 1920.'

Jack was a multi-instrumentalist, and one of the most versatile of bandleaders. He had two brothers in the band—Tommy, his manager and drummer, and Jay, the saxophonist. His father was one of the pioneer dance musicians. Jack, of course, was a Liverpudlian, born and bred. At the age of sixteen he formed his own band—a semi-pro outfit. During the day he worked for a South African produce broker and, at night, he led the band. Later, he became a motor engineer and in his spare time he learned to play the saxophone. When he wasn't working he was either leading the band or playing football.

Music and sport were his twin interests, and it was inevitable that he soon decided to give up motor engineering. His problem was whether to go full time in football, as he was no mean player, or branch out in the dance band world. That was where the legendary Dixie Dean came in. It was only some sage advice from the Everton and England centre-forward that prevented him from becoming a professional footballer. At the time, he was playing for Everton's 'A' team.

When he broached the subject of turning pro, Dixie was realistic. 'Look at me, Jack', he said, 'I'm as famous a footballer as there is in the country. But all I make is £8 a week—and for how long? How much can you make in music?' 'Who knows?' replied Jack, 'If the breaks come there's no limit.' 'Then stick to music,' advised Dixie, and Jack saw the sense of it. He'd already won half a dozen semi-pro dance band championships, including the North of England championship, when he decided to turn professional entirely. That was in 1929, when he was nearly 24. He started at the Rialto Ballroom, Liverpool. Later came sessions at the West End Ballroom, Birmingham, the State Restaurant, Liverpool, the Plaza, Manchester, Shanklin Pier, Sherry's in Brighton, the Hammersmith Palais in London, and the Regent, Brighton. In 1935 he came to the Astoria Ballroom in Charing Cross Road, and was there for several years as second band to the popular Joe Loss combination.

But let's go back to the 1920s and relate the story as Jack told it to me: 'At that time, most of the churches used to hold whist drives and dances—whist until 9.30 and then dancing to eleven o'clock. We played for many of them, and soon started to spread our wings. I think we played in every dance hall from Southport to Runcorn—Acacia House, Peppers, Peel Hall in Dingle, Guild Hall in Toxteth, Stanley Hall Bootle, the Green Lane Pavilion, Derwent Hall, the Assembly Rooms in Mount Pleasant, and, last but not least, St. Martin's Hall in Scotland Road.

'Then there were the cafes—Reece's, the Yemen Cafe in Bold Street, the Edinburgh Cafe, the Bears Paw, Bon Marche, Owen Owens, Lewis's, and Blackler's—not to mention the shipping companies' staff dances at the Liver Building, Cunard Building, and the Mersey Docks and Harbour Board Building—also all sections of Liverpool University. Like a good semi-pro band we played everywhere and anywhere. During those years, 1920 to 1929, we won the Liverpool Dance Band Championship, the Lancashire Dance Band Championship, and the North of England Championship—twice!

'We turned professional in September, 1929, when we went to the Rialto Ballroom. The band comprised George Johnston, piano, Stan Stanton, trumpet, Tom White, drums, Tony Morris, alto sax and vocalist, my other brother Jay, tenor sax, and myself on tenor sax. We were still together when the war started in 1939. With the exception of Stan Stanton we all joined up again in 1946, when we returned to the Astoria Ballroom, London. Going back to our Liverpool days, we played at the Rialto from September, 1929, to September, 1931, then moved to the West End Ballroom, Birmingham. We didn't like Birmingham and soon returned to Liverpool and started at the State Restaurant in February, 1932, and played there until December, 1934.

'Sam Bonner was the biggest name in Liverpool. He was one

of the greatest chaps I knew, and would always put himself out to help you if he could. Henry Hall and Billy Cotton were big names in Liverpool at the time, and we were just a small local band. Nevertheless, when Bill Cotton did a stage show, we took his place in the ballroom. It was the same with Henry Hall. People used to book the Adelphi Hotel and Henry's band. They played in the Sefton Lounge from 11 p.m., and we used to play until they took over.

'My sister, Kay, played quite a lot with local bands when their pianist was ill, and I think the first time she formed her own band was in 1940 when she played for Littlewood's social events. Eventually, Littlewoods took over the State Restaurant for their clubroom, and Kay provided the band. She also played at Atlantic House during the war, and it was from there that I heard her broadcasting'.

Jack himself made many broadcasts. He retired in September, 1957, but the BBC persuaded him to continue his 'Music While You Work' broadcasts, and his last was the Christmas one of 1969. When I asked him what was his greatest moment, he told me, with obvious pleasure, 'When I switched on the radio and heard my sister broadcasting from Liverpool. That was really something!'

I first met Jack Pettit at the old Radio Merseyside studios a few years ago when I interviewed him about his dance band activities. If ever there was a thorough gentleman it was Jack. He was almost completely blind then but he was full of good humour, and I realised there and then why he was so popular with all his fellow musicians during his long career. He was a lovable man.

Jack Pettit started his colourful career in 1922 with the then resident band at the Grosvenor Hotel, Chester, did the opening season at the Prestatyn Beach Ballroom in 1926, and in 1928 was at the Adelphi Hotel with Henry Hall's band. Then, early in 1929, he formed his own five-piece band called 'The Florida Five' at the old Edinburgh Cafe in Lord Street, where they appeared continuously until the end of 1932 when the premises were closed.

He went back to the Grosvenor for a spell, then did the summers of 1935 and 1936 with Jack Gordon at the Grafton Rooms, whilst Wilf Hamer took his band to Rhyl. At that time, almost every Friday night was 'Big Band Night' at the Grafton, and they had the pleasure and privilege of sharing the stand with all the big bands—Ambrose, Roy Fox, Carroll Gibbons, Lew

Stone, Jack Jackson, Harry Roy, and Geraldo. And it was Jack Pettit who sent a promising young singer named Eric Whitley to the Rialto Ballroom in 1934 with a letter advising Jack McCormack to audition him—Eric's first step to national fame.

When Jack played with Henry Hall's Band at the Adelphi Hotel in 1928 it was a six-piece, and the instrumentation was typical of the type of combination playing for dancing in the large provincial hotels at the time. It comprised, in this instance, piano-leader, violin, alto sax, clarinet, banjo, string bass and drums, with one or two of the musicians 'doubling', of course. The pianist-leader was Dick Steele, who could never have guessed at the time that he'd still be playing at the Adelphi some forty years later. The violinist was Norman Elwin, the banjoist Ned Owens, the saxophonist Harold Greatbanks, the bass player Jim Howarth, with Jack Pettit himself on drums.

Jack told me that in the middle and late 30s he did a lot of work for the man whose name was familiar to everyone on Merseyside—the great Sam Bonner. Sam had the services of dozens and dozens of local musicians in his day, and quite often had seven or eight dance combinations playing for him in all parts of Merseyside on the same night. Jack regarded Sam as Liverpool's Jack Hylton. Sam's own band used to do a lot of cine-variety—playing at local cinemas for about twenty minutes every night during the interval. Readers may remember Teddy Jones, Sam's singing drummer, who was extremely popular. Teddy retired to the Isle of Man and died there in 1973.

Jack Pettit became a close friend of a virtually unknown fiddle player, and they often found themselves playing a 'gig' in the same four or five-piece unit. While this character wasn't exactly a Joe Venuti on the violin, his sense of humour was simply out of this world. Yes, you've guessed it—I'm back to Charlie Olden again. Charlie eventually left the dance band scene and went on the stage. As I mentioned in a previous chapter, he simply reversed his surname and the billing was—'Nedlo—Fiddle and Feet'. If he had a week's 'rest', as they called a lay-off in the profession, he always came back to Liverpool, when it was always get-together time for Charlie and Jack Pettit.

Coming home on one of these 'rests', and having been told that Jack was playing at the Adelphi Hotel's daily afternoon tea dance with Henry Hall's band, Charlie entered the main lounge, and somehow managed to get to the back of the band platform without Jack spotting him. As the band was in the middle of a

214

brand-new number, he opened the drapes which hung immediately behind Jack's chair and whispered a typical Nedlo wisecrack into his unsuspecting ear.

The result was exactly as he'd anticipated. Trying to control a spontaneous belly-laugh, Jack lost the beat, the band rocked perilously close to chaos for about four bars, then by some miracle Jack managed to recover the beat and everything went on smoothly to the end of the number. Immediately, the leader turned round in his chair demanding to know what had gone wrong. Jack tactfully told him that he'd almost dropped one of his sticks. Fortunately, Henry Hall hadn't up till then arrived to play second piano, as he invariably did on Wednesday and Saturday afternoons.

Jack told me: 'From my own personal experience, I can say in all sincerity that Henry Hall, or "H.R.H.", as his boys affectionately christened him, was one of nature's gentlemen, and undoubtedly the best guv'nor I ever had the privilege of working for. But a few years later, he pinched the tenor sax player from my 'Florida Five' Band. This was George Dickenson, who was also a fine guitarist, and it was in this capacity that Henry had been using him in his Gleneagles Hotel Broadcasting Band at the Adelphi for the previous few months, and I'd been releasing George for these weekly broadcasts. He went on to enjoy six years with Henry Hall's BBC Dance Orchestra and his later band.'

George Dickenson did his first 'gig' in 1927 at the Empress Ballroom, New Brighton, playing there on Saturdays for a season. Then he formed his own five-piece band and did the occasional dances and spots in cinemas between films—at the Empress, Tuebrook, and the Rice Lane Cinema in Walton, etc. Later, George fixed up with a touring show—Madame Hayley's Juveniles, before joining Billy Cotton's Band, working in Liverpool and Preston for about eighteen months.

Bill Cotton then moved to London but, owing to domestic problems, George didn't go with him. So Bill fixed him up with Howard Baker, who was just about to put the first band in the Palais, in Kensington, where he worked for a season. Then followed a summer season in Aberdeen, and back to the Edinburgh Cafe with Jack Pettit. When George went to London to audition for Henry Hall he was in competition with hundreds of musicians, but he got the job. He stayed with Henry's orchestra right through the memorable broadcasting years until just before the war. And when I chatted with George at Radio Merseyside not so long ago I very soon discovered yet another who considered Henry to be a perfect gentleman in every way.

I'm still asked about the identity of the Liverpool dance band musician who was driving a bus-load of war workers either to or from their factory when the vehicle was attacked and machine-gunned by a low-flying enemy aircraft. Well, I've always maintained that it was Hal Graham, and it was Jack Pettit who vouched for this when he told me: 'In the summer of 1945, I was playing with the Benny Boyd Band at the Rialto Ballroom, where Hal Graham succeeded us with his band in the early autumn. From what I gathered at the time, it was indeed, Hal Graham who was driving the bus concerned. It seems he took the only avoiding action he could under the circumstances, by immediately swinging his bus to right and left, which was successful. For this rather hair-raising exploit, Hal earned himself the nickname of "Zig-Zag Smith" among his colleagues.' Hal Graham was his professional name as a bandleader. I believe his real name was Smith.

Jack Terry was another of those gifted dance musicians who provided such great music for dancing in Liverpool's halls in the 30s. Jack was a member of Norman Trafford's Bandits—Norman was the pianist and leader, and readers will no doubt recall that he eventually started the children's shows at New Brighton each summer. Jack really went to town as a musician, and played at the Aintree Institute, Barlow's Lane, Fazakerley, Alexandra Hall, Crosby, the main hall of India Building, the Mecca Cafe in that same building, Holyoake Hall, the Co-op Hall in Walton Road, Bootle Town Hall, Star of the Sea in Seaforth, Francis's Cafe in Clayton Square, and many church halls.

Jack Terry, incidentally, went to school with Bill Shankland, brother of Jimmy Shankland, of Billy Cotton and Sydney Lipton fame, and Bill later had drum lessons from Arthur Haydock, who was with Jack McCormack's Ambassadors at the Rialto Ballroom. Jack Terry became a drummer in 1932, and he also had lessons from Arthur—and so did that famous Liverpool comedian, Deryck Guyler.

Many readers who dined at Lewis's Restaurant in the 30s will remember Ronnie O'Dell's fine band which played there from September 1934, to January, 1936. Ronnie was leader, pianist and vocalist. It was a ten-piece band—two trumpets, trombone, three saxes, double bass, drums, piano and guitar.

It was formed at the request of Sir Frederick Marquis, the chief of Lewis's—later to become Lord Woolton. Sir Frederick had been most impressed with Lew Stone's famous band in London, and asked Lew to supply one to play his own particular brand of music. Lew duly obliged, and also supplied some of the arrangements he used himself. Nat Gonella's younger brother, Bruts, used to impersonate Nat with his trumpet playing and vocals. Another well-known musician in the band was Arthur Maden. Lew Stone travelled up specially from London to introduce the band for the first time to the diners in the Tudor Restaurant. When Ronnie O'Dell's Band left they were replaced by Leonardi and his Orchestra, who were introduced by a special guest artist—none other but the great Mantovani.

Merseyside was abundantly blessed with musicians and bands of the highest calibre. There was the Liverpool All-Saxophone Band. Local musician, Cyril Wookey, later with Henry Hall's Orchestra, and who formerly played saxophone in Jack McCormack's Ambassadors Band, and later managed a musical instrument shop for Jack Heyworth Ltd., in Renshaw Street, started the All-Saxophone Band. They used to play at the David Lewis Theatre and many other venues, and were immensely popular.

Bernard Sheridan was a member of this band, and he told me its full name was the Paramount All-Saxophone Orchestra, named after the trade mark of Jack Heyworth Ltd. They rehearsed on Sunday mornings in Colquitt Street. The highlight of the orchestra's life was a Sunday concert in Bolton, where they opened the programme in support of the legendary Coleman Hawkins, accompanied by a Jack Hylton unit which included Joe Crossman on clarinet. Jack Terry played drums with this all-saxophone band.

Bert Yates was the popular bandleader at the New Brighton Tower Ballroom for many years, and thousands of dancers used to throng that famous ballroom. Bert came to the Tower Ballroom from Sherry's, Brighton, with Archie Craig's Band in 1938, but, owing to the outbreak of war, and the consequent closure of dance halls, the band broke up. So Bert formed his own band when the American troops arrived and the Tower Ballroom opened its doors again. He alternated with big bands such as Harry Roy, Lew Stone, and Joe Loss. The signature tune Bert adopted epitomised the wish of everyone during those grim war years—'The world is waiting for the sunrise'.

A Liverpool family provided the leading sax player for one

of Britain's first radio broadcasting bands—the legendary Savoy Orpheans, in the 20s. He was Arthur Lally. The Lallys certainly were a musical family. They lived at No. 7 Dodge Street, off Wavertree Road—now demolished. There were three sons— Jimmy, who was a pianist at the New Brighton Tower Ballroom for a number of years and later became a brilliant arranger for some of Britain's leading bands; Albert, another pianist with the local bands in Liverpool, and the most famous of the three, Arthur, who, after his years with the Savoy Orpheans, became leader of Ambrose's 'second band'—the Blue Lyres, at the Dorchester Hotel in the early 30s. Arthur later formed his own band which he called 'Arthur Lally and his Million-Airs'.

A well-known Liverpool all-girls band was Jennie Miller's Lady Syncopators, who were going strong from early 1928 onwards, and often played at Holyoake Hall, Smithdown Road, among many other places. Edie Ledsham was their banjoist, and another member of the band was a Miss Thorpe, who ran a music shop next to the police station in Prescot Street.

The late Alf Sergeant, himself a well-known local bandleader, told me that it was Edie Ledsham who taught him to play jazz in 1928, and thus putting him on the road to meeting hundreds of celebrated dance musicians. Incidentally, Jennie Miller came from Garmoyle Road, in Wavertree. Hers was certainly a lively little band. Liverpool's Ivy Benson!

Alf Sergeant enjoyed an exciting and varied career. After entertaining throughout the 30s he found himself on the 'Queen Mary' in 1940 with one of the finest jazz groups formed impromptu from the Services, which included top-liners from the London West End bands. Alf then formed an outfit in Jerusalem to perform on a regular programme—'Strike up the Band' over the Forces network. After the war he formed a 12-piece band for Littlewoods which re-opened the State Restaurant in Dale Street, then going on to 'Workers Playtime' for the BBC from Littlewoods large canteen in Walton Hall Avenue.

I wonder whether any readers remember Patrizov and his Orchestra who used to play at the Futurist Cinema before the talkies arrived! They were featured in a 15-minute interval spot when the 'Great Patrizov', in the full glare of the spotlights, would play a terrific violin solo in a wild gypsy style. Not many people knew that 'Patrizov' was a local lad named Patsy Collins!

About the same time, there was another musician around named Delmonte, who ran about six bands at the local 'hops', and also a show band of about twelve musicians. They used to tour three cinemas every night, playing for about twenty minutes at each one. They'd pack up their instruments after each performance, hop into a coach, change into different jackets, and on to the next cinema.

Delmonte was a great showman. Whether he was a good musician is open to question, for all he used to play himself was a little clog dance called 'Handel Wakes' on piano. Then came the talkies—out went the cinema orchestras, and hundreds of musicians were thrown out of work.

Bob Jenkins was known to thousands with his 'Jenkins Jazz Band'. Bob was at his peak in 1929 when he was making a steady £40 a week, which was a splendid wage in those days. He had very definite views on dancing, and said the difference in the night-life scene in the 20s and 30s was that there weren't any clubs to speak of in those days. Dance halls were where the customers went —Claremont House, Acacia House, Daulby Hall, St Martin's Hall, Swainsons Ballroom—and it was usually a very much more polite and formal affair than the 'd'ye wanna dance den?' discos the youngsters go for these days. 'Chaps would actually bow when they asked a girl for a dance', Bob said, fondly, 'and there was none of this gyrating and shuffling twenty feet away from each other'.

Going back to when he got his first booking as a 16-year-old pianist at the Lytton Hall in Everton, he said they were dancing the Valeta, the Ladbrooke, and the Jazz Twinkle. The foxtrot and the quickstep hadn't even been invented. Bob claims to have introduced 'The Shiek of Araby' three years before the song became a hit. He played for Jessie Matthews, reckons boxing champion Nel Tarleton was the best dancer he ever saw, and happily admits that 'all we musicians knew in those days were lines and spaces, flats and sharps'. Even so, Jenkins Jazz Band was great to dance to.

Many people's favourite dance hall was Burton Chambers, on the corner of Spellow Lane Terminus—a stone-throw from Goodison Park. The resident band was that of Stan Roberts. Stan played drums, and his brother, Les, also played in the band. Eddie Lyons was on saxophone, and Wally Hale was pianist for seven years—a very talented pianist who would have graced many a bigger and more famous band.

Stan also had a singer named Reg Pye, who won the Teddy Joyce Cup for a Bing Crosby impersonation, which earned him the title of 'Liverpool's Bing Crosby'. Lillian Ross, the All-England Ballroom Champion, judged dancing competitions at Burton Chambers, apart from her afternoon instruction classes. And the hall was open seven days a week for well over twenty years, even during the war. Many folk have the happiest of memories dancing to Stan Roberts' Band at Burton Chambers.

Even better known than Jennie Miller's Lady Syncopators was Lily Lettiss and her Band. Lily started playing for dances in 1914, when she was a schoolgirl. She decided to form her own band in 1919 and her first engagement was at a Dancing Class for Beginners at a well-known hall called 'Sammy Cartledge's' in Hillside Road, Tranmere.

Her own band comprised violin, saxophone, banjo and drums, with herself on the piano, of course. As time passed, tangos became popular in the dance halls, so she engaged a couple of accordion players. The band played almost every night of the week around the Birkenhead area—sometimes small sixpenny 'hops' and other times at special functions at the Lady Lever Art Gallery for the late Lord Hesketh Leverhulme.

These were very important engagements indeed for Lily's up-and-coming band. Lord Leverhulme always requested her to play 'Stumbling', which was his favourite foxtrot.

Lily Lettiss had many good stories to tell me. She said: 'In the 20s I had a standing engagement once a year, every February, to play for the Cheshire Regimental Ball at their headquarters in Grange Road West, Birkenhead. This used to be a grand affair, starting at eight o'clock in the evening and finishing at four o'clock next morning.

'Most of the officers and wives and friends, including Lord Leverhulme, attended every year—and, of course, all ranks of the Cheshire Regiment. There's one particular night I'll never forget. It was at the Battle of Meanee Ball. The stage was situated in the centre of the massive drill-hall. My band of six started at eight o'clock with the first waltz. All went smoothly until 8.45—dancers packing the floor, when, suddenly, the entire hall was plunged into complete darkness.

'Can you imagine the stampede?' Lily chuckled. 'There were people trying to scramble back to their seats in total blackness. Someone came to our aid with a few candles, some of which found their way into the officers' mess, and a few in the sergeants' mess. I was in a bit of a mess myself. I was given one solitary candle in the middle of the stage. My one concern was how I'd be able to keep things going. No-one would dance in complete darkness so, on my own, while the rest of my band were imbibing in the sergeants' mess, I started up community singing.

'This continued until midnight, until the fault had been repaired. But there was more comedy to come. When the lights suddenly came on again without warning, there were ladies frantically smoothing down their dresses, straightening their hair and powdering their noses—gents combing their hair, straightening their ties, and wiping lipstick from their faces. It must have been one great cuddle in the dark!

'Anyhow, things got sorted out, and the band came back, very much the worse for wear and in no fit state to continue playing at their best. I remember Lord Leverhulme coming across to shake my hand and, later, I received a special letter of thanks from the adjutant at Chester Castle. It was a night to remember!' I think Lily deserved a medal as well as that letter of commendation.

Lily decided to call it a day as a bandleader in 1950, and changed from dance music to playing piano in the various clubs. For well over twenty years she was resident pianist at various clubs on Merseyside, and even in her eighties, continued to give immense pleasure at senior citizens meetings. She was quite a lady!

And Jack Kincey told me: 'I was a friend of Bertini, who used to be at the Blackpool Tower Ballroom and the Winter Gardens Ballroom with his broadcasting band. During the late 20s and early 30s I had a six-piece band myself known as Jack Kincey's Vienna Band, and I must have played in most halls on my side of the river, and quite a few in Liverpool. I was living in Rock Ferry in those days. Two of our special bookings were the staff dances on the old "Conway", which used to be moored in the Mersey, off Rock Ferry, and the Cheshire Regiment's Annual Ball. My signature tune was "Happy days are here again", and we used to close with "Goodnight Sweetheart".' I trust Jack never experienced the same kind of 'blackout' as Lily Lettiss did when she played for those same annual balls!

The countless Merseyside folk who took their holidays in the Isle of Man will no doubt remember Doug Swallow's Band before the war. Doug was a Liverpool man and his first engagement in Douglas (in the very early 30s) was at the Derby Castle, the site of the ill-fated 'Summerland' Pleasure Centre. For the next couple of years he played at the Palace Ballroom where, for 1/6d, you could dance all evening, or watch the variety show and dance afterwards.

Doug also played for afternoon concerts in the grounds of the Palace, and accompanied such artistes as Florrie Forde. His programme always opened with his signature tune which was, naturally enough, 'Follow the Swallow'. Doug Swallow, by the way, was the composer of that famous tune, danced to by hundreds of thousands of people—'The St. Bernard's Waltz'.

Merseysiders had some justification in claiming that Bertini was one of their bands, as hordes of trippers from this area must have danced to the music of Bertini and his Band at the Blackpool Tower Ballroom in the dancing 30s. On occasions the band was enhanced by the accompaniment of Reginald Dixon on the famous organ.

No, Bertini wasn't an Italian, in spite of the name. He was a cockney, born within the sound of Bow Bells, and his real name was Bert Gutsell. Unlike our well-known local bands, however, Bertini recorded extensively, mainly on those wonderful little eight-inch records on the Eclipse label which you could buy at Woolworths for sixpence.

I've always considered it an enormous pity that Wilf Hamer, Mrs. Wilf Hamer, and Merseyside's other splendid bands never made any records for us to sit back now and enjoy their delightful music. We just have the memories, but in Bertini's case, we can still enjoy his attractive band on the many records still in existence.

Looking back to my Blackpool trips, I can still visualise Bertini's Band playing in that famous ballroom under a group of palm trees, with a large letter 'B' on the tall centre tree. And talking of Blackpool, Larry Brennan's Band is also well-remembered—a wonderful band and, for many people, superior to Bertini's Band.

It was Jack Pettit who told me that the last time he met Eric Whitley was in 1937, when Jack was playing at the Empress Ballroom, in Whitley Bay, and Eric was with the Peter Fielding Band at the Oxford Galleries in Newcastle, just a few miles away. I mentioned that it was Jack, who, in 1934, sent Eric to the Rialto Ballroom, Liverpool, with a letter advising Jack McCormack to audition this young singer as, and I'm using Jack's own words to me here: 'In my opinion Eric was one of the best vocalists I'd ever heard'.

This was only a couple of days after the disastrous fire at the New Brighton Assembly Rooms, which had put bandleader Jack

Gordon, Eric, and many others out of work with dramatic suddenness. It was especially unfortunate for Eric, coming when he'd only completed a couple of days of his engagement—his very first job.

After singing with Jack McCormack, Peter Fielding, Teddy Joyce, Geraldo, Carroll Gibbons, Harry Roy, and other big name bands, Eric became lead tenor singer with the Black and White Minstrel Show which toured Australia. Jack Pettit's shrewd judgement proved to be right. And when Eric sang at a recent Radio Merseyside Dance at the Grafton Rooms he was still in excellent voice.

There was a happy sequel at that Grafton dance. I said the fire that destroyed New Brighton's Pico Ballroom took place in 1934. During the many long years after, Eric Whitley and Jack Gordon never set eyes on each other. Then we had the Radio Merseyside dance a couple of years ago. There, waiting to greet Eric on the steps of the Grafton was Jack Gordon. A happy re-union indeed after 48 years. Needless to say they hurried off to the nearest pub to celebrate!

I mustn't leave out Wally Poole's Band which played for many years in Wallasey. It was Wally who gave a young local songstress named Enda Carefull her first big chance, and, as Eve Lombard, she went on to a successful career with Carroll Gibbons, Harry Roy, and other bands. The stories she told me of her experiences with the inimitable Harry Roy were quite hilarious. She was fired by the little maestro on innumerable occasions, but he'd always completely forgotten about it by the next morning. And Eve's another singer who recently graced our Radio Merseyside Grafton Rooms dances, and her voice was still good enough to delight the dancers there.

Many readers will have spent many a cosy night dancing at the Queen Mary Ballroom in Renshaw Street in the 30s. Syd Hall and his Band used to play in what was described as 'Britain's Finest Ballroom', and they used to advertise a 'Modern Partners Night'—a lady and gent together—1/6d for the two.

And then there was Bennie Boyd whose band played at such popular venues as the Rialto Ballroom, the Ocean Club, the Bears Paw, the Grafton, the Ritz, the Golden Goblet, and the Kingsland, Birkenhead. And older readers will remember Ernest Zeffer's Premier Band in the 20s, who played all over Merseyside, and their talented drummer, Jack Rooney. I'm pleased to say that Bennie, Ernie and Jack are all fit and well, and in touch with me.

All of which reminds me of the world featherweight boxing contest at Anfield in the 30s between the Liverpool idol, Nel Tarleton, and the American, Freddy Miller, in front of a packed Spion Kop. The contestants were in the ring, and the usual celebrities were being introduced from the ring.

Roy Fox, whose band was playing at the Empire Theatre that week, and who was an avid boxing enthusiast, stepped into the ring, immaculate as ever in tails. His name was announced, and most people recognised him instantly. But the amplification was poor, and one 'scouser' said to his mate: 'Oo de 'ell was dat?' 'Aw sum geezer named Guy Fawkes, I tink!' was the reply. Obviously no followers of dance music!

Some more Merseyside dance halls—the Balfe, situated over a pub in Nelson Street, Dayne's in Chatham Street, which was almost a marriage bureau as so many couples met there for the first time and married, Marmaduke Hall, known as the 'Marmy', Swainson's, King's Hall, Blair Hall, Tagus Hall, the Carlton— by the wash-house at the corner of Bevington Bush, admission twopence, Winstanley's in Richmond Row, popularly called 'Winnie's' for short, and the 'Wilkie Hop' in Arkwright Street. Also the Central in Stanley Road, County Hall in Oriel Road, Ridgeways Cafe, the 'Memo' in Northumberland Terrace, Quine's Ballroom in Mill Street, where you always danced to Victor Silvester's records, 'Gussie's' in Shaw Street, Hulme Hall, and the Albion. Many only boasted three-piece bands, but they certainly knew how to play.

And some more local bands—Mick Devine, Tommy Finnigan, Bill Gregson, Al Vine, Tom Hughes, Bob Oakley, Freddy Gordon, Pierre Bethell, Bill Morton, Nick Kearsley, Bob Easson, and the Blue Ribbon Band.

So many fine bands, so many cosy dance halls, so many delightful memories. These were the names that were part of the scene when Merseyside danced, in the true sense of the word, to the swinging and melodic bands of the 20s and 30s. I wonder whether we'll ever see the like again?